COVID and Climate Emergencies in the Majority World

The COVID-19 pandemic has amplified the hardships people are experiencing from human-induced climate change and its impact on weather extremes. Those in the Majority World are most affected by such global crises, and the pandemic has exposed the vulnerabilities of these populations while highlighting the differences between them and those fortunate to live in the Minority World. This book presents an overview of the impact of the climate emergency punctuated by a pandemic, discussing the expanding inequalities and deteriorating spaces for democratic public engagement. Pandemic responses demonstrate how future technological, engineering, political, social, and behavioural strategies could be constructed in response to other crises. Using a critical analysis of these responses, this book proposes sociotechnical alternatives and just approaches to adapt to cascading crises in the Majority World. It will be valuable for social science students and researchers, policymakers, and anyone interested in inequality and vulnerability in developing countries.

Laurence L. Delina is assistant professor of environment and sustainability at the Hong Kong University of Science and Technology. He is a Filipino academic working on just energy transition and resilient climate adaptation, especially in the Majority World, in response to the accelerating anthropogenic climate crisis.

'Laurence Delina has done an excellent job of linking all the major global crises facing mankind today. None of them can be dealt with in isolation and so a joined-up approach is essential which this book provides an excellent blueprint for.'

Saleemul Huq, International Center for Climate Change and Development, Bangladesh

'A comprehensive and fascinating look at the way our crises are overlapping now – as the author realizes, this makes the moment hard, but also rich with opportunity to set the world on new footings.'

Bill McKibben, author The End of Nature

'Laurence Delina takes you on a grand tour of world crises, injustice and hope, from colonialism to overconsumption and climate nationalism to indigenous epistemology. Delina draws on knowledge from his native Philippines to highlight challenges facing the Majority World, for which rich countries are primarily responsible. With diverse topics and extensive referencing, this is a treasure trove of ideas and sources for navigating the future.'

Brian Martin, University of Wollongong, Australia

'This is the book the world needs right now! Laurence Delina connects the dots in a powerful way by linking responses to intersecting global crises and offering realistic, yet optimistic, mechanisms to mobilize systemic change.'

Jennie C. Stephens, Northeastern University, author Diversifying Power: Why We Need Antiracist, Feminist Leadership on Climate and Energy

'The world is confronted by cascading crises, as Laurence Delina describes very well in this book. No country or region is spared from the impacts of such threats as the COVID pandemic and the climate emergency. But developing countries, which constitute the majority world, are specially challenged. This book presents not only an integrated analysis of these challenges but also proposes comprehensive responses to them.'

Antonio Gabriel M. La Viña, Manila Observatory

COVID and Climate Emergencies in the Majority World
Confronting Cascading Crises in the Age of Consequences

LAURENCE L. DELINA

The Hong Kong University of Science and Technology

Shaftesbury Road, Cambridge CB2 8EA, United Kingdom

One Liberty Plaza, 20th Floor, New York, NY 10006, USA

477 Williamstown Road, Port Melbourne, VIC 3207, Australia

314–321, 3rd Floor, Plot 3, Splendor Forum, Jasola District Centre, New Delhi – 110025, India

103 Penang Road, #05–06/07, Visioncrest Commercial, Singapore 238467

Cambridge University Press is part of Cambridge University Press & Assessment, a department of the University of Cambridge.

We share the University's mission to contribute to society through the pursuit of education, learning and research at the highest international levels of excellence.

www.cambridge.org
Information on this title: www.cambridge.org/9781108838344

DOI: 10.1017/9781108974455

© Cambridge University Press & Assessment 2023

This publication is in copyright. Subject to statutory exception and to the provisions of relevant collective licensing agreements, no reproduction of any part may take place without the written permission of Cambridge University Press & Assessment.

First published 2023

A catalogue record for this publication is available from the British Library.

ISBN 978-1-108-83834-4 Hardback
ISBN 978-1-108-97880-4 Paperback

Cambridge University Press & Assessment has no responsibility for the persistence or accuracy of URLs for external or third-party internet websites referred to in this publication and does not guarantee that any content on such websites is, or will remain, accurate or appropriate.

To Emo and Shawn

Contents

Preface		*page* ix
Acknowledgements		xii
1	**Portrait of a Grief**	1
2	**Collapsing Dominoes**	11
3	**Vulnerabilities Amplified**	19
4	**Walled World**	26
5	**Obscene Opulence**	33
6	**Climate Nationalism**	47
7	**Toggling the System**	62
8	**Decluttering Consumption**	73
9	**Confronting Neo-Liberalism**	84
10	**Ceasing Arrogance**	93
11	**Making Amends**	101
12	**Collective Solidarities**	110
13	**Decolonising from Within**	116
14	**Indigenous Epistemology**	123
15	**Communicating Risks**	129
16	**The Hubris of Control**	135
17	**Mobilising the 3.5 Per Cent**	147
	Index	155

Preface

The COVID-19 pandemic declared by the World Health Organization in March 2020 – which continues to strike as this text is written in the last week of July 2022 – ushered in two different new worlds: a world under control and surveillance on the one hand, and a world experiencing cascading crises on the other. I write these words on quarantine near Hong Kong airport, where I arrived from my home country, the Philippines, two days ago. Hong Kong remains one of the very few countries on Earth still seeking zero COVID infection. Others have opened their borders already. My seven-day quarantine is a control mechanism that was ubiquitous the world over during the first two years of the pandemic. This is not my first; I was also quarantined for twenty-one days upon returning to Hong Kong in August 2021. Also, as these words are written, hell has descended upon Europe. Thermometer readings on the continent reached more than 40°C; Spain and Portugal were on fire; the runway at London Heathrow melted. At the same time, Russia's invasion of Ukraine is still in full force. The global economy is also bleeding. Many countries, including mine, have turned to populist governments. Overall, we see a cascade of changes, from climate to politics to economics.

While cascading crises are not new, what we are seeing now portends a plausible future juxtaposed by parallel, and serial, intensifying global crises. The natural world, which we continue to plunder, is hurling back at us. The impacts of fossil fuel–powered industrialisation of the Minority World are now felt hard and fast by many vulnerable countries in the Majority World. Natural systems, especially the climate, are now reaching their tipping points. Once crossed, the models predict these systems will likely collapse. Once collapse occurs, our civilisation will be in danger. The ramifications of weather extremes to human societies, for example, are already far-reaching. Accelerating climate change is an existential crisis. While some may survive, many will not.

The majority of those who will suffer and perish from the extremes brought about by these cascading crises are, unfortunately, those who have little capacity to adapt. Most of these vulnerable populations live in the Majority World – the very sources of the natural resources that powered industrialisations in countries in the colonial Minority World.

The climate injustices suffered (and that will be most suffered) by people living in the Majority World will not be the only injustices they will experience. If the COVID-19 pandemic foretells policy response in a heated world, we can see more future injustices occurring. The gap in terms of early access to COVID-19 vaccines, for instance, is very glaring. While the Minority World rushed to get their citizens vaccinated, the Majority World waited until its turn. In the same fashion, as rich countries experience extreme weather events, their primary task is to secure the safety of their citizens first. Those in miserable conditions in the Minority World will make do with what they can mobilise among themselves. The fragilities of those who are already climate vulnerable will most likely increase as countries in the Minority World erect fences to keep climate migrants out. We already see this happening in the migration crisis in Europe, where people fleeing from war-torn countries in the Middle East, Africa, and South Asia are subjected to harsh border control. Contrast that to how the Majority World took care of white migrants during the Russian invasion of Ukraine.

The task ahead – to address accelerating climate change while also addressing other global issues – is immense. No country can tackle the climate crisis alone. It takes multilateral action to push for an accelerated global transition to renewables and curtail unfettered consumption in the Minority World. With many governments captured by multinational fossil fuel businesses and the top 1 per cent of the world's wealthiest people living in untethered opulence, the only hope for action seems to be a strengthened transnational climate action movement. Calling for a just social transformation requires moving beyond changes in energy generation engineering systems. The challenge is so entrenched that we also need social re-engineering of energy social infrastructures and our consumption behaviours. Politics and economics must be attuned to the need to respond to cascading crises now and in the future.

Recognising historical and present injustices brought about by colonialism and neo-colonialism is a crucial way forward in sociotechnical re-engineering. Unless former colonialists in the Minority World acknowledge that their centuries of plunder of resources, the genocide of peoples, and erasures of cultures has resulted in the mess we are all in, we cannot have just social transformations. In addition to the need for recognition of these injustices, restorative justice is also imperative. As the world heats up and the vulnerabilities of those living in the Majority World increase, people in this part of the world must demand restitution. Due to past transgressions by the Minority World, climate damages in the Majority World should be remedied through debt forgiveness and unconditional grants for climate adaptation and mitigation.

As crises cascade, indigenous knowledge about coping and surviving offers new hinges on which to hang future processes and strategies of knowing and doing. Management approaches devised in the Minority World will not work in the context of vulnerable communities in the Majority World. Centuries, if not millennia, of local and Indigenous Peoples' knowledge offer wellsprings of new ideas for surviving emergent and cascading crises. The control of risk, which is very salient and even dogmatic in many western management approaches, will not work in the future just as it does not work in pandemic situations. We saw first-hand how one type of coronavirus alone can elude control. When biology and nature strike, we have to adapt better.

COVID and Climate Emergencies in the Majority World contains these ideas and more. Compared with my previous books on what we can learn from histories of mobilisation for the Second World War and non-violent social movements in designing contemporary climate action, I admit that I am being pessimistic in this prose. I write this book at the same time as I experience personal crises, which also cascaded in a matter of less than a year. If the COVID-19 pandemic yielded some positive effects for me, it was the opportunity to know myself better and, most importantly, to value what matters to me the most: my family, my well-being, and my small, intimate circle of supportive friends. I trust many would find that my experience resonates with theirs.

Acknowledgements

Since leaving the Philippines for postgraduate studies in 2008, the pandemic years of 2020 and 2021 were the longest time I have spent at home. I got to enjoy my nieces – Michaela Marie, Sophia Lucylle, Michelle Lorraine – and nephews – Matheo Rain and Ian Gabriel. I also appreciated my *nanay* (mother), Lucy, more during this time, as well as my *tatay* (father), Rito Sr, my brothers, Michael and Rito Jr, and my sisters-in-law, Brendaly and May. I am always grateful to them for letting me pursue my passion despite it entailing that I work thousands of miles from home.

I am grateful to be given the opportunity to write *COVID and Climate Emergencies in the Majority World*. I am grateful that my publisher, Cambridge University Press, my commissioning editor, Matt Lloyd, and my editorial assistant, Sarah Lambert, did not give up on me during the entire process of writing, production, and marketing.

I am also very thankful to my proposal reviewers, Brian Martin and an anonymous colleague, for their comments on the book proposal. The manuscript also received comments from my postgraduate students at the Hong Kong University of Science and Technology. Olivia Anne Perez and Dane Ellice Ancheta read some chapters as I churned them out, often after meals we shared at my home in the winter of 2022. I am very grateful for the insights of these smart and grateful students, who I have the privilege of mentoring. I am also thankful to my colleagues and supervisors, Kira Matus, King Chow, and Alexis Lau, who, during my trying times, lent me their full support.

Friends who are like family are hyacinths for the soul. I have a few. I am grateful to know Aynee Triunfante, Aileen Rondilla, Oneal Mendoza, Allan Lao, Vipra Kumar, Albert Salamanca, Jong de Castro, Alma Dolot, Charmae Andas, and Ever Pinon-Simonsson. I wonder if authors acknowledge their cats in their work? Regardless, I thank my cats, Emo and Shawn, for providing a much-needed emotional tonic during these trying times, that is, the pandemic.

Acknowledgements

In this book, I write about fond memories of my childhood, growing up in a rice-farming *barrio* (village) in southern Philippines, my life as a development banker in South Cotabato, my time as an international student in Auckland and Sydney, and my travels. I had the opportunity to see places despite the limitations of my Majority World passport. The people I encountered over the years, in the Philippines and elsewhere – many of whom were not merely passers-by – and the experiences I shared with them shaped who I am today. I do not have the space to name and thank them all here. They know who they are, and I am grateful to be part of their lives.

In closing, *COVID and Climate Emergencies in the Majority World* does not promise a silver bullet for emerging and cascading crises. Instead, this book is my humble contribution to ongoing discussions, stocktaking, and future-charting to decolonise and ensure the just acceleration of climate action.

1
Portrait of a Grief

We assault the living world from every angle, and all at the same time. As we remember this onslaught, we grieve. Reminiscing is a powerful act. In grieving, we consider the state of our natural environment and take the necessary actions to rectify our abuse of the living planet.

Natural systems change from state to state, and we are failing to pay attention. When I was nine or ten, I recall native freshwater fishes – *toragsoy* and *poyo* – and snails – *agihis* and *igi* – were so typical we caught and collected them in streams and even in the small canal across from our home. I barely paid attention to this abundance. But ecosystems are now collapsing, almost year on year, and this has made me think and ask: where are those fishes and snails (Jackson et al., 2001; Peterson, Carpenter, and Brock, 2003; Crispin and Simonetty, 2015)?

Globally, industrial-scale meat production, mining, and fishing continue to swell as the face of the Earth is ransacked clean. Industrial-scale looting of the natural environment is the *fons et origo* of biological obliteration embodied in the bewildering disintegration of our oceans (Hughes et al., 2019; Pratchett et al., 2021), extinction of vertebrate species (Ceballos, Ehrlich, and Dirzo, 2017; Ceballos, Ehrlich, and Raven, 2020), the sprint to chop remaining virgin forests (Barlow et al., 2016), dying coral reefs (Pratchett et al., 2021), melting glaciers and sea ice (Gobbi et al., 2021), and contracting and drying lakes and wetlands (Pham-Duc et al., 2020).

The root of this rapid species decline is no secret. If my village in the southern Philippines is a microcosm of this accelerating change, the decimation can be traced back to rapid changes in the natural environment. Inorganic agricultural practices proliferated (Agboola and Bekun, 2019; Olanipekun, Olasehinde-Williams, and Alao, 2019); the number of mouths to feed increased (Wang and

Dong, 2019; Khan, Hou, and Le, 2021). Economists trumpet this as development, but we should label it as it is: a pillage, an act of plunder. Our natural world is *in extremis*. We are devouring the planet beyond its capacity to replace.

As the COVID-19 pandemic raged, we learned new things about our nearest neighbour in the universe. There is now evidence that flowing water once existed on Mars and that subterranean aquifers might be present on the red planet (Salese et al., 2019; Balme et al., 2020). This is an irresistible find for astrobiologists looking for prospects of life in the universe. As human ingenuity continues to seek new knowledge, we cannot even begin to contemplate other marvels that are set to unwrap in years to come. The idea of life other than on our planet has captivated our species since perhaps the first time our ancestors in the savannahs of Africa gazed at the night sky. Why does it seem that we have lost interest in the species that live on our own planet?

Consider what would be different if we accorded the same importance to the water on Earth as we do to the potential of finding water on Mars. Only 3 per cent of all water on our planet is fresh water, and two-thirds of it is stored in ice (Postel, Daily, and Ehrlich, 1996). Potable water is a crucial resource, but not every country has ready access to it. Hong Kong, where I live, imports most of its water supply from mainland China. Despite this, we continue to think that fresh water is easily accessible, when in fact, many of our streams, lakes, and groundwater supplies are already depleted (Hogeboom, 2020; Chen et al., 2018) and the water left in these areas is often so polluted that it poses health risks to people who continue to use it (Yaleliere, Cobbina, and Duwiejuah, 2018; Mekonnen and Hoekstra, 2018).

On Earth, when we find salty water – like what was presumably found on Mars – we show our gratitude by going on a rampage and destroying everything in it. In an undergraduate class I teach, one of our early class activities is the fish banks game. Developed by Massachusetts Institute of Technology Sloan School, in this multiplayer, web-based simulation my students play the role of fishers seeking to maximise their net worth as they compete against each other and deal with different volumes and prices of fish stocks and their catch. The simulation provides students with the opportunity to manage resources sustainably in a common-pool resource setting, given the changing dynamics of the available common-pool resource: in this case, fish stocks. As is often the case in real life, we would end the simulation with fish stocks almost depleted. All this occurred as 'fishers' sought to maximise their catch and increase their net worth. This, of course, came with a price. Fisheries were pushed to the brink due to decisions that unfolded over time.

I am a pescetarian. General Santos City is a seafood capital, on the mouth of Sarangani Bay, south of my home province and about a two-hour drive from home. Every September, the city hosts a tuna festival. I am now wondering whether these festivities were indeed homage to the bounty of the year's catch or a memorial to once abundant ocean species. The Pacific bluefin tuna, which spawns in the northern part of the Philippine Sea south of Japan and Taiwan and migrates to the eastern and southern Pacific, is threatened. Despite having formerly populated the oceans in their countless millions, this species of tuna, according to the latest estimate, is now less than 50,000 (Geib, 2022). Yet, they are still actively hunted by fishers since they fetch very high prices.

Also in my country, the West Philippine Sea is not only a military hotspot but also a paradise – for now – for Chinese fishers dragging their trawls in the waters. No one knows the extent to which these trawling operations impact the rich marine diversity of these waters. The West Philippine Sea is not only a space that provides fish for Filipinos; it also serves as spawning grounds for schools that populate the seas of South East Asia. As climate change accelerates, coral reefs are also under so much strain (Pratchett et al., 2021), and it is possible that by the middle of this century – that is, in less than thirty years from now – most of these reefs may no longer exist (Goreau and Hayes, 2021).

The best approach that governments have found to handle the problem of the devastation of the natural world, thus far, is to step back and let the market decide. The proliferation of corporate sustainability branding and Environment, Social, and Governance (ESG) standards signals how governments are leaving the problem of dwindling and disappearing resources up to consumers' consciences (Albert, 2020; McLennan and Banks, 2019). Because so little knowledge is available, the onus is left on our shoulders. It is now up to us to determine what we should take from other species and from other people. It is also up to us to decide what we should keep for ourselves or pass on to the generations who will come after us. This is a recipe for destruction.

Dredging, drilling, excavating, and polluting appear – it seems to me – to be preconditions for ensuring humans have access to the full range of human experience. Ingenious methods of destroying things are developed every year. And every year, humans grow more desensitised to the imbecilic exploitation of our planet's valuable resources. As economies become wealthier, it will no longer be a surprise to learn that those living in affluent countries in the Minority World – including Hong Kong – are almost becoming less concerned about the impacts of their actions on the living Earth. I live in Hong Kong, where almost everything the city consumes is imported. I tried to grow okra on my windowsill, but I failed.

The loss of biodiversity and ocean acidification are called slow-onset climate change hazards. If there is one thing we know about the impending climatic collapse, it is that the processes leading to the catastrophe will not be linear or smooth. Our climate system will take the load for a time, then – most likely without warning – abruptly flip (Alley et al., 2003). However, adaptation programmes adopted worldwide to prevent climate shocks are straight, seamless, and gradual. Accelerated and swift climate action given the possibility of surprise is an absolute need right now.

The problem with the unhurried and piecemeal climate action approaches in current proposals is that they were designed on the assumption that a climate system functions as a simple system. The climate system is considered as if it is a washbasin, in which one can stop the tap until the input is less than the outflow. But the climate system is a complex one. All systems seek equilibria, meaning that systems flip quickly into another state when pushed too far out of their balance.

Often, complex systems have the characteristic that pushing them beyond their tipping points will be far more straightforward than pulling them back from those points. When change has already occurred, it is impossible to go back in time and undo it. Once it has flipped to a new equilibrium, the climate system will not be as it was. At the end of his 1925 poem *The Hollow Men*, T. S. Eliot tells us: 'This is the way the world ends, not with a bang but a whimper.' Perhaps, and more likely, it will be the other way around.

What is worrisome is not only that fish stocks are dwindling and coral reefs are bleaching but also that we build our assumptions of the Earth's tipping points as being a long way off. These are dangerous assumptions. In February 2021, at the height of the COVID-19 pandemic, it was found that the Atlantic meridional overturning circulation, often known as the mechanism that drives the Gulf Stream and responsible for distributing heat all over the globe, may now be nearing a crucial change (Caesar et al., 2021). This circulation has experienced several phases of 'on' and 'off' over prehistoric periods, which has resulted in extreme cold in northern Europe and eastern North America, increased temperatures in tropical regions, and disruption of monsoon patterns. The article by Caesar et al. (2021) strongly suggests that this heat redistribution mechanism is now at its weakest state in over a millennium. Juxtaposing present evidence with prehistoric shifts and their impacts, the future seems to be bleak.

Other systems might also be reaching their thresholds within a generation or two, including the West and East Antarctic ice sheets (Ge et al., 2022), the Amazon rainforest (Amigo, 2020), the Arctic tundra (Foley, 2005; Lenton, 2012), and the boreal forests (Lenton, 2012). These ecosystems are fast depleting the carbon they store, which drives a cycle of increased global heating. The Earth systems do not remain confined to their designated spaces; hence, it is possible that as these systems transition into their new states, they will cause changes in other states. It will be a snowball effect (Lenton et al., 2019). This means that even a temperature increase of just 1.5 or 2°C might still bring about abrupt changes in present conditions.

Increasing volatility is a classic indicator that complex systems are getting close to their tipping points (Scheffer et al., 2009). Volatility indicates that systems have begun to fluctuate. The weather extremes observed, felt, and experienced in 2020, 2021, and, as this chapter is written, in 2022 are, to put it bluntly, scary. Fires and floods became familiar events. While some parts of the world baked, other places were inundated with rain. If the Earth's systems start to tilt due to global heating, taking insufficient action, or none, will not make much of a difference in the long run. All that we have done and everything that we have been – the intricacies of human knowledge, our experiences, our stories, our love, our fury, and our hope, will be reduced to relics.

The goal that most countries have now set for climate action – reaching net zero by the year 2050 or even earlier for some – starts to appear insensible and insecure (Lin, 2022; cf., Hale et al., 2022). It is correct that some kind of net zero is our only chance of preventing a climatic breakdown of catastrophic proportions. Greenhouse gas emissions must be decreased by decarbonising economies and removing carbon dioxide from the atmosphere. Without achieving both, it is already too late to meet the temperature objectives set in the 2015 Paris Agreement. There are, therefore, two aspects that governments should be concerned with: pace and authenticity of climate action. The transition must be accomplished quickly before systems spin out of control; and climate action must be truthful and honest. This means facing up to the challenge directly.

At its worst, the goal of achieving net-zero emissions by some future year is a vehicle for countries and nations to shuffle the blame temporally and spatially. Those in power now attempt to shift the burden of their responsibilities onto those who will be in charge tomorrow. A number of these plans depend on either technologies or the natural world to collect the carbon they want to continue emitting. These methods include carbon capture and storage. One of the technologies involves collecting emissions from power plants and cement and steel factories and depositing them in rock layers. Another technology is via direct air capture: containing carbon directly from the atmosphere and burying these emissions too. Although carbon capture and storage has been discussed over the last twenty years, it is improbable that these technologies will ever be implemented at a large scale (Low and Schäfer, 2020; Haikola, Hansson, and Anshelm, 2019). The reason for this cynicism is that these technologies are not yet being implemented at large scale today, because of constraints that we already knew.

The only thing that is left in this technocentric approach is to manipulate nature by banking on the ability of the world's biological systems to soak up the gases that humans emit. The problem, however, is there is not enough land in the world to fulfil the commitments made by governments to reduce emissions. Farmers and farm owners would also prefer someone else to be responsible for dealing with the gases produced by their properties. This preference contrasts with governments' net-zero promises that require farms to first achieve significant reductions, including ceasing industrial livestock and grain farming practices.

Let us be honest here. The prospect of a climate system restored to its safe levels is derailed by governments' inability to halt fossil fuel combustion and replace energy systems with renewables speedily and at scale. Even in a scenario of the most optimistic future, when governments deploy all of the planned technological solutions, the climate action we now have in place is still set to condemn us to a disastrous increase in global heating of 3°C. A mere 2°C heating could already flip the system. Changes cannot be undone when that point is reached. Relying on technologies that have not yet been developed and on capabilities that do not yet exist is a recipe for disaster.

The only way to halt the full-spectrum attack we are launching on Earth systems is to scale down the aggression we are hurling at the planet. The sheer magnitude of economic activity powered by the wanton burning of fossil fuels is the root cause of all of these impacts (Kallis, 2011). We are overdoing almost everything, and the Earth's biological systems are struggling to keep up with us. However, since we cannot perceive the big picture, we will be unable to address the climate catastrophe in a systemic and successful way. When we pigeonhole the climate dilemma, our attempts to find a solution to one facet of the emergency make another facet of the crisis worse.

When coral reefs are harmed by human activities such as overfishing, trawling, and the coral bleaching induced by global heating, the appropriate response is to harvest the bounty of the sea sustainably (Melnychuk et al., 2021). This entails letting ocean resources recover before they are harvested again. The droughts and fires inflicted on the landscapes by climate disruption can be addressed by reining in livestock grazing and industrial agriculture (Bezner-Kerr et al., 2011). Reducing, if not curtailing, human activities on the seas and lands has to be paired with efforts to intensify the reduction of present and future emissions.

Indeed, a rapid mitigation project to curtail emissions is essential. This means deploying market-ready and cost-effective renewable energy systems to replace extant coal, oil, and gas power plant facilities while reducing energy consumption of all sources. Suppose we were to construct direct air capture devices instead of transitioning to renewables. The critical challenge is not only that we do not have these technologies ready for deployment, despite decades of research, but this moment in history – when the world is in the midst of a pandemic – offers governments an opportunity to make the transition – both technologically in our energy systems and in the ways we consume things.

If we do not reduce the amount of economic activity that is taking place, we have no chance of escaping the climate crisis (Victor, 2012). To keep our life-support systems running, we need to do less of almost everything. There may be a more significant number of bicycles and electric cars plying the roads; however, there are also more aircraft and internal combustion engines. It makes no difference how many positive things we do; the only way to stop the environment from breaking down is to curtail economic activities, particularly in the Minority World.

One cannot just gloss over this underlying issue. Economic progress, the power that pulled millions out of deprivation, provided education, and treated diseases, is now tipping us back. It is difficult to challenge ideals such as economic growth, consumption, and materialism, especially since they are questioned the least in many Minority World societies. However, the notion that this existential crisis is not taking place is the most remarkable kind of denial. It is a disservice to humanity.

Then what to do? We start a conversation. The resolve of campaigners, organisers, and activists to shift public attitudes around contentious issues was a significant contributor to the sea change in views that has taken place in recent years. Regardless of how uneasy it makes us, and those around us, feel about the climate emergency, we need to discuss major taboo topics: not just the deterioration of the environment but also the rise of unfettered consumerism – especially by the uber wealthy – widening inequalities, and the decline of the culture of care, empathy, and respect.

References

Agboola, M. O., & Bekun, F. V. (2019). Does agricultural value added induce environmental degradation? Empirical evidence from an agrarian country. *Environmental Science and Pollution Research*, *26*(27), 27660–27676.

Albert, M. J. (2020). Capitalism and Earth system governance: An ecological Marxist approach. *Global Environmental Politics*, *20*(2), 37–56.

Alley, R. B., Marotzke, J., Nordhaus, W. D., Overpeck, J. T., Peteet, D. M., Pielke Jr, R. A., ... & Wallace, J. M. (2003). Abrupt climate change. *Science*, *299*(5615), 2005–2010.

Amigo, I. (2020). When will the Amazon hit a tipping point? *Nature*, *578*(7796), 505–508.

Balme, M. R., Gupta, S., Davis, J. M., Fawdon, P., Grindrod, P. M., Bridges, J. C., ... & Williams, R. M. (2020). Aram Dorsum: An extensive mid-Noachian age fluvial depositional system in Arabia Terra, Mars. *Journal of Geophysical Research: Planets*, *125*(5), e2019JE006244.

Barlow, J., Lennox, G. D., Ferreira, J., Berenguer, E., Lees, A. C., Nally, R. M., ... & Gardner, T. A. (2016). Anthropogenic disturbance in tropical forests can double biodiversity loss from deforestation. *Nature*, *535*(7610), 144–147.

Bezner-Kerr, R., McGuire, K. L., Nigh, R., Rocheleau, D., Soluri, J., Perfecto, I., & Hemming, D. (2011). Effects of industrial agriculture on climate change and the mitigation potential of small-scale agro-ecological farms. *Animal Science Reviews*, *69*, 1–18.

Caesar, L., McCarthy, G. D., Thornalley, D. J. R., Cahill, N., & Rahmstorf, S. (2021). Current Atlantic meridional overturning circulation weakest in last millennium. *Nature Geoscience*, *14*(3), 118–120.

Ceballos, G., Ehrlich, P. R., & Dirzo, R. (2017). Biological annihilation via the ongoing sixth mass extinction signaled by vertebrate population losses and declines. *Proceedings of the National Academy of Sciences*, *114*(30), E6089–E6096.

Ceballos, G., Ehrlich, P. R., & Raven, P. H. (2020). Vertebrates on the brink as indicators of biological annihilation and the sixth mass extinction. *Proceedings of the National Academy of Sciences*, *117*(24), 13596–13602.

Chen, B., Han, M. Y., Peng, K., Zhou, S. L., Shao, L., Wu, X. F., ... & Chen, G. Q. (2018). Global land-water nexus: Agricultural land and freshwater use embodied in worldwide supply chains. *Science of the Total Environment*, *613*, 931–943.

Crespin, S. J., & Simonetti, J. A. (2015). Predicting ecosystem collapse: Spatial factors that influence risks to tropical ecosystems. *Austral Ecology*, *40*(4), 492–501.

Foley, J. A. (2005). Tipping points in the tundra. *Science*, *310*(5748), 627–628.

Ge, S., Chen, Z., Liu, Q., Wu, L., Zhong, Y., Liu, H., ... & Zhang, Q. (2022). Dynamic response of East Antarctic ice sheet to Late Pleistocene glacial–interglacial climatic forcing. *Quaternary Science Reviews*, *277*, 107299.

Geib, T. (2022). The overfished Pacific bluefin tuna: The tragedy of a highly migratory fish species. *Sustainable Development Law & Policy*, *21*(2), Art. 4.

Gobbi, M., Ambrosini, R., Casarotto, C., Diolaiuti, G., Ficetola, G. F., Lencioni, V., ... & Caccianiga, M. (2021). Vanishing permanent glaciers: Climate change is threatening a European Union habitat (Code 8340) and its poorly known biodiversity. *Biodiversity and Conservation*, *30*(7), 2267–2276.

Goreau, T. J., & Hayes, R. L. (2021). Global warming triggers coral reef bleaching tipping point. *Ambio*, *50*(6), 1137–1140.

Haikola, S., Hansson, A., & Anshelm, J. (2019). From polarization to reluctant acceptance – bioenergy with carbon capture and storage (BECCS) and the post-normalization of the climate debate. *Journal of Integrative Environmental Sciences*, *16*(1), 45–69.

Hale, T., Smith, S. M., Black, R., Cullen, K., Fay, B., Lang, J., & Mahmood, S. (2022). Assessing the rapidly-emerging landscape of net zero targets. *Climate Policy*, *22*(1), 18–29.

Hogeboom, R. J. (2020). The water footprint concept and water's grand environmental challenges. *One Earth*, *2*(3), 218–222.

Hughes, T. P., Kerry, J. T., Baird, A. H., Connolly, S. R., Chase, T. J., Dietzel, A., ... & Woods, R. M. (2019). Global warming impairs stock–recruitment dynamics of corals. *Nature*, *568*(7752), 387–390.

Jackson, J. B., Kirby, M. X., Berger, W. H., Bjorndal, K. A., Botsford, L. W., Bourque, B. J., ... & Warner, R. R. (2001). Historical overfishing and the recent collapse of coastal ecosystems. *Science*, *293*(5530), 629–637.

Kallis, G. (2011). In defence of degrowth. *Ecological Economics*, *70*(5), 873–880.

Khan, I., Hou, F., & Le, H. P. (2021). The impact of natural resources, energy consumption, and population growth on environmental quality: Fresh evidence from the United States of America. *Science of the Total Environment, 754,* 142222.

Lenton, T. M. (2012). Arctic climate tipping points. *Ambio, 41*(1), 10–22.

Lenton, T. M., Rockström, J., Gaffney, O., Rahmstorf, S., Richardson, K., Steffen, W., & Schellnhuber, H. J. (2019). Climate tipping points – too risky to bet against. *Nature, 575,* 592–595.

Lin, A. C. (2022). Making net zero matter. *Washington and Lee Law Review, 79,* 679–768.

Low, S., & Schäfer, S. (2020). Is bio-energy carbon capture and storage (BECCS) feasible? The contested authority of integrated assessment modeling. *Energy Research & Social Science, 60,* 101326.

Magnus, G. K., Celanowicz, E., Voicu, M., Hafer, M., Metsaranta, J. M., Dyk, A., & Kurz, W. A. (2021). Growing our future: Assessing the outcome of afforestation programs in Ontario, Canada. *The Forestry Chronicle, 97*(2), 179–190.

McLennan, S., & Banks, G. (2019). Reversing the lens: Why corporate social responsibility is not community development. *Corporate Social Responsibility and Environmental Management, 26*(1), 117–126.

Mekonnen, M. M., & Hoekstra, A. Y. (2018). Global anthropogenic phosphorus loads to freshwater and associated grey water footprints and water pollution levels: A high-resolution global study. *Water Resources Research, 54*(1), 345–358.

Melnychuk, M. C., Kurota, H., Mace, P. M., Pons, M., Minto, C., Osio, G. C., ... & Hilborn, R. (2021). Identifying management actions that promote sustainable fisheries. *Nature Sustainability, 4*(5), 440–449.

Olanipekun, I. O., Olasehinde-Williams, G. O., & Alao, R. O. (2019). Agriculture and environmental degradation in Africa: The role of income. *Science of the Total Environment, 692,* 60–67.

Peterson, G. D., Carpenter, S. R., & Brock, W. A. (2003). Uncertainty and the management of multistate ecosystems: An apparently rational route to collapse. *Ecology, 84*(6), 1403–1411.

Pham-Duc, B., Sylvestre, F., Papa, F., Frappart, F., Bouchez, C., & Crétaux, J. F. (2020). The Lake Chad hydrology under current climate change. *Scientific Reports, 10*(1), 1–10.

Postel, S. L., Daily, G. C., & Ehrlich, P. R. (1996). Human appropriation of renewable fresh water. *Science, 271*(5250), 785–788.

Pratchett, M. S., Heron, S. F., Mellin, C., & Cumming, G. S. (2021). Recurrent mass-bleaching and the potential for ecosystem collapse on Australia's Great Barrier Reef. In J. Canadell & R. Jackson (Eds.), *Ecosystem Collapse and Climate Change* (pp. 265–289). Springer, Cham.

Salese, F., Pondrelli, M., Neeseman, A., Schmidt, G., & Ori, G. G. (2019). Geological evidence of planet-wide groundwater system on Mars. *Journal of Geophysical Research: Planets, 124*(2), 374–395.

Scheffer, M., Bascompte, J., Brock, W. A., Brovkin, V., Carpenter, S. R., Dakos, V., ... & Sugihara, G. (2009). Early-warning signals for critical transitions. *Nature, 461*(7260), 53–59.

Victor, P. A. (2012). Growth, degrowth and climate change: A scenario analysis. *Ecological Economics, 84,* 206–212.

Wang, J., & Dong, K. (2019). What drives environmental degradation? Evidence from 14 sub-Saharan African countries. *Science of the Total Environment*, *656*, 165–173.

Yeleliere, E., Cobbina, S. J., & Duwiejuah, A. B. (2018). Review of Ghana's water resources: The quality and management with particular focus on freshwater resources. *Applied Water Science*, *8*(3), 1–12.

2
Collapsing Dominoes

> *Civilisational collapse could occur. The cascading risks attached to climate change could happen within decades or half a century, so it is no longer the next generation that will carry the burdens of the climate emergency. Before the dominoes collapse, we must take climate risks seriously and act accordingly. If we act now, climate risks can be minimised, if not avoided.*

Robust science now supports the possibility of a global collapse. Peer-reviewed journal articles (e.g., Turner, 2012; Peterson, Carpenter, and Brock, 2003; Harries-Jones, 2009) suggest several tipping points towards a catastrophe. This chapter presents an account of the risks of civilisational collapse to foster discussions in the public sphere beyond the confines of academia, think tanks, and institutions. Risks have to be understood so that we can plan and prepare. Since these are urgent and vital issues and the general public need to engage in meaningful conversations, the discourse on catastrophic risks should move beyond the confines of scholars and independent experts alike.

For all the misery it brought, the COVID-19 pandemic opened up the necessity to study risks seriously, including the most extreme among them: the collapse of civilisation as we know it. The pandemic has shown us how life could go out of control, suggesting that we now have to prepare for more civilisational risks. Risks that could emerge include abrupt impacts of the climate emergency and its cascading impacts, such as the mass extinction of species (Wake and Vredenburg, 2008; Ceballos et al., 2015), multiple breadbasket failures (Gaupp et al., 2019, 2020), and geoengineering schemes that may be deployed but go out of control. Nuclear winter is another extreme scenario. These risks could appear in parallel, devastating livelihoods and killing millions of people. Most of the populations vulnerable to these risks live in the Majority World.

The cascading risks attached to climate change could occur within decades or half a century. It is no longer the next generation that will carry these emergent burdens. This means the family you provide food for and the children you see on the street are all at risk. The topic of cascading risks is, in all honesty, scary. But these risks are so life-threatening that they merit the most attention.

If you live in a city with a fire brigade and they tell you that your house could burn and kill your family, you do not keep quiet and call them alarmists. Most likely, you take this warning seriously. You manage the risk presented to you. You take out fire insurance and have your appliances checked. You clear escape routes and install smoke detectors and extinguishers. By all means possible, you would attempt to ensure that your home will not burn down. You make plans to avert the fire.

The collapse of civilisation is a subject that must be understood from the lens of uncertainty (Shue, 2018). We cannot be 100 per cent sure about the future; nevertheless, our knowledge of the impacts of these risks has been expanding almost daily. Since the collapse of civilisation is an existential risk, we do not have the luxury of experiencing it first-hand. Making society collapse to be 100 per cent sure that it can indeed collapse is ridiculously impossible.

Climate science has advanced considerably during the last decade. Yet, scientists have been continually engaging in never-ending scientific discussions instead of moving towards preparation for the eventualities their scenarios have predicted. The Intergovernmental Panel on Climate Change's (IPCC) continuing work on assessing the physical basis of climate change is a testament to this seemingly perpetual quest to close all gaps in the science of the climate system: making all uncertainties sure. This quest persisted even when science was already more than 95 per cent close to establishing that the climate system has been changing due to human-instigated practices and activities, and that the impacts of these perturbations all point to a possibility of societal collapse. These scientific uncertainties have been used, in turn, by policymakers to make excuses for not wholly acting or simply ignoring the climate emergency (Porritt, 2020).

We are now almost sure that civilisational collapse could happen in the future. Risks have been cascading, from the COVID pandemic to the various manifestations of the climate emergency, to the natural environment, and to our societies. It is high time to take these risks seriously and act accordingly. If we act now, these risks can be minimised, if not avoided.

Not doing something about an imminent planetary catastrophe is unacceptable. Precaution is better than any cure, especially when we do not know what that cure is or what it might be (Foster, Vecchia, and Repacholi, 2000). This is a matter of the precautionary principle. When human health or the environment is threatened with harm, precautionary actions should be taken even if some of the causes and effects of these harms are not fully known or not fully established by science.

Several societies in the past have collapsed (e.g., Middleton, 2012; Butzer and Endfield, 2012). Many models have also projected that our industrial civilisation could collapse (e.g., Meadows and Randers, 2012; Motesharrei, Rivas, and Kalnay, 2014). The natural environment that makes life on Earth possible could also collapse – including the climate system (e.g., Steffen et al., 2018; Lenton et al., 2019). Human societies cannot survive if the biosphere fails.

The idea of the collapse of our civilisation is now widespread. Scientists have warned about it (e.g., Heleno, Ripple, and Traveset, 2020; Ripple et al., 2019) and the military has also made a case for addressing it (e.g., Guy, 2020; Barnett, 2003). We could not choose to save only our civilisation without ensuring the security of the natural environment. The climate emergency will most likely result in the collapse of civilisation.

In 2020, as the pandemic began to ravage the world, governments were still concerned to safeguard fossil fuel interests and increase consumption. Twelve top climate scientists issued a distressing statement. Publicly, they said: 'It is game over for preventing dangerous climate change now that governments are planning the cheapest and quickest return to consumption. Riding on the wave of cheap oil and fossil-fuel bailouts is incompatible with keeping the average global temperature rise below 2C, let alone 1.5C.' (Knorr et al., 2020).

Addressing the risks of the climate emergency requires serious mitigation efforts now. Since the lion's share of greenhouse gas emissions is from the energy sector, deep mitigation requires total decarbonisation of energy systems. Energy transition – the shift from the combustion of fossil fuel, including coal, oil, and gas, to generate energy towards using low-carbon, renewable, and sustainable energy resources, especially from sunlight, wind, and water – must happen fast and deep. Our consumption patterns also need to change. Economies should move from being carbon-intensive towards zero carbon.

Accelerating energy transition and quickly achieving sustainable consumption and production requires hard work. These wicked problems require profound imagination regarding how they could be achieved.

Failing to act now, and within the next few years, means accepting the era of climate consequences, and suggests we have to prepare for colossal efforts at global adaptation. Sea walls must be built as sea levels rise, and coastal communities must be relocated. While relocation is essential, it has to be done in ways in which the vulnerabilities of people at risk and their communities are addressed. As stronger typhoons become more frequent, evacuation shelters also need to be more permanent. As more extended droughts and seasons without rain persist, agriculture must shift elsewhere and resilient crops must be developed. As people are forced to move due to rising sea levels and decimated landscapes, just migration has to be reconsidered globally.

These dire prospects are due to the impacts of extreme weather events alone, but there are other global systemic risks – their tipping points and nexuses that are not yet factored in. As planetary boundaries are breached, more suffering can be expected, especially by the Majority World's poor and marginalised communities. Despite the imminence of these global catastrophes, governments remain unable to deal with them, and society at large continues to live as if it is not in danger.

These risks exist. Precaution demands that we now act as if it is our most likely future.

As we think over these threats, it is crucial to consider the question: how do we continue to live with the fact that we are in an age characterised by these chronic and acute mega risks? As we admit the reality of our present circumstances, emotions will be high. Fear will be mixed with grief, and sadness with guilt.

A truthful and honest response to emerging risks requires a candid acknowledgement of our species' interdependence with the biosphere. Our anguish, fear, misery, and rage should be transformed and translated into action. We should use these unpleasant emotions to stay alert (Soroya et al., 2021; Yang and Kahlor, 2013), refine our risk perceptions (Leiserowitz, 2006; Kitt et al., 2021), and turn apathy into urgency (Thomas, McGarty, and Mavor, 2009; Bührle and Kimmerle, 2021). While further studies are needed, psychology research on fear suggests that appeals that use fear effectively influence intentions and behaviours (Bigsby and Albarracín, 2022; Tannenbaum et al., 2015). As long as it is coupled with information on solutions, fear can nudge people into action. Yet again, an important caveat is that further research that considers specific contexts remains necessary.

Another crucial question that arises from this view of the future is: how do we respond and ensure that we reduce suffering from this dystopia? *Just* adaptation is imperative. This means embedding justice into coping, bouncing back, and building better. Doing so necessitates four things. First, we must recognise that injustices in the present are due to the built-in structural indifference that co-produces anthropocentric societies. This includes underlining inequalities that are due to generations of colonisation and imperialism by the Minority World and the impacts on the well-being of people in their colonies in the Majority World. Second, the burdens of these new challenges and any benefits from solutions to address them must be equitably distributed. In this vein, special consideration must be afforded to ensure the needs of the most vulnerable, especially those historically marginalised such as Indigenous Peoples, poor people, women, children, and the differently abled in the Majority World, are met. Third, spaces for truthful public engagement in charting different futures should pay attention to mechanisms of honest deliberation and transparent procedures. Four, restoring lost opportunities is essential, including fair repatriation of loss and damages incurred to climate-vulnerable populations who have contributed the least to the climate crisis. Just adaptation requires devising new policies of resilience that bring front and centre the needs of the most vulnerable, especially those in the Majority World, to cope with the turbulence of cascading risks in the era of climate consequences, manage societal collapse, and imagine a future built on justice.

The COVID-19 pandemic provides a preview of how cascading risks could manifest. When the pandemic broke out, an atmosphere of fear prevailed (Ornell et al., 2020), sending governments into emergency mode. Economic activity slowed down. Medicines and masks were in short supply. Central banks injected massive amounts of liquidity into financial markets to avoid an economic downturn. The risk was anathema.

As the pandemic brought intense pressures on our globalised economy, this moment in history also provided a mirror by which we can view what matters most. It was a practice, a dress rehearsal for future disasters and the psychological impacts they will bring, including fear, anxiety, and despair. As half the world went into lockdown, the natural environment demonstrated that it can self-generate quickly. Nature can exist sans humans.

While the concept of contemporary societal collapse may remain theoretical and abstract for some, pandemic outbreaks, notably, have been on the radar of the United Nations for a while (e.g., Drake, Chalabi, and Coker, 2012). Disruptions from extreme weather events are already happening in many societies, especially in the Majority World. Five hundred-year typhoons have become more frequent, such as those experienced by Filipinos (Takagi and Esteban, 2016), including during the pandemic (Lucero-Prisno et al., 2020). Due to the El Niño phenomenon, droughts now extend not just in months but in years. Flooding and wildfires have also become more frequent in affluent societies such as Australia, the United States (California), and Canada (British Columbia).

Talk of technofixes is now fast becoming standard. According to this discourse, the climate crisis can be abated through geoengineering techniques. These proposals include reflecting the sun's radiation into space by spraying aerosols in the atmosphere. Geoengineering technofixes are now being normalised as they are introduced by science academies and the agencies of the United Nations (Stephens et al., 2021). Some billionaires are even trying space escapism (Jackson, 2021). And preppers are building underground bunkers (Garrett, 2021).

However, options are limited for most people, especially those in the Majority World, where mitigation and adaptation matter the most. Although our window of opportunity for mitigation is now rapidly closing, the imperative of energy transition remains. Preparing for the consequences already here and those arriving soon makes the case for just adaptation more serious. The collapse of civilisation must remain an imagined future.

References

Barnett, J. (2003). Security and climate change. *Global Environmental Change*, *13*(1), 7–17.
Bigsby, E., & Albarracín, D. (2022). Self-and response efficacy information in fear appeals: A meta-analysis. *Journal of Communication*, *72*(2), 241–263.
Bührle, H., & Kimmerle, J. (2021). Psychological determinants of collective action for climate justice: Insights from semi-structured interviews and content analysis. *Frontiers in Psychology*, *12*, Art. 695365.
Butzer, K. W., & Endfield, G. H. (2012). Critical perspectives on historical collapse. *Proceedings of the National Academy of Sciences*, *109*(10), 3628–31.
Ceballos, G., Ehrlich, P. R., Barnosky, A. D., García, A., Pringle, R. M., & Palmer, T. M. (2015). Accelerated modern human-induced species losses: Entering the sixth mass extinction. *Science advances*, *1*(5), e1400253.
Drake, T. L., Chalabi, Z., & Coker, R. (2012). Cost-effectiveness analysis of pandemic influenza preparedness: What's missing? *Bulletin of the World Health Organization*, *90*, 940–941.
Foster, K. R., Vecchia, P., & Repacholi, M. H. (2000). Science and the precautionary principle. *Science*, *288*(5468), 979–981.
Garrett, B. (2021). Doomsday preppers and the architecture of dread. *Geoforum*, *127*, 401–411.
Gaupp, F., Hall, J., Mitchell, D., & Dadson, S. (2019). Increasing risks of multiple breadbasket failure under 1.5 and 2°C global warming. *Agricultural Systems*, *175*, 34–35.
Gaupp, F., Hall, J., Hochrainer-Stigler, S., & Dadson, S. (2020). Changing risks of simultaneous global breadbasket failure. *Nature Climate Change*, *10*(1), 54–57.
Guy, K. (2020). *A Security Threat Assessment of Global Climate Change: How Likely Warming Scenarios Indicate a Catastrophic Security Future*. The Center for Climate and Security, Washington, DC.
Harries-Jones, P. (2009). Honeybees, communicative order, and the collapse of ecosystems. *Biosemiotics*, *2*(2), 193–204.
Heleno, R. H., Ripple, W. J., & Traveset, A. (2020). Scientists' warning on endangered food webs. *Web Ecology*, *20*(1), 1–10.
Jackson, T. (2021). Billionaire space race: The ultimate symbol of capitalism's flawed obsession with growth. *The Conversation*, 20 July.
Kitt, S., Axsen, J., Long, Z., & Rhodes, E. (2021). The role of trust in citizen acceptance of climate policy: Comparing perceptions of government competence, integrity and value similarity. *Ecological Economics*, *183*, 106958.
Knorr, W., Rignot, E., Leemans, R., Morse, A., Baldocchi, D., Hickler, T., ... & Dyke, J. G. (2020). After coronavirus, focus on the climate emergency. *Guardian*, 10 May.

Leiserowitz, A. (2006). Climate change risk perception and policy preferences: The role of affect, imagery, and values. *Climatic Change*, 77(1), 45–72.

Lenton, T. M., Rockström, J., Gaffney, O., Rahmstorf, S., Richardson, K., Steffen, W., & Schellnhuber, H. J. (2019). Climate tipping points – too risky to bet against. *Nature*, 575, 592–595.

Lucero-Prisno, D. E., Bernardino, G. D., Camua, A. A. R., Lin, X., & Adebisi, Y. A. (2020). Philippines braces for the typhoon season amidst COVID-19. *The Lancet Regional Health–Western Pacific*, 1, Art. 100003.

Meadows, D., & Randers, J. (2012). *The Limits to Growth: The 30-year Update*. Abingdon, UK: Routledge.

Middleton, G. D. (2012). Nothing lasts forever: Environmental discourses on the collapse of past societies. *Journal of Archaeological Research*, 20(3), 257–307.

Motesharrei, S., Rivas, J., & Kalnay, E. (2014). Human and nature dynamics (HANDY): Modeling inequality and use of resources in the collapse or sustainability of societies. *Ecological Economics*, 101, 90–102.

Ornell, F., Schuch, J. B., Sordi, A. O., & Kessler, F. H. P. (2020). 'Pandemic fear' and COVID-19: Mental health burden and strategies. *Brazilian Journal of Psychiatry*, 42, 232–235.

Peterson, G. D., Carpenter, S. R., & Brock, W. A. (2003). Uncertainty and the management of multistate ecosystems: An apparently rational route to collapse. *Ecology*, 84(6), 1403–1411.

Porritt, J. (2020). *Hope in Hell: A Decade to Confront the Climate Emergency*. London: Simon & Schuster.

Ripple, W., Wolf, C., Newsome, T., Barnard, P., Moomaw, W., & Grandcolas, P. (2019). World scientists' warning of a climate emergency. *BioScience*, 70(1), 8–12.

Shue, H. (2018). Mitigation gambles: Uncertainty, urgency and the last gamble possible. *Philosophical Transactions of the Royal Society A: Mathematical, Physical and Engineering Sciences*, 376 (2119), 20170105.

Soroya, S. H., Farooq, A., Mahmood, K., Isoaho, J., & Zara, S. E. (2021). From information seeking to information avoidance: Understanding the health information behavior during a global health crisis. *Information Processing & Management*, 58(2), 102440.

Steffen, W., Rockström, J., Richardson, K., Lenton, T. M., Folke, C., Liverman, D., ... & Schellnhuber, H. J. (2018). Trajectories of the Earth System in the Anthropocene. *Proceedings of the National Academy of Sciences*, 115(33), 8252–8259.

Stephens, J. C., Kashwan, P., McLaren, D., & Surprise, K. (2021). The dangers of mainstreaming solar geoengineering: A critique of the National Academies report. *Environmental Politics*, 1–10.

Takagi, H., & Esteban, M. (2016). Statistics of tropical cyclone landfalls in the Philippines: Unusual characteristics of 2013 Typhoon Haiyan. *Natural Hazards*, 80 (1), 211–222.

Tannenbaum, M. B., Hepler, J., Zimmerman, R. S., Saul, L., Jacobs, S., Wilson, K., & Albarracín, D. (2015). Appealing to fear: A meta-analysis of fear appeal effectiveness and theories. *Psychological Bulletin*, 141(6), 1178–1204.

Thomas, E. F., McGarty, C., & Mavor, K. I. (2009). Transforming 'apathy into movement': The role of prosocial emotions in motivating action for social change. *Personality and Social Psychology Review*, 13(4), 310–333.

Turner, G. M. (2012). On the cusp of global collapse? Updated comparison of The Limits to Growth with historical data. *GAIA-Ecological Perspectives for Science and Society*, *21*(2), 116–124.

Wake, D. B., & Vredenburg, V. T. (2008). Are we in the midst of the sixth mass extinction? A view from the world of amphibians. *Proceedings of the National Academy of Sciences*, *105* (Supp. 1), 11466–11473.

Yang, Z. J., & Kahlor, L. (2013). What, me worry? The role of affect in information seeking and avoidance. *Science Communication*, *35*(2), 189–212.

3
Vulnerabilities Amplified

The pandemic, coupled with weather extremes and the possibility of violent global conflicts, evokes the wicked nature of contemporary human challenges. These cascading risks reveal the true character of the social fabric and expose its frailties. With vulnerabilities amplified, we are catapulted to a world of miseries.

During the second week of May 2020, just as most of the Philippines went into strict lockdowns, Typhoon Vongfong made landfall bringing torrential rains and strong winds at a speed of 155 kilometres per hour (Lucero-Prisno et al., 2020). As Vongfong pounded a country under lockdown, the Philippine health system was tested. It was a perfect storm: a super typhoon during a devastating pandemic. Due to floods and landslides, hundreds of thousands of homes and valuables were destroyed, rendering thousands of Filipinos homeless. Coronavirus infections rose as evacuation centres became overcrowded and physical distancing could not be observed. Since the pandemic began, twenty-two typhoons have made landfall in the Philippines as this is written in February 2022. The cascading impacts of climate change chapter and the pandemic provide a sobering signal of what lies ahead.

Other than my own country, the Pacific nation of Fiji braced two tropical cyclones in 2020, Harold in April and Yasa in December (Shelledy, 2021). As these words are written, both were the strongest cyclones on record to make landfall in Fiji. Yasa destroyed more than 8,000 homes, displaced tens of thousands in a country of less than a million, triggered flash flooding, and ruined crops. Harold first hit Vanuatu, where it destroyed eight in every ten homes in Espiritu Santo in the northern islands and another nine in ten homes in Pentecost, before it moved to Fiji and then Tonga. Harold displaced more than 10,000 people in Fiji.

Already burdened with pandemic-related issues, the weight of misery carried by the peoples of the Pacific became increasingly heavier (Shelledy, 2021).

Harold arrived just as travel restrictions were implemented in mid-March 2020, hindering foreign aid workers bringing food and medicine. Governments in Pacific Island nations closed their seaports and schools, while non-essential businesses placed restrictions on gatherings and imposed curfews. As a result, humanitarian assistance was limited, and the delivery of life-saving supplies was significantly delayed. With domestic food supplies jeopardised, including through damage to gardens producing home-grown produce and roads washed away by storms, many people experienced food insecurity (Shelledy, 2021).

While the Pacific was flooded, Zimbabwe experienced drought in 2018 and 2019, leaving close to seven million people in acute food and water insecurity (Mupepi and Matsa, 2021). More than four million live in rural areas. Access to critical services, such as water, sanitation, hygiene, health, and education, was severely hampered by drought and economic constraints. Their vulnerability to infectious diseases also increased. Many women and girls also became at risk of gender-based violence. At the time of writing, more than 20,000 refugees in Zimbabwe, fleeing from eastern Democratic Republic of the Congo, are also at risk.

In many parts of the world, thermometers are expected to exceed their usual readings, due to global heating. In the summer of 2022, thermometers read more than 40°C in many parts of Europe; forests burnt in Spain and London Heathrow's runway melted (Landler, 2022). Heatwaves will continue to disrupt public health and power supplies, especially in more densely populated places, like cities. Hong Kong, for example, where I work, experienced fifty hot nights and forty-seven scorching days in 2020, the highest number of hotter than normal days and nights on record. With movement restricted and people spending more time at home during the pandemic, residential electricity use in Hong Kong increased by about 9 per cent compared to 2019. An emerging climate challenge is that energy demand for cooling is expected to increase with global heating (Mastrucci et al., 2019; Van Ruijven, De Cian, and Wing 2019). If this demand is not met, heat-related illnesses could exacerbate the vulnerabilities of poor people, especially those who are homeless, those with disabilities, those who do not have access to air conditioning, and those with pre-existing health issues (Hamstead, Farmer, and McPhearson, 2018).

Wildfires are another consequence of weather extremes (Jones et al., 2020; Sun et al., 2019). These events occur when oxygen, fuel, and the temperature required for ignition are available at the same time, as land use, vegetation, and climate work in concert. The effects of air pollution, as a consequence of wildfires, were exacerbated during the pandemic: it is likely to exacerbate morbidity, and an outbreak can further strain public health systems (Bo et al., 2020). The Australian bushfires, which began to rage barely two months after the start of the pandemic, showed how air pollution could interact with the pandemic response (Yu et al., 2020). From a simple health perspective, if one has been seriously ill with COVID-19, one's response to bushfire smoke is likely to be more severe, and vice versa. Since bushfire smoke causes respiratory symptoms, people with existing respiratory or heart ailments are at high risk. A study in New South Wales, Australia has shown the likelihood of more COVID-19 cases in bushfire-burned areas than in unburnt areas (Cortes-Ramirez et al., 2022). However, the link between bushfires and COVID-19 is complex since symptoms overlap.

The above experiences tell us that disasters and crises reveal and amplify the vulnerabilities of societies where these miseries occur. The effects of these events already differ widely between poor and affluent communities. As discussed above, there is a worrying body of evidence indicating that hazards are born of the climate crisis, and its impacts are increasing in intensity and frequency. These impacts will likely intersect with existing and emergent social, economic, and geopolitical pressures.

As this chapter is written in late February 2022, a geopolitical crisis has surfaced at a scale that has not been seen in Europe since the Second World War. Europe and the West changed into emergency mode as Russia invaded Ukraine. Close to 800,000 Ukrainians hurried westward to Poland for safety and most were welcomed with open arms (Higgins, 2022), but not all. Students of colour, particularly Africans studying for degrees in Ukraine, reported being turned away at train stations near the border (Armangue, 2022). Escaping Ukraine became a process drawn along racial lines. The risks carried by the 'minorities' from the Majority World, it appeared, are far more intense than those by the 'majority' in the Minority World.

The intensity of risks compounded by war and climate displacements, aggravated by the COVID-19 pandemic, is most experienced by the displaced Rohingya (Jalais, 2021). In August 2017, Myanmar's military started a campaign and drove this Muslim minority, numbering hundreds of thousands, from their homes in Rakhine state, beginning their unrivalled agony. About 900,000 Rohingya now live in cramped refugee tents in southern Bangladesh. Their situations have deteriorated as a consequence of the reduction of humanitarian assistance during the pandemic and the monsoon floods and major fires caused by inclement weather (Jalais, 2021; Ahmed et al., 2021). The Rohingya were robbed of their citizenship and subjected to an apartheid-like system of segregation and marginalisation.

The cascading risks exhibited by the pandemic, coupled with weather extremes and the possibility of violent global conflicts, suggest the wicked nature of contemporary human challenges. These cascades require that policies are adjusted to address the crises and their potential collisions and intersections with other national, regional, and global crises, including climate change and wars.

Cascading risks can be defined as sequences of hazards governed by cause–effect relationships (Pescaroli and Alexander, 2018). Identifying the degree of causality between the elements or nodes of these sequences is the first task in assessing the cascades. Disasters and crises are often rare events since they represent the slender ends of normal probabilistic curves. Yet, there are fat-tailed events, which are unlikely to happen and difficult to predict but can occur.

Fat tails are the most underappreciated in our general understanding of climate impacts. Global heating has a heavy-tailed or fat-tailed distribution, with more areas under the extreme right end of the probability curve than would be predicted for a normal distribution (Wagner and Weitzman, 2018). We are now increasingly observing the occurrences of several fat tails that are cascading with other risks as this book is written: a raging pandemic, weather extremes, and a significant war. Vulnerabilities we previously identified as independent are now accumulating and suddenly tethering. The line of causality between these variegated crises and their impacts now indicates a cascade. Our present experience of these cascading crises has arisen mainly because of the dependencies and complexities of our modernity.

We can no longer neglect the existence of risks and their likelihood of cascading. The compounding crises they produce are also no longer negligible. Perennial and intersecting racial, social, and economic inequalities within countries and regions are likely to worsen with these cascades of risks and crises. They will plausibly subject specific populations, particularly those with extant vulnerabilities, to an amplified level of risk, compromising their opportunity to recuperate from all these miseries. This burden will fall disproportionately on peoples and communities in the Majority World.

The inability of vulnerable populations in the Majority World to deal with these cascades is directly attributable to their extensive history of social inequality. During the pandemic, these inequities were revealed in the disparities between those who stayed on the payroll while working from home and those who were not paid until they physically reported to their workplaces (Nomani and Parveen, 2022). Inequities were also demonstrated between households with ample access to nutritious food versus those who experienced food insecurity and poverty (Morales, Morales, and Beltran, 2021; Benfer et al., 2019). People with medical insurance also stood in a better position than those without (Khatana and Groeneveld, 2020). The securely housed were indubitably advantaged compared with the precariously housed and the homeless (Barocas, Jacobson, and Hamer, 2021). These inequities were observed due solely to the pandemic. Grave injustices, including growing economic precarity as traditional livelihood sources – especially agriculture – disintegrate, are amplified by weather extremes.

Cascading crises reveal the true character of the social fabric and expose its frailties. While the poor and the Majority World bear the consequences of these disasters, the rich became more affluent during the pandemic. Amazon's Jeff Bezos, Microsoft's Bill Gates, and Tesla's Elon Musk, like many of the world's richest people, became even wealthier during this period, according to a report by Oxfam (Ahmed et al., 2022). The world's ten wealthiest billionaires have seen their wealth grow by US$540 billion – money that is more than enough to pay for universal vaccination (Ahmed et al., 2022). A world with global heating may also mean creating wealth for the rich and continuing misery for the poor and the already vulnerable.

Despite the present lack of documentation about the pandemic's wider repercussions, it is probable that they will resemble those of earlier disasters (Ishiwatari et al., 2020). Those with extant vulnerabilities will have their risks increased. Vulnerable people will be further pushed onto the peripheries. Their historical marginalisation will become more acute as they tend to their newfound miseries. Those living in places vulnerable to the impacts of climate change stand to experience more suffering than those in other places.

The structural risks and systemic inequities magnify the risks from cascading crises faced by people in the Majority World. One way to reduce these amplified vulnerabilities is to provide affordable universal health coverage (Verguet et al., 2021). Medical insurance for all provides a remedy for people's unequal access to health care. The right to health is a critical component of addressing climate change (Friel, 2020; Phillips et al., 2020). Solutions that emphasise building people's resilience must be based on justice, equity, and human rights. Integrating these solutions with rights-based cooperation among communities, countries, and governments can help address cascading crises.

References

Ahmed, N., Marriott, A., Dabi, N., Lowthers, M., Lawson, M., & Mugehera, L. (2022). *Inequality Kills*. Oxford: Oxfam.

Ahmed, S., Simmons, W. P., Chowdhury, R., & Huq, S. (2021). The sustainability–peace nexus in crisis contexts: How the Rohingya escaped the ethnic violence in Myanmar, but are trapped into environmental challenges in Bangladesh. *Sustainability Science*, *16*(4), 1201–1213.

Armangue, B. (2022). International students are facing challenges as they try to evacuate Ukraine. *NPR*, 3 March.

Barocas, J. A., Jacobson, K. R., & Hamer, D. H. (2021). Addressing the COVID-19 pandemic among persons experiencing homelessness: Steps to protect a vulnerable population. *Journal of General Internal Medicine*, *36*(5), 1416–1417.

Benfer, E. A., Mohapatra, S., Wiley, L. F., & Yearby, R. (2019). Health justice strategies to combat the pandemic: Eliminating discrimination, poverty, and health disparities during and after COVID-19. *Yale Journal of Health Policy, Law & Ethics*, *19*, 122–171.

Bo, M., Mercalli, L., Pognant, F., Berro, D. C., & Clerico, M. (2020). Urban air pollution, climate change and wildfires: The case study of an extended forest fire episode in northern Italy favoured by drought and warm weather conditions. *Energy Reports*, *6*, 781–786.

Cortes-Ramirez, J., Michael, R. N., Knibbs, L. D., Bambrick, H., Haswell, M. R., & Wraith, D. (2022). The association of wildfire air pollution with COVID-19 incidence in New South Wales, Australia. *Science of The Total Environment*, *809*, 151158.

Friel, S. (2020). Climate change and the people's health: The need to exit the consumptagenic system. *The Lancet*, *395*(10225), 666–668.

Hamstead, Z. A., Farmer, C., & McPhearson, T. (2018). Landscape-based extreme heat vulnerability assessment. *Journal of Extreme Events*, *5*(04), 1850018.

Higgins, A. (2022). At the Polish border, tens of thousands of Ukrainian refugees. *New York Times*, 26 February.

Ishiwatari, M., Koike, T., Hiroki, K., Toda, T., & Katsube, T. (2020). Managing disasters amid COVID-19 pandemic: Approaches of response to flood disasters. *Progress in Disaster Science*, *6*, 100096.

Jalais, A. (2021). Bangladesh in 2020: Debating social distancing, digital money, and climate change migration. *Asian Survey*, *61*(1), 194–201.

Jones, M. W., Smith, A., Betts, R., Canadell, J. G., Prentice, I. C., & Le Quéré, C. (2020). Climate change increases the risk of wildfires. *ScienceBrief Review*, January.

Khatana, S. A. M., & Groeneveld, P. W. (2020). Health disparities and the coronavirus disease 2019 (COVID-19) pandemic in the USA. *Journal of General Internal Medicine*, *35*(8), 2431–2432.

Landler, M. (2022). U.K. Heatwave: Britain sets new record on a second day of scorching temperatures. *New York Times*, 20 July.

Lucero-Prisno, D. E., Bernardino, G. D., Camua, A. A. R., Lin, X., & Adebisi, Y. A. (2020). Philippines braces for the typhoon season amidst COVID-19. *The Lancet Regional Health–Western Pacific*, *1*, Art. 10003.

Mastrucci, A., Byers, E., Pachauri, S., & Rao, N. D. (2019). Improving the SDG energy poverty targets: Residential cooling needs in the Global South. *Energy and Buildings*, *186*, 405–415.

Morales, D. X., Morales, S. A., & Beltran, T. F. (2021). Racial/ethnic disparities in household food insecurity during the COVID-19 pandemic: A nationally representative study. *Journal of Racial and Ethnic Health Disparities*, *8*(5), 1300–1314.

Mupepi, O., & Matsa, M. M. (2021). Spatio-temporal dynamics of drought in Zimbabwe between 1990 and 2020: A review. *Spatial Information Research*, *30*, 117–130.

Nomani, M. Z. M., & Parveen, R. (2022). Socioeconomic disparities in times of COVID-19 pandemic in India. *Environmental Justice*, *15*, 330–336.

Pescaroli, G., & Alexander, D. (2018). Understanding compound, interconnected, interacting, and cascading risks: A holistic framework. *Risk Analysis*, *38*(11), 2245–2257.

Phillips, C. A., Caldas, A., Cleetus, R., Dahl, K. A., Declet-Barreto, J., Licker, R., . . . & Carlson, C. J. (2020). Compound climate risks in the COVID-19 pandemic. *Nature Climate Change*, *10*(7), 586–588.

Shelledy, K. N. (2021). *Tropical cyclones and COVID-19: How disaster managers can help prevent COVID-19 outbreaks after severe tropical cyclones in Oceania* (Master's thesis). University of Washington, Seattle, WA.

Sun, Q., Miao, C., Hanel, M., Borthwick, A. G., Duan, Q., Ji, D., & Li, H. (2019). Global heat stress on health, wildfires, and agricultural crops under different levels of climate warming. *Environment International, 128*, 125–136.

Van Ruijven, B. J., De Cian, E., & Sue Wing, I. (2019). Amplification of future energy demand growth due to climate change. *Nature Communications, 10*(1), 1–12.

Verguet, S., Hailu, A., Eregata, G. T., Memirie, S. T., Johansson, K. A., & Norheim, O. F. (2021). Toward universal health coverage in the post-COVID-19 era. *Nature Medicine, 27*(3), 380–387.

Wagner, G., & Weitzman, M. L. (2018). Potentially large equilibrium climate sensitivity tail uncertainty. *Economics Letters, 168*, 144–146.

Yu, P., Xu, R., Abramson, M. J., Li, S., & Guo, Y. (2020). Bushfires in Australia: A serious health emergency under climate change. *The Lancet Planetary Health, 4*(1), e7–8.

4
Walled World

When governments restricted travel and closed borders in efforts to control the COVID-19 pandemic, we had a preview of how the world will most likely respond to intense global heating. Nations in the Minority World will probably erect visible and invisible walls to stop refugees and migrants from the Majority World, who will have been forced to flee their homes because of climate impacts, from entering.

When borders closed in 2020 because of the COVID-19 pandemic, I was forced to stay at home in my village in the southern Philippines. It was a blessing for me and my family. After years of being away from home, the pandemic lockdowns provided us with an opportunity to spend time together for an extended period. I thought I would be able to return to Hong Kong after a month or so, but it was only after eighteen months that I was finally able to cross international borders. To get into Hong Kong, however, I had to pass through a third country. I was lucky that my visit visa was still valid in the United States. I had to spend a month with a friend and her family before I was finally allowed to enter Hong Kong. On arrival, I had to spend another twenty-one days in hotel quarantine.

Travel restrictions and border closures during the pandemic portend a future, under intense global heating, with a walled world . Nations in the Minority World will most likely erect visible and invisible walls to stop those forced to flee their homes because of climate impacts from getting into their territories. The border crisis at the United States–Mexico border in 2020 is illustrative of this scenario (Correa and Simpson, 2022). When farmers from El Salvador and other South American countries fled north from weather extremes – either intense storms or prolonged drought or, worse, a combination – that devastated their crops and decimated their livelihoods, they were met at the United States border not with a warm welcome but with intense surveillance (Reichman, 2022; Andrasko, 2022).

According to the United Nations High Commissioner for Refugees (United Nations, 2022), the number of persons forcibly displaced around the world has increased significantly over the past ten years, reaching at least 100 million people. The organisation's estimations suggest that the number of refugees falling within its purview has roughly quadrupled since 2012 due to several wars, such as those in Ukraine and Syria, and the Rohingya crisis in Myanmar (United Nations, 2022).

Because of war, economic instability, and the effects of climate change, an increasing number of people are being driven from their homes against their will. With the climate crisis, this trend is expected to continue (Askland et al., 2022; Siddiqui, 2022). The number of forced climate migrants is already increasing at a rate even faster than that at which the global population is growing. Instead of focusing on establishing policies to protect refugees and migrants, a number of nations have strengthened their borders to keep out migrants (Turner and Bailey, 2022).

In the last fifty years, more than fifty walls have been built along international borders – or even within inside occupied regions (Linebarger and Braithwaite, 2022). Governments in Australia, the European Union, and the United States have progressively outsourced the management of their borders to other nations, preventing displaced individuals from entering their territories. In addition, they have been monitoring borders, which has led to the unjust deportation and harsh treatment of migrants and refugees (Heidbrink, 2022; Panter-Brick, 2021). Since governments now increasingly rely on artificial intelligence and biometrics to defend their borders, the obstacles to entry are now both physical and digital (Smith and Miller, 2022; Radziwinowiczówna, 2022; Nedelcu and Soysüren, 2022).

Businesses that profit from providing border facilities exert pressure on governments to adopt more militarised migration policies (Akkerman, 2021; Panebianco, 2022; Correa and Simpson, 2022). The border and surveillance sector is so lucrative that it is now much-needed by major investment corporations, which invest on behalf of university endowments and pension funds (Akkerman, 2021).

Private companies are fighting for, supporting, and benefitting from an expanded border and surveillance sector, despite governments putting in place laws restricting these border operations. Indeed, the administration of international borders is now increasingly being contracted out to private corporations that specialise in the provision of surveillance technologies and services (Akkerman, 2021).

Due to the privatisation of border control, refugees and migrants are subjected to increasingly severe human rights violations (Akkerman, 2021; Panebianco, 2022; Correa and Simpson, 2022). In contrast, the actors implicated in continuing these violations are being held less responsible. The levels of violence and abuse of refugees and migrants at borders are at an all-time high, and, in many instances, there are no checks and balances in place.

Contemporary migration has been depicted as a danger to national security by politicians and corporations on the political right who have business interests and a motivation to see the border security sector flourish (McConnon, 2022). In the European Union, and more broadly in the Minority World, migration is being portrayed as a risk to 'their' economic success and to national identity. Describing the entry of migrants and refugees as a threat to economies and security necessitates a security response, which the border security sector is, of course, best positioned to supply (McConnon, 2022).

Branding immigrants as threats to national security has therefore led to a meteoric rise in the border and surveillance business (McConnon, 2022; Akkerman, 2021). This expansion has been supported by a boom in immigration and border control funding, which saw a surge of more than 6,000 per cent in the United States alone during the last decade (Akkerman, 2021). The industry that deals with borders and surveillance is growing in four ways. The first is via border security, as the production and acquisition of equipment and technology increases to police borders and deter refugees from entering. The second is via biometrics with cutting-edge technology for fingerprinting, iris scans, and social media surveillance. The third is via consulting, including lobbying governments to implement stricter border policies. The fourth is via migrant detainment and expulsion (Akkerman, 2021).

People who have been forced to leave their homes are most affected by the growing border and surveillance sector. Refugees and migrants are now being watched at the borders by drones in the sky (Koslowski, 2021) or by their online activity on social media (Bankston, 2021). The militarisation of borders in the Minority World has made migrants more vulnerable to violence and forced them to take more dangerous routes (Correa and Simpson, 2022; Akkerman, 2021). There have also been many complaints about the violation of refugees' and migrants' human rights while in custody (Costello and Mann, 2020).

Holding border and surveillance corporations responsible is more challenging, since these private businesses are not subject to the legal requirements typically imposed on government agencies. It would also be difficult to hold governments liable for contracting out border surveillance to the private sector. Demanding that investment corporations remove pensions and university endowments from businesses that perpetuate the abuse of migrants and refugees is the most effective course of action (Halcoussis and Lowenberg, 2019). Firms depend on investors' funds to stay afloat, especially those in the border and security sector. A decision to diversify their holdings would make it more difficult for them to continue their business. The fossil fuel divestment movement illustrates how social, political, and economic pressure can be exerted for the institutional divestment of bonds and stocks in companies involved in border and surveillance operations (Cojoianu et al., 2021).

However, the Minority World–Majority World divide is not only manifested in terms of physical walls. There is also a widening data gap. As the COVID-19 pandemic spread worldwide, data and statistics were reported in the news. We kept track of the number of tests that have been conducted. We monitored the increase in the overall number of people who tested positive for the virus. We expressed our sorrow for the deceased by looking at the daily death toll.

These figures and statistics, however, are firmly buried in their socio-economic and political geographies. This is not only due to the virus following its unique transmission trajectories, but also to the uniqueness in the way nations and institutions gather their statistics. It is evident that the facts that get computed come to exist in public policy and in people's imaginations. Our capacity to sympathise, show compassion for one another, and contribute to relief operations is influenced by numbers. For an issue to exist, and for a nation or a particular social reality to be located on the world map of concerns, numbers must also be available. However, the vast majority of countries in the Majority World are almost entirely missing from the numbered narrative of the pandemic (Naudé and Vinuesa, 2021; Milan and Treré, 2020).

The absence of reliable statistics from the Majority World during this time of misery indicates how the number of climate migrants and populations affected by weather extremes now and in the future could simply be erased. If the significance of the pandemic and other crises is directly proportional to the number of affected people, we need to pay attention to the ability – and inability – of many countries in the Majority World to produce reliable statistics.

What is evident is the perilous equation of 'no data equals no issue' (Milan and Treré, 2020). The lack of reliable statistics underlines the inability of governments in the Majority World to provide adequate medical care for their citizens. The challenge is not only due to the data gap but also the questionable quality of the data itself. Even in 'normal' circumstances, it is challenging to secure accountability from Majority World governments. One can only imagine how it could be when emergencies cascade.

The lack of Majority World governments' capacity to produce reliable data risks their countries falling victim to the burgeoning genetic testing industry (cf., Degiuseppe et al., 2021). Private businesses may fill the void created by governments by mapping communities in danger, all the while making money from this data (e.g., Oliver et al., 2020). Private actors could also offer essential services, such as food resources, that resource-starved nations in the Majority World cannot provide for their citizens. The skewed and sometimes covert goals of profit-driven players, however, shed light on the inadequacies and risks associated with these actors.

The absence of trustworthy numbers that can correctly reflect the state of the crisis – the pandemic, in this case – as it extends to the Majority World also provides fertile ground for misleading and harmful narratives that can be mobilised for political objectives (e.g., McKee et al., 2021; Gerbaudo, 2021). Populist leaders, such as the Philippines' Rodrigo Duterte, who used the pandemic to amass more power and to crack down on rights and freedoms, delayed early lockdowns claiming that COVID-19 was just ordinary flu when the evidence at the time already pointed to the contrary. Because there is a shortage of reliable data and testing, potentially harmful statements, assumptions, and attitudes have arisen (Gallotti et al., 2020).

The lack of reliable data from the Majority World also proved detrimental to effective pandemic response. As a result, modelling the spread of the virus has been challenging (Naudé and Vinuesa, 2021). There was a strong temptation to 'import' models and 'appropriate' projections based on the socio-economic realities of other nations and then to establish local policies and actions based on them (Naudé and Vinuesa, 2021). It is easy, particularly in these times of global uncertainty, to 'universalise' the issues and the remedies. When one universalises a concept, however, erroneous assumptions are made that the problem occurs in precisely the same way in every location, ignoring regional specifics and 'alternative' methods of solving it.

Experts in open data, researchers, life science scholars, and activists for digital rights, to name but a few, must contribute to 'fixing' the widening data divide. This gap in knowledge severely weakened any local efforts to curb the expansion of the pandemic to populations already at the margins. The same will be said when weather extremes become typical in the climate emergency era. Addressing data divide issues is about providing much-required resources and designing mechanisms for governments to work together. This means expediting the process of enhancing the capacity of developing nations to engage in the activity of counting.

References

Akkerman, M. (2021). *Financing Border Wars: The Border Industry, Its Financiers and Human Rights*. Transnational Institute.

Andrasko, B. (2022). Looking ahead: A human security perspective to tackling the potential for widespread environmental migration in Latin America. In H. Gupta, F. Kruidbos, & A. Parlow (Eds.), *The Climate–Conflict–Displacement Nexus from a Human Security Perspective* (pp. 71–110). Cham: Springer.

Askland, H. H., Shannon, B., Chiong, R., Lockart, N., Maguire, A., Rich, J., & Groizard, (2022). Beyond migration: A critical review of climate change induced displacement. *Environmental Sociology*, *8*(3), 267–278.

Bankston, J. (2021). Migration and smuggling across virtual borders: A European Union case study of internet governance and immigration politics. In *Digital Identity, Virtual Borders and Social Media*. Cheltenham, UK: Edward Elgar Publishing.

Cojoianu, T. F., Ascui, F., Clark, G. L., Hoepner, A. G., & Wójcik, D. (2021). Does the fossil fuel divestment movement impact new oil and gas fundraising? *Journal of Economic Geography*, *21*(1), 141–164.

Correa, J. G., & Simpson, J. M. (2022). Building walls, destroying borderlands: Repertoires of militarization on the United States–Mexico border. *Nature and Culture*, *17*(1), 1–25.

Costello, C., & Mann, I. (2020). Border justice: Migration and accountability for human rights violations. *German Law Journal*, *21*(3), 311–334.

Degiuseppe, J. I., Roitman, K. L., Rivero, K. A., & Stupka, J. A. (2021). Norovirus passive surveillance as an alternative strategy for genetic diversity assessment in developing countries. *Journal of Infection and Public Health*, *14*(8), 990–993.

Gallotti, R., Valle, F., Castaldo, N., Sacco, P., & De Domenico, M. (2020). Assessing the risks of 'infodemics' in response to COVID-19 epidemics. *Nature Human Behaviour*, *4*(12), 1285–1293.

Gerbaudo, P. (2021). *The Great Recoil: Politics After Populism and Pandemic*. London: Verso Books.

Halcoussis, D., & Lowenberg, A. D. (2019). The effects of the fossil fuel divestment campaign on stock returns. *North American Journal of Economics and Finance*, *47*, 669–674.

Heidbrink, L. (2022). 'How can I have a future?': The temporal violence of deportation. *Journal of Intercultural Studies*, *43*(4), 480–496.

Koslowski, R. (2021). Drones and border control: An examination of state and non-state actor use of UAVs along borders. In M. MacAuliffe (Ed.), *Research Handbook on International Migration and Digital Technology* (pp. 152–165). Cheltenham: Edward Elgar Publishing.

Linebarger, C., & Braithwaite, A. (2022). Why do leaders build walls? Domestic politics, leader survival, and the fortification of borders. *Journal of Conflict Resolution*, *66*(4–5), 704–728.

McConnon, E. (2022). People as security risks: The framing of migration in the UK security–development nexus. *Journal of Ethnic and Migration Studies*, *48*(6), 1381–1397.

McKee, M., Gugushvili, A., Koltai, J., & Stuckler, D. (2021). Are populist leaders creating the conditions for the spread of COVID-19? Comment on 'A scoping review of populist radical right parties' influence on welfare policy and its implications for population health in Europe'. *International Journal of Health Policy and Management*, *10*(8), 511–515.

Milan, S., & Treré, E. (2020). The rise of the data poor: The COVID-19 pandemic seen from the margins. *Social Media + Society*, *6*(3).

Naudé, W., & Vinuesa, R. (2021). Data deprivations, data gaps and digital divides: Lessons from the COVID-19 pandemic. *Big Data & Society*, *8*(2), 20539517211025545.

Nedelcu, M., & Soysüren, I. (2022). Precarious migrants, migration regimes and digital technologies: The empowerment–control nexus. *Journal of Ethnic and Migration Studies*, *48*(8), 1821–1837.

Oliver, N., Lepri, B., Sterly, H., Lambiotte, R., Deletaille, S., De Nadai, M., ... & Vinck, P. (2020). Mobile phone data for informing public health actions across the COVID-19 pandemic life cycle. *Science Advances*, *6*(23), eabc0764.

Panebianco, S. (2022). The EU and migration in the Mediterranean: EU borders' control by proxy. *Journal of Ethnic and Migration Studies*, *48*(6), 1398–1416.

Panter-Brick, C. (2021). Solidarity, social justice, and faith: Humanitarian action on the US–Mexico border. *Journal of Refugee Studies*, *34*(4), 3688–3709.

Radziwinowiczówna, A. (2022). Bare life in an immigration jail: Technologies of surveillance in US pre-deportation detention. *Journal of Ethnic and Migration Studies*, *48*(8), 1873–1890.

Reichman, D. R. (2022). Putting climate-induced migration in context: The case of Honduran migration to the USA. *Regional Environmental Change*, *22*(3), 1–10.

Siddiqui, T. (2022). Climate change and displacement: Locating the most vulnerable groups. In H. Khondker, O. Muurlink, & A. Bin Ali (Eds.), *The Emergence of Bangladesh* (pp. 259–272). London: Palgrave Macmillan.

Smith, M., & Miller, S. (2022). The ethical application of biometric facial recognition technology. *AI & Society*, *37*(1), 167–175.

Turner, J., & Bailey, D. (2022). 'Ecobordering': Casting immigration control as environmental protection. *Environmental Politics*, *31*(1), 110–131.

United Nations (2022). UNHCR: A record 100 million people forcibly displaced worldwide. *UN News*, 23 May.

5
Obscene Opulence

As the climate emergency worsens, the wealthiest will suffer from it the least. This is despite the disproportionate contribution of the uber rich in the Minority World – most of whom live obscenely in their opulence – to the continuing climate crisis. In contrast, poor-people – most of them living in the Majority World – will be hit hardest and most severely by the effects of rapid global heating.

During the first wave of the COVID-19 pandemic, the wealth of the world's 2,000 billionaires surged by more than a quarter between April and July 2020, when the pandemic was at its peak (Ahmed et al., 2022). This global inequality data is based on the Forbes Billionaires List as well as the annual Credit Suisse Global Wealth report, which gives the distribution of global wealth dating back to 2000 (Ahmed et al., 2022). Amazon.com provides a perfect illustration of who benefitted from the pandemic as shoppers, trapped in their homes, flocked to the online shopping website (Hunter and Nida, 2021). The company's profit in the first three months of 2021 was a record US$8.1 billion, more than triple what it was in the same period during 2020 (Ahmed et al., 2022). This indicates the persistence of the neo-liberal paradigm that allows the wealthiest to gain obscenely excessive amounts of money.

Neo-liberalism, which rose to prominence towards the end of the 1970s, is being pursued by the majority of countries today. China's authoritarian capitalism is on a comparable path (Petry, 2021). Transnational businesses – the most visible evidence of neo-liberalism at work – may include certain multi-stakeholder projects, but they seldom participate in democratic change (Boissiere, 2022). Countries have taken economic action at the state level, including increased public sector spending (Busemeyer, 2021; Romer, 2021; Hartman et al., 2022), yet the private sector typically benefits the most from these economic trends.

Inequality grows as the rich get richer and the poor get poorer (Piketty, 2015). There are no boundaries when it comes to amassing wealth. However, it does appear to be a universal truth that there is always a significant crime preceding a considerable fortune. Those who possess enormous wealth inevitably have massive impacts on the natural environment, regardless of whether or not they intend to do so (Fairbrother, 2013; Alcott, 2008). The extremely wealthy are responsible for ecological genocide, and this is almost always the case, without exception.

Income is, by a significant margin, the most crucial factor in determining the impact on the natural environment. It makes no difference how environmentally conscious one believes one is. If one has extra money, it is spent on fuel for transportation, energy for the home, and other materials that people consume.

The psychological effects of wealth only compound the already disastrous effects of spending power on the individual. Studies have shown that a person's ability to connect with others decreases in direct proportion to their level of wealth (cf., Sun et al., 2019; Kraus et al., 2012). Affluence is thus a barrier to empathy.

As the climate emergency worsens, the wealthy will suffer the least – and less severely from it – even though they are disproportionately responsible for the crisis (Mendelsohn, Dinar, and Williams, 2006). By contrast, poor people will suffer the most and be hardest hit by the impacts of accelerating global heating.

Even those with the best intentions can have their perspectives narrowed by their wealth, which is another problem. For example, in an interview with *The Financial Times* in September 2019, billionaire Bill Gates argued that divesting from fossil fuels is a waste of time. Instead, Gates argued that it would be more prudent to invest in innovative new technologies that produce fewer emissions. While it is true that climate action requires the deployment of renewable energy technologies, as Gates advocates, he has still missed the most critical point. In the fight to avert a climate catastrophe, what matters most is not what you do but what you refrain from doing. This is where the fossil fuel divestment movement, a branch of the global climate action movement, matters. Take, for example, the case of a homeowner putting up solar photovoltaic panels on their rooftop. It makes no difference how many panels they set up if they do not also turn off their gas stoves. Gas is a fossil fuel that needs to be replaced with cleaner cooking fuel sources.

This is the situation just in the home. Magnify it to the context of a city or a country. There is little chance that global heating can be prevented from exceeding 1.5°C if coal-fired power plants already in operation are not shut down before the end of their useful lives. An honest and genuine energy transition requires the replacement of fossil fuel assets with market-ready renewable energy solutions. Furthermore, deploying solar and wind farms will not make sense if efforts to discover and develop new fossil fuel reserves, including natural gas, are continued.

Structural changes must be made to achieve a true and just energy transition. This shift necessitates both political and technological innovation: two concepts which, unfortunately, are loathed by the billionaire class. Very few of them – if any at all – will admit that money is not a magic wand that can make the climate crisis disappear.

The neo-liberal idea that everyone works to increase their wealth to the greatest extent possible is the foundation upon which many governments and economists base their policies. If we complete that mission of making everyone wealthy, we will unavoidably destroy the systems that are keeping us alive in the first place. If the middle class lived like oligarchs, everything would fall apart. The relentless quest for riches in a world with plenty, albeit extremely unequally distributed, is a recipe for widespread impoverishment.

There is a great deal of innovative thinking coming to the forefront in many countries due to advocacy for more equitable economic systems. This thinking addresses superfluous opulence and asks what it means to have enough and how we will know when we have enough. Belgian philosopher Ingrid Robeyns (2022) calls this *economic limitarianism*. Robeyns (2022) contends that social improvement can be achieved by placing a specific limit on personal wealth. Capping this wealth means regulating the total income and wealth an individual can accumulate.

A limitation to wealth corresponds well w the widely understood concept of 'limit to poverty'. Limitarianism acknowledges rich and poverty lines: the latter is the minimum below which no one should fall; the former is the maximum over which no one should climb. The unfortunate reality is that the wealthy are only able to live the lifestyles they do because others are unable to do so as well. There is simply not enough room, physically or ecologically, for everyone to seek extreme opulence. With this limit recognised, everyone should be working towards achieving individual sufficiency. Moderation is thus essential to the continuation of life on Earth.

In a community inside Pa Deng, Thailand's oldest national park, households claim to practice living in self-sufficiency and moderation. This community lives according to what is called in Thai *sethakit por piang*, loosely translated as 'sufficiency economy', guided by the principles of 'MoSo' or 'moderation society'. During my field work in Pa Deng in 2016, I observed how a network of around 100 households joined together to pursue sustainable energy projects. The network adopted community-based economics based on principles of mutual help and trust to expand the scope and scale of household-based biogas cooking fuel and solar home systems (Delina, 2021, 2022). The impacts of this transition to renewable energy systems were varied. These included increased household savings, new employment opportunities (especially for women), the acquisition of new skills, and improved community cohesion (Delina, 2022).

The Pa Deng MoSo network is one of many self-help organisations in the world. It is very encouraging to learn that 12 per cent of the world's population belongs to at least one of the three million cooperatives that are in operation (cf., Candemir, Duvaleix, and Latruffe, 2021). Before moving to academia, I was a development banker in the Philippines, extending funding and institutional support to cooperatives, most of which were agricultural. Doing development work in the Philippine countryside was a meaningful experience. It made me appreciate how people can converge for mutual objectives and seek opportunities to improve their well-being.

While a number of these groups eventually succeed and thrive (e.g., Pahnke, 2015), it is important to note that there are also those whose existence is quickly cut short due to funding issues (e.g., Basterretxea, Cornforth, and Heras-Saizarbitoria, 2022). Nevertheless, this does not suggest that 'failure' means losing hope. In contrast, it only suggests that more work is needed to ensure that cooperatives and other mutual assistance groups thrive. Renewable energy cooperatives have proved to be important organisations in the energy transition (e.g., Heras-Saizarbitoria et al., 2018; Yildiz et al., 2015; Huybrechts and Mertens, 2014). Scaling them and ensuring that more cooperatives support the transition are important.

Public knowledge on environmental sustainability, especially climate action, has significantly increased in several countries, including in the Majority World. People's recurrent experiences of severe weather events are finally influencing public opinion (e.g., Brosch, 2021). As understanding of climate change and the need to mitigate its impacts by shifting to renewables increases, it is notable that renewable energy technologies have also advanced rapidly, at the same time as their costs have declined.

The crucial obstacle to expanding the scale and scope of renewable energy deployment is that the neo-liberal system has not reacted quickly enough to take advantage of innovation and cost declines. Political cooperation between governments is still hopelessly constrained, especially with regard to technology and funding transfer from the Minority World to the Majority World (Roberts et al., 2021).

In addition, the military–industrial complex also continues to be deeply ingrained in the control paradigm (Alic, 2021; Dunlap, 2011). The war-promoting military–industrial complexes have a strong position in the cultures of many countries, including the United States, China, Russia, the United Kingdom, France, India, and other large economies. In 2021, at the height of the pandemic, the United States, Australia, and the United Kingdom were able to move from failing in Afghanistan to fighting a trade war with China in just over a month. This was a big accomplishment for the military–industrial complex. If resources can be made available for the armed forces, why are they not readily available for the climate emergency?

The current trajectory, epitomised by increased militarisation, continues while the world is on fire. In this scenario, the 2020s will, first and foremost, be marked by the persistent issue of nationalism, perversely powered by the fuel of neoliberalism (cf., Lueck, Due, and Augoustinos, 2015). Already, the COVID-19 pandemic has revealed, in full view, the vast inequality between those who have the resources and those who do not (Ahmed et al., 2020; Yamin, 2022). Testing and vaccination became key inequity issues, separating the Minority World from the Majority World (Tatar et al., 2021; Oehler and Vega, 2021). And even within countries, the gap between the haves and the have-nots became wide and clear (DiRago et al., 2022). As the climate system continues to break down, revealed in more extreme weather occurrences, other gaps and inequalities will lead to catastrophic loss of life and chronic suffering (Cappelli, Costantini, and Consoli, 2021). Those in the Majority World stand to experience this misery more harshly than those whose past actions led to accelerating global heating.

There will be attempts to fix inequality, but they will not work out the way people in the Majority World want. By the end of the 2020s, the world will probably be a lot less safe than it is now. The anger and resentment of the majority of people who are left out (e.g., Sherman, 2021), especially the hundreds of millions in the Majority World, will make people, regardless of where they live, feel even less safe (e.g., Nyiwul, 2021; Ujunwa et al., 2021). Global insecurity makes it even more important to act quickly; yet, the pressures associated with human migration will only strengthen the 'build the wall' mindset of wealthy countries in the Minority World (Ahuja, 2021).

The cumulative effects of these trends will cause marginalised groups to stage much more widespread uprisings, which will most likely result in profound instability that will be confronted with force, further exacerbating people's rage. We saw this most recently in Sri Lanka, where, at the height of the COVID-19 pandemic, the Sri Lankan people mobilised against the government of Gotabaya Rajapaksa (Biyanwila, 2022). This mobilisation was the result of Rajapaksa's alleged mismanagement of the Sri Lankan economy, which led to an economic crisis and severe inflation, and, in turn, resulted in a decline in the supply of essential items, including fuel and electricity (Biyanwila, 2022).

Soon, the situation worldwide will further deteriorate to such an extent that societies, including those that are particularly affluent and powerful, will be compelled to undergo profound transformations. The pressure of change will become too tremendous to resist. However, this will only be the case when an alternative dilemma is too awful even to consider, and there will already have been several disasters. A world becoming increasingly hotter portends miseries, violence, and conflict.

The genuinely important work, therefore, is to quicken the pace of sociotechnical transitions – and the remaining years of this decade will be crucial. Either we continue down the path we are currently on, bringing about some improvements that are desirable but moving at a pace that is far too slow to avert disaster, or we speed up the processes that need to be carried out to bring about a more just and sustainable world order sooner, with fewer casualties and fewer adverse effects on the environment. The choice is ours.

Moving forward, we must redesign the economic system that opened the floodgates to vast inequality. To that end, we need a tax structure that helps ensure a fair recovery from crises and keeps up with the rapid speed of the required transition (cf., Gunderson and Fyock, 2022). Those impacted the hardest during the COVID-19 pandemic should not be forced to pay more. This also includes those already carrying the burden of extreme weather events, such as those living in typhoon-prone areas and those forced to migrate away from their previously productive lands.

Several proposals have been made to improve our current method of levying taxes. The first is the imposition of a one-time windfall tax on earnings gained during the pandemic (MaCartney, Montgomerie, and Tepe, 2022; Berkey, 2021; Azémar et al., 2022). There is nothing novel about windfall taxes. In my work on what can be learned in respect of climate policy from the mobilisations for the Second World War, I noted that taxes on excess profits were instituted to support the war effort (Delina, 2016; Delina and Diesendorf, 2013). In a global climate emergency, initiating this type of levy on the wealthy, on a similar basis, is one option.

The Green New Deal is another approach to the climate crisis, as well as post-pandemic recovery. One example is the European Green Deal, which was adopted by the European Commission to reduce the continent's carbon emissions to net zero by 2050 (Bloomfield and Steward, 2020). Nevertheless, any proposal for a Green New Deal must be examined closely. One criticism, for example, contends that Franklin Delano Roosevelt's original New Deal, which served as the theoretical foundation for Green New Deals, was mainly geared towards preserving social order during the Great Depression and, as a consequence, maintained the capitalist status quo. Similarly, some doubt Green New Deals because they do not challenge the underlying underpinnings of the neo-liberal economic paradigm (Samper, Schockling, and Islar, 2021).

Another point at issue is that Green New Deals continue to hold to the notion that it is feasible to entirely decouple economic development from the effects that economic production has on the environment. In short, the Green New Deal strategy assumes we can achieve green growth while significantly lowering our emissions.

A third contentious issue with Green New Deals is their over-reliance on technological innovation and deployment, in the absence of a thorough assessment of what it entails (White, 2020). Although renewables are superior to fossil fuels, renewable energy systems open up challenges around the shortage of and competition for rare earth metals (Månberger and Johansson, 2019; Lee et al., 2020; Li et al., 2020). Since most of these metals are concentrated in the Majority World, which is already harmed by extractivism, the energy transition could exacerbate these ongoing vulnerabilities (Luckeneder et al., 2021; Sovacool, 2021).

Yet another issue with Green New Deals is that they tend to put private benefit ahead of the public interest. The emphasis on the private sector may push businesses to accelerate their greenwashing efforts to portray themselves as essential participants in the energy transition (Aşıcı and Bünül, 2012; McCollum, 2022). Consequently, other participants, such as small and medium-sized enterprises, are eliminated from the process. Most often, Green New Deal proposals have timetables that are too short, require massive investment, and are replete with cumbersome processes that make them less attractive to small-scale players.

There are alternatives to Green New Deal proposals that are better attuned to the needs of the greater good. The Southern Ecosocial Deal, established in Latin America, for example, prioritises the cancellation of foreign debt, tax reforms, public health care systems, universal basic income programmes, and a move away from extractive industries towards decentralised, de-commodified, and democratic renewable energy systems (Ajl, 2021).

Although some Green New Deal proposals have seemingly been co-opted by neo-liberalism, it does not follow that they should not be supported. We need a rapid transition to renewable energy, and these proposals are our best shot at this point. Some – for example, the European Green Deal – have already been adopted, and the fact that Green New Deals have the potential to reach a large and varied audience in a short amount of time is a quality that, given the amount of time we have to prevent a climate disaster, cannot be understated.

The wisest course of action is thus to adopt a two-track approach rather than obstinately choosing sides. We must work towards enhancing current Green New Deals while also lending our support to those who call for a more comprehensive reorganisation of our economy along the lines of justice and equality for all. If one recalls history, the aspirational goals of Roosevelt's New Deal were inspired by working-class mobilisations in the United States. The same is true with the emergence of many Green New Deal proposals during a period of unprecedented climate mobilisation.

One of the critical tenets of any Green New Deal, including those proposed by more progressive groups, is security of livelihoods and income (Cha et al., 2022). The COVID-19 pandemic has revealed how many people need economic assistance. Thus, some level of income security is essential when reorganising economic systems. To that end, a universal basic income (UBI) programme offers a desirable policy option (Ståhl and MacEachen, 2021). This programme gives people monetary relief at a time when governments, organisations, and individuals are struggling to comprehend quickly changing realities, face those challenges, and find their way through them. In a world already altered by the pandemic, and that will continue to be changed by other crises, the implementation of UBI programmes allows for some degree of financial certainty.

Payments made by governments to their citizens in the form of a UBI are intended to serve several purposes (Bidadanure, 2019). A UBI programme seeks to reduce poverty, accelerate economic growth, promote entrepreneurship, and restore employment opportunities eliminated as a result of technological advancement (Bidadanure, 2019). For these programmes to be practical, lessons from prior iterations suggest two essential criteria that need to be met: first, payments should be made to all regardless of their financial circumstances, and second, payments should be made without any condition. I make this case below.

Some countries, including India, Kenya, Canada, Brazil, Finland, and Switzerland, have entertained the idea of implementing UBI programmes. The State of Alaska has the longest-running UBI programme in the United States (Berman, 2018; Feinberg and Kuehn, 2020). With support from oil money, the programme resulted in a decrease in poverty, primarily among Indigenous Peoples. This does not mean, however, that while a UBI programme tends to offer more help for the most vulnerable members of a population than the middle or higher classes, the programme should be limited to them. Universal basic income programmes can also assist middle-class households, especially when the income-earner is in severe sickness or has lost a job, for example. In the absence of a basic income, these situations may lead to financial collapse for many families. A universal basic income, in its most basic definition, thus reduces the amount of insecurity in one's financial future and gives assurances that are not contingent on any particular set of circumstances.

Unemployment and anxieties over future job prospects can arise in a climate emergency. A regular stream of income provided by a UBI programme could offer essential assistance for individuals, including not only the jobless or the underemployed, but also those with higher incomes. In respect of the latter, the programme provides a safety net, allowing people to spend their money more freely if their work situation changes. A UBI programme would thus result in improved confidence and increased expenditure on the part of consumers. As technologies continue to radically alter the concept of work, with automation most likely replacing many in the workforce, a UBI programme can also help in this transition, including those furloughed from their jobs.

The COVID-19 pandemic provided an impetus, showing how this social programme could be undertaken (Ståhl and MacEachen, 2021). This does not mean, however, that UBI programmes will not have repercussions. Redistributing wealth – which is, in a way, what a UBI programme does – can have impacts on other welfare programmes, such as public access to universal education and health. However, the economic advantages of UBI programmes should not be discounted. As already mentioned in respect of the Alaskan case, these include lifting people out of poverty and generating demand from consumers. Over the long run, UBI programmes would, however, incur high costs; hence, designing them properly is important.

With regard to work, the change that the COVID-19 pandemic caused in terms of how we see the benefits of mobility has also been profound. Before the pandemic, travelling across international boundaries was considered a perk for those with high skill levels. The pandemic, however, ushered in a new kind of privilege: immobility. People with specialised knowledge were at an advantage in terms of work opportunities. In 2020, those with resources or talents that enabled them to be mobile, while not suffering economically, hopped the world to ride out the storm (Lustig et al., 2020; Bonaccorsi et al., 2020). Those who did not have these resources or skills remained stationary. People who lack financial resources but have the necessary skill set and a reliable internet connection can now take advantage of newly developed policies, especially those related to working remotely.

When the year 2020 came along and I was stuck in the Philippines, I was also forced to work from home. Because the borders were now blocked, I could not return to Hong Kong. During my time in the Philippines, however, I was able to carry out my teaching and research online. I was there for nearly eighteen months in total. My students would often enquire about whether we were in a farm setting when they heard the sounds of cooing chickens and barking dogs during our Zoom classes.

A new phenomenon thus emerged due to the pandemic: people staying put to work on their terms. The advantage of mobility evolved into the privilege of immobility, the ability to choose to remain in one place while maintaining one's safety (Lazreg and Garnaoui, 2020; Bissell, 2021). Those who had the financial means to carry out their tasks from home could do so. So those whose employers allowed virtual work remained in their homes. I was one of the lucky few.

This luxury of immobility is further shown by the widespread practice of recruiting workers from other nations without requiring them to relocate (Martin and Bergmann, 2021). Employers find it easier to hire staff to work remotely or in virtual offices, while employees find it easier to adapt to their new working conditions. Thus, the expansion of work that may be done from home across many time zones is one of the most significant uncharted territories in the post-pandemic labour market.

As these words are written, two and a half years since the COVID-19 pandemic was declared, it remains too soon to assess the full impact that the pandemic will have on the mobility of people with highly specialised skills. This is due mainly to the fact that data on mobility is not yet fully accessible, and studies are still being conducted. One of the pandemic's most significant repercussions – as it now seems – will be its effect on the future of highly skilled mobility (Kramer and Kramer, 2020). It is possible that, as businesses transition towards virtual office models, international recruiting will become obsolete and the talent competition will shift exclusively to the online sphere. This does not mean, however, that a worker in the Majority World would be paid the same salary that a worker doing the same work in the Minority World receives (Collings and Sheeran, 2020; Gamlen, 2020). This is an injustice that technological improvement and shifting work environments bring.

Thus, as work is de-globalised, inequities will expand. Addressing these inequalities requires capping the profits made by individuals in the Minority World, especially those who profit from the work done by workers in the Majority World and those profiting from any future crisis. Taxing the rich and ensuring that everyone has access to some form of guaranteed basic income is significantly important in addressing this inequality.

References

Ahmed, F., Ahmed, N. E., Pissarides, C., & Stiglitz, J. (2020). Why inequality could spread COVID-19. *The Lancet Public Health*, *5*(5), e240.

Ahmed, N., Marriott, A., Dabi, N., Lowthers, M., Lawson, M., & Mugehera, L. (2022) *Inequality Kills*. Oxfam.

Ahuja, N. (2021). *Planetary Specters: Race, Migration, and Climate Change in the Twenty-First Century.* UNC Press Books.

Ajl, M. (2021). A people's Green New Deal: Obstacles and prospects. *Agrarian South: Journal of Political Economy*, *10*(2), 371–390.

Alcott, B. (2008). The sufficiency strategy: Would rich-world frugality lower environmental impact? *Ecological Economics*, *64*(4), 770–786.

Alic, J. A. (2021). The US Politico–Military–Industrial Complex. In *Oxford Research Encyclopedia of Politics*. Oxford University Press. https://doi.org/10.1093/acrefore/9780190228637.013.1870.

Aşıcı, A. A., & Bünül, Z. (2012). Green New Deal: A green way out of the crisis? *Environmental Policy and Governance*, *22*(5), 295–306.

Azémar, C., Desbordes, R., Melindi-Ghidi, P., & Nicolaï, J. P. (2022). Winners and losers of the COVID-19 pandemic: An excess profits tax proposal. *Journal of Public Economic Theory*, *24*(5), 1016–1038.

Basterretxea, I., Cornforth, C., & Heras-Saizarbitoria, I. (2022). Corporate governance as a key aspect in the failure of worker cooperatives. *Economic and Industrial Democracy*, *43*(1), 362–387.

Berkey, B. (2021). Pandemic windfalls and obligations of justice. *Erasmus Journal for Philosophy and Economics*, *14*(1), 58–70.

Berman, M. (2018). Resource rents, universal basic income, and poverty among Alaska's indigenous peoples. *World Development*, *106*, 161–172.

Bidadanure, J. U. (2019). The political theory of universal basic income. *Annual Review of Political Science*, *22*, 481–501.

Bissell, D. (2021). A changing sense of place: Geography and COVID-19. *Geographical Research*, *59*(2), 150–159.

Biyanwila, J. (2022). Sri Lanka: Behind the popular uprising. *Green Left Weekly*, (1344), 20.

Bloomfield, J., & Steward, F. (2020). The politics of the Green New Deal. *Political Quarterly*, *91*(4), 770–779.

Boissiere, M. A. (2022). Transnational corporate power. *Class, Race and Corporate Power*, *10* (1), Article 3.

Bonaccorsi, G., Pierri, F., Cinelli, M., Flori, A., Galeazzi, A., Porcelli, F., ... & Pammolli, F. (2020). Economic and social consequences of human mobility restrictions under COVID-19. *Proceedings of the National Academy of Sciences*, *117*(27), 15530–15535.

Brosch, T. (2021). Affect and emotions as drivers of climate change perception and action: A review. *Current Opinion in Behavioral Sciences*, *42*, 15–21.

Busemeyer, M. R. (2021). Financing the welfare state in times of extreme crisis: Public support for health care spending during the COVID-19 pandemic in Germany. *Journal of European Public Policy*, 1–20.

Candemir, A., Duvaleix, S., & Latruffe, L. (2021). Agricultural cooperatives and farm sustainability – A literature review. *Journal of Economic Surveys*, *35*(4), 1118–1144.

Cappelli, F., Costantini, V., & Consoli, D. (2021). The trap of climate change-induced 'natural' disasters and inequality. *Global Environmental Change*, *70*, 102329.

Cha, J. M., Stevis, D., Vachon, T. E., Price, V., & Brescia-Weiler, M. (2022). A Green New Deal for all: The centrality of a worker and community-led just transition in the US. *Political Geography*, *95*, 102594.

Collings, D. G., & Sheeran, R. (2020). Research insights: Global mobility in a post-COVID world. *Irish Journal of Management*, *39*(2), 77–84.

Delina, L. L. (2016). *Strategies for Rapid Climate Mitigation: Wartime Mobilisation as a Model for Action?* Abingdon, UK: Routledge.

Delina, L. L. (2021). Participation in nondemocracies: Rural Thailand as a site of energy democracy. In A. M. Feldpausch-Parker, D. Endres, T. Rai Peterson, & S. L. Gomez (Eds.), *Routledge Handbook of Energy Democracy* (pp. 270–279). Abingdon, UK: Routledge.

Delina, L. L. (2022). Co-producing just energy transition in everyday practices: Sociotechnical innovation and sustainable development in the Thailand–Myanmar border. *Local Environment, 27*(1), 16–31.

Delina, L. L., & Diesendorf, M. (2013). Is wartime mobilisation a suitable policy model for rapid national climate mitigation? *Energy Policy, 58*, 371–380.

DiRago, N. V., Li, M., Tom, T., Schupmann, W., Carrillo, Y., Carey, C. M., & Gaddis, S. M. (2022). COVID-19 vaccine rollouts and the reproduction of urban spatial inequality: Disparities within large US cities in March and April 2021 by racial/ethnic and socioeconomic composition. *Journal of Urban Health, 99*(2), 191–207.

Dunlap Jr, C. J. (2011). The military–industrial complex. *Daedalus, 140*(3), 135–147.

Fairbrother, M. (2013). Rich people, poor people, and environmental concern: Evidence across nations and time. *European Sociological Review, 29*(5), 910–922.

Feinberg, R. M., & Kuehn, D. (2020). Does a guaranteed basic income encourage entrepreneurship? Evidence from Alaska. *Review of Industrial Organization, 57*(3), 607–626.

Gamlen, A. (2020). Migration and mobility after the 2020 pandemic: The end of an age. Working Paper No. 146, Centre on Migration, Policy and Society, University of Oxford.

Gunderson, R., & Fyock, C. (2022). Are fossil fuel CEOs responsible for climate change? Social structure and criminal law approaches to climate litigation. *Journal of Environmental Studies and Sciences, 12*(2), 378–385.

Hartman, M., Martin, A. B., Washington, B., Catlin, A., & National Health Expenditure Accounts Team. (2022). National health care spending in 2020: Growth driven by federal spending in response to the COVID-19 pandemic. *Health Affairs, 41*(1), 13–25.

Heras-Saizarbitoria, I., Sáez, L., Allur, E., & Morandeira, J. (2018). The emergence of renewable energy cooperatives in Spain: A review. *Renewable and Sustainable Energy Reviews, 94*, 1036–1043.

Hunter, R. E., & Nida, R. A. (2021). Compulsive shoppers flourish on Amazon during COVID-19 pandemic. *Journal of Medical Science and Clinical Research, 9*(03), 87–93.

Huybrechts, B., & Mertens, S. (2014). The relevance of the cooperative model in the field of renewable energy. *Annals of Public and Cooperative Economics, 85*(2), 193–212.

Kramer, A., & Kramer, K. Z. (2020). The potential impact of the COVID-19 pandemic on occupational status, work from home, and occupational mobility. *Journal of Vocational Behavior, 119*, 103442.

Kraus, M. W., Piff, P. K., Mendoza-Denton, R., Rheinschmidt, M. L., & Keltner, D. (2012). Social class, solipsism, and contextualism: How the rich are different from the poor. *Psychological Review, 119*(3), 546–572.

Lazreg, H. B., & Garnaoui, W. (2020). Reversal of (im)mobility privilege and borders during COVID-19. *E-International Relations*, 18 May.

Lee, J., Bazilian, M., Sovacool, B., Hund, K., Jowitt, S. M., Nguyen, T. P., ... & Kukoda, S. (2020). Reviewing the material and metal security of low-carbon energy transitions. *Renewable and Sustainable Energy Reviews*, *124*, 109789.

Li, J., Peng, K., Wang, P., Zhang, N., Feng, K., Guan, D., ... & Yang, Q. (2020). Critical rare-earth elements mismatch global wind-power ambitions. *One Earth*, *3*(1), 116–125.

Luckeneder, S., Giljum, S., Schaffartzik, A., Maus, V., & Tost, M. (2021). Surge in global metal mining threatens vulnerable ecosystems. *Global Environmental Change*, *69*, 102303.

Lueck, K., Due, C., & Augoustinos, M. (2015). Neoliberalism and nationalism: Representations of asylum seekers in the Australian mainstream news media. *Discourse & Society*, *26*(5), 608–629.

Lustig, N., Pabon, V. M., Sanz, F., & Younger, S. D. (2020). *The Impact of COVID-19 Lockdowns and Expanded Social Assistance on Inequality, Poverty and Mobility in Argentina, Brazil, Colombia and Mexico*. Center for Global Development, Washington, DC.

Macartney, H., Montgomerie, J., & Tepe, D. (2022). A windfall at the top. In H. Macartney, J. Montgomerie, & D. Tepe (Eds.), *The Fault Lines of Inequality* (pp. 37–55). Cham: Palgrave Macmillan.

Månberger, A., & Johansson, B. (2019). The geopolitics of metals and metalloids used for the renewable energy transition. *Energy Strategy Reviews*, *26*, 100394.

Martin, S., & Bergmann, J. (2021). (Im)mobility in the age of COVID-19. *International Migration Review*, *55*(3), 660–687.

McCollum, J. (2022). Avoiding the pitfalls of capitalism in the Green New Deal. In J. McCollum (Ed.), *Routledge Handbook on the Green New Deal* (pp. 73–87). Abingdon, UK: Routledge.

Mendelsohn, R., Dinar, A., & Williams, L. (2006). The distributional impact of climate change on rich and poor countries. *Environment and Development Economics*, *11*(2), 159–178.

Nyiwul, L. (2021). Climate change adaptation and inequality in Africa: Case of water, energy and food insecurity. *Journal of Cleaner Production*, *278*, 123393.

Oehler, R. L., & Vega, V. R. (2021). Conquering COVID: How global vaccine inequality risks prolonging the pandemic. *Open Forum Infectious Diseases*, 8 (10), ofab443.

Pahnke, A. (2015). Institutionalizing economies of opposition: Explaining and evaluating the success of the MST's cooperatives and agroecological repeasantization. *Journal of Peasant Studies*, *42*(6), 1087–1107.

Petry, J. (2021). Same, but different: Varieties of capital markets, Chinese state capitalism and the global financial order. *Competition & Change*, *25*(5), 605–630.

Piketty, T. (2015). *The Economics of Inequality*. Cambridge, MA: Harvard University Press.

Roberts, J. T., Weikmans, R., Robinson, S. A., Ciplet, D., Khan, M., & Falzon, D. (2021). Rebooting a failed promise of climate finance. *Nature Climate Change*, *11*(3), 180–182.

Robeyns, I. (2022). Why limitarianism? *Journal of Political Philosophy*, *30*(2), 249–270.

Romer, C. D. (2021). The fiscal policy response to the pandemic. *Brookings Papers on Economic Activity*, (Spring), 89–110.

Samper, J. A., Schockling, A., & Islar, M. (2021). Climate politics in green deals: Exposing the political frontiers of the European Green Deal. *Politics and Governance*, *9*(2), 8–16.

Sherman, J. (2021). *Dividing Paradise: Rural Inequality and the Diminishing American Dream*. Oakland: University of California Press.

Sovacool, B. K. (2021). Who are the victims of low-carbon transitions? Towards a political ecology of climate change mitigation. *Energy Research & Social Science*, *73*, 101916.

Ståhl, C., & MacEachen, E. (2021). Universal basic income as a policy response to COVID-19 and precarious employment: Potential impacts on rehabilitation and return-to-work. *Journal of Occupational Rehabilitation*, *31*(1), 3–6.

Sun, R., Vuillier, L., Hui, B. P., & Kogan, A. (2019). Caring helps: Trait empathy is related to better coping strategies and differs in the poor versus the rich. *PLoS One*, *14*(3), e0213142.

Tatar, M., Shoorekchali, J. M., Faraji, M. R., & Wilson, F. A. (2021). International COVID-19 vaccine inequality amid the pandemic: Perpetuating a global crisis? *Journal of Global Health*, 12, 3072.

Ujunwa, A., Okoyeuzu, C., Nkwor, N., & Ujunwa, A. (2021). Potential impact of climate change and armed conflict on inequality in Sub-Saharan Africa. *South African Journal of Economics*, *89*(4), 480–498.

White, D. (2020). Just transitions/design for transitions: Preliminary notes on a design politics for a Green New Deal. *Capitalism Nature Socialism*, *31*(2), 20–39.

Yamin, D. (2022). Vaccine inequality benefits no one. *Nature Human Behaviour*, *6*(2), 177–178.

Yildiz, Ö., Rommel, J., Debor, S., Holstenkamp, L., Mey, F., Müller, J. R., ... & Rognli, J. (2015). Renewable energy cooperatives as gatekeepers or facilitators? Recent developments in Germany and a multidisciplinary research agenda. *Energy Research & Social Science*, *6*, 59–73.

6
Climate Nationalism

An isolated approach to climate action hinged on nationalism and built on the superiority complexes of countries in the Minority World will not be enough to address the climate emergency. Climate multilateralism, despite its imperfections, remains a potent tool for addressing the tragedies of our commons.

On June 21, 2021, in my village centre in the southern Philippines, I got my first shot of the COVID-19 vaccine, which came from the small number of Sinovac doses that have made it to the Majority World. As someone with more than one underlying illness (I have asthma), I was in my country's 'priority sector' and was able to get the vaccine. At that time, less than 0.5 per cent of Filipinos were fully vaccinated, while about 40 per cent of Americans were fully vaccinated (cf., Asundi, O'Leary, and Bhadelia, 2021). I was one of those who got lucky.

By the end of that month, more than a billion doses of the COVID-19 vaccine had already been given. Over 80 per cent of these were given to people in the Minority World, while only 0.2 per cent went to people in the Minority World, like me (cf., Burki, 2021). During this time, India suffered a horrifying surge of the virus, with over 4,000 deaths recorded daily. Only 2 per cent of India's population had been fully vaccinated at that time.

At times of global misery, countries in the Majority World have unfair access to life-saving tools – in this case, vaccines. Nationalistic views took priority over international cooperation (Nhamo et al., 2021; Zhou, 2022). In parallel, populists have been ascending to political power, championing economic nationalism clothed with protectionist schemes advocated via xenophobic speech (Elias et al., 2021; Nourbakhsh et al., 2022). Populists sketch the 'national interest' as outside the purview of international peace and inclusive development in an interdependent world. Nationalists gape at global institutions with cynicism, if not hostility, ignoring the significance of international cooperation. Projecting superiority, nationalists champion isolationism in the hope of attaining lost glory (Milner, 2021; Yasmin, 2022).

Before the global COVID-19 pandemic started in 2020, the United Nations Secretary-General, António Guterres (2018), told the Security Council in November 2018 that the world needs to cooperate and intensify international relations in confronting emerging global threats. Guterres (2018) emphasised that the rise of nationalism has put multilateralism in bad shape and under a lot of stress. Nationalism, according to Guterres, threatens decades of life-saving lives progress in development.

While a nationalist administration was defeated in the United States when Joseph Biden defeated Donald Trump in the presidential elections of 2020, nationalism remains an acute threat to multilateralism (Agwu, 2021; Linn, 2017). It has successfully halted the United Nations Security Council from having a stance on the overthrow of elected leaders in Myanmar by a military coup, the civil war in Tigray, and regarding the climate emergency as a global security threat.

I love my country. Despite opportunities and pathways to acquire 'new' citizenship elsewhere, I chose to remain Filipino. For me, this is virtuous, not only patriotic. But one's love for country does not mean nationalism has no limits. Loving blindly has its issues. There is no persuasive argument for blind love except an emotional one. But passive patriotism is now seen by nationalists as inadequate. One must now demonstrate ardent patriotism as enthusiastically as possible. And doing so sometimes means loathing the country of a perceived enemy. As the COVID-19 pandemic commenced its rage worldwide, public odium and animus towards Asians and Asian-looking people in the United States and Europe – as those allegedly responsible of the virus – is proof of this (Gover, Harper, and Langton, 2020; Ziems et al., 2021). Now and then, Asian hate still continues to register in many news accounts.

There is a fine line between being a patriot and flaunting one's nationalism, between being an ardent nationalist and elevating the significance of one's country and culture above others. By forging flawed beliefs of superiority and national pride, nationalist leaders avow unity, bringing their people together. Trump's 'America First' slogan carries this superiority complex (Lee, 2020). However, the resultant notion and attitude of 'us' versus 'them' also marshals undue bigotries, intolerances, and prejudices not only against 'other' countries but also political opponents and parties. Most of these vitriols now occur on social media (Bhat and Klein, 2020; Siegel et al., 2021), where opponents are regarded as enemies and, worse, as forces deterring national progress.

Nationalists take their nationalism as a licence to hurt people branded as 'the others'. Politicians continue to spawn lies and distort history to produce a delusion of regaining the fancied glory of the past (cf., Hameleers, van der

Meer, and Vliegenthart, 2021). In turn, nationalist discourses precipitate and legitimise control of a supposedly independent media, tyrannising the judiciary, and demolishing the rule of law (Waisbord, 2018).

As a result of over-enthusiastic nationalism, disinformation displaces reality. Any vestige of opposition is squeezed. Convinced they have exclusive and superior power over others, nationalists advocate militarism and agitate discord with other peoples and countries (Diaz and Mountz, 2020). Believing themselves to be special, nationalists disregard the community of nations. President Donald Trump pulling the United States out of the Paris Agreement on climate change is one example of this (Jotzo, Depledge, and Winkler, 2018).

Egocentric and myopic benefits and the pompous show of power are the ardent nationalists' main impetus in foreign policy. National interests, seen through restricted and limited lenses, supplant moral responsibilities, global peace, and the obligation to international agreements. This was fully displayed, for example, when Philippine President Rodrigo Duterte threatened to pull out of the Paris Agreement. As a political strategy, excessive patriotism and unmerited nationalism go against the grain of international cooperation and multilateralism.

As ardent, yet unmerited, nationalism has gained ground, countries have been pushed to take unilateral actions and flout the norms of multilateralism. The presidency of Donald Trump provided a mirror of how international cooperation could be brought to a state of bewilderment as a significant party backed out of the Paris Agreement (Fehl and Thimm, 2019; Weiss, 2018). As the pandemic raged – it still does, as these words are written – the world under the climate emergency continues to grow in scale and complexity and is therefore coming under intense pressure. A solitary approach by nationalist forces will never be enough to address this emergency, and multilateralism remains critical in sustaining an international climate action regime.

Multilateralism may not be an end, but it is a requisite avenue to collective global climate action (cf., Alexandroff, Bradford, and Tiberghien, 2020). Collective intelligence – only achievable via multilateralism – needs to be developed and strengthened to confront nationalism. Giving multilateralism a new substance in this age of nationalistic fervour is consequential in steering the idea of global cooperation on climate action. The case of COVAX, which has provided a global response to an indiscriminate pandemic, imparts new lessons for international cooperation (Eccleston-Turner and Upton, 2021).

In 1918, the Spanish Flu took hold of war-torn Europe. A lot has changed over the last century, and, since that pandemic, the science and research enterprise publicly unveiled its renewed vigour to triumph over the unseen risk of another pandemic. The year 2020 arrived, and, with it, a novel coronavirus that spurred a pandemic. That year, the scientific enterprise was in a rush to develop vaccine candidates against SARS-CoV-2. Their purview was to develop vaccines to immunise the vast majority of the global population. Widespread immunisation – which is only possible with guaranteed equitable access to vaccines regardless of a country's economic status – is, however, foregrounded in the capacity of political leaders to collaborate and commit to a global vaccine development programme. COVAX was established along these lines.

COVAX is the world's most extensive and diverse portfolio of COVID-19 vaccines. A World Health Organization-backed programme, COVAX is available to governments willing to participate in developing and producing vaccines to ensure their people get equitable access to them. It was created in partnership with the Global Alliance of Vaccines and Immunization and the Coalition for Epidemic Preparedness Innovations (Eccleston-Turner and Upton, 2021). Through this facility, resources were pooled, thus ensuring greater efficiencies in vaccine production while incurring cost savings since competition among countries was neutralised. COVAX addressed the gaps between global demand for COVID vaccines and available doses. COVAX envisions making two billion doses of the vaccines available in middle- and low-income developing countries, covering some 20 per cent of their total populations (Eccleston-Turner and Upton, 2021).

It was clear at the outset that without engagement from wealthy countries, COVAX would be less efficacious. When nationalist forces were gaining ground in the United States and elsewhere, global superpowers were competing to ensure their countries were at the front of the queue for the much-needed vaccine and steering clear of the COVAX programme (Nhamo et al., 2021). In addition to the US government, for example, Australia, European countries, Japan, and the United Kingdom were all in independent negotiations with suppliers of potential COVID vaccines. These countries were able to secure rights to some 130 million doses of potential vaccines. Vaccine nationalism thus became the de facto option of the Minority World, despite rich countries having the technological, scientific, and financial capacity to cover research and production costs (Wagner et al., 2021).

Vaccine nationalism is not new. During the H1N1 epidemic of 2009 to 2010, some rich countries cooperated to conduct vaccine research (Zhou, 2022). In the end, some of them stockpiled successful vaccines. Poorer countries were only given access to these vaccines after the needs were met in rich countries, by which time the H1N1 epidemic had already ended. Because of this, vaccines were wasted. Vaccine nationalism, it turned out, proved to be a costly contest (Zhou, 2022).

The spread of COVID-19 ignores a person's nationality and dismisses nation-state boundaries. A multilateral facility for vaccine production and distribution thus poised a clear challenge to vaccine nationalism (Katz et al.,

2021; Bollyky and Bown, 2020). The greater the number of societies reaching herd immunity, and the earlier this happened, the greater the hope for moving out of the pandemic. This can only be done through widespread immunisation by vaccination, which is a function of greater international cooperation through multilateralism (Bollyky and Bown, 2020). Multilateralism in vaccine access, therefore, aligns with protecting a nation's economy and public health security. COVAX – multilateralism at work – remains the only global programme that works with governments and vaccine manufacturers to ensure the global availability of vaccines regardless of a country's income status (Eccleston-Turner and Upton, 2021).

But it does not follow that COVAX will undoubtedly be successful. The factors that promote nationalism also endanger its efficacy. First, international cooperation is imperative, and not only among nations with research and production facilities. Collaboration among public health agencies and the communities that will eventually use the vaccines worldwide is equally important (Katz et al., 2021). Ignoring these critical actors, especially at the early stages of the process, may result in vaccines being ill-suited for use in certain places. Second, the COVID-19 pandemic could not be addressed single-handedly by just one country. Global cooperation is important in equitable vaccine distribution, where people at highest risk should take precedence in immunisation, irrespective of residence. No vaccine is effective if only the needs of a particular country are met (Rutschman, 2021). Participation in the COVAX facility by the world's leading public health funders, such as the United States, is therefore a must. Third, vaccine dispatch in poorer countries requires international support, especially given the persistent challenges of their transport sectors.

Vaccine multilateralism, not nationalism, proved effective in countering a global pandemic (Katz et al., 2021). Through the COVAX facility, COVID-19 vaccines have saved lives in more than 100 countries since the first doses were delivered to Ghana on 24 February 2021 (Grenfell and Oyeyemi, 2022). AstraZeneca, Pfizer–BioNTech, and the Serum Institute of India supplied these doses across six continents.

Multilateralism has also proved crucial in addressing environmental issues. Fifty years ago, in 1972, the United Nations held its first conference in Stockholm to tackle challenges to the natural environment (Paglia, 2021). More than 100 nations and over 400 government and non-governmental organisations gathered at the conference to explore the emerging global problems of ecological degradation and environmental change. The United Nations Conference on the Environment, as the meeting was called, was the first worldwide gathering to debate water, desertification, and the use of pesticides in agriculture.

The Declaration of the United Nations Conference on the Environment, adopted on 6 June 1972, became the original seed from which the concept of a new type of development – mindful of the natural environment – was born. The declaration was a success despite no consensus or final agreement being reached due to opposition from the wealthiest countries at the time. The event ushered in many firsts. It created the United Nations Environment Programme as a new major global environmental organisation. Also, non-governmental organisations were welcomed to a global conference for the first time. The 1972 conference in Stockholm also contributed to broader systemic changes. These included the importance of science-based environmental policymaking. In addition to putting problem interconnectedness on the environmental agenda, the conference promoted environmental awareness and, most critically, engaged a wide range of non-state actors in environmental governance (Bernstein, 2002; Najam, 2005).

Since 1972, the global environmental landscape has evolved extensively. Multilateralism fuelled this change. Twenty years after that first United Nations–sponsored meeting on the environment, Rio de Janeiro hosted the Earth Summit in 1992. This event was a major turning point in the history of environmental multilateralism. Biodiversity and climate change problems were codified in Agenda 21 (Andonova and Hoffmann, 2012). A blueprint for international action on the environment, Agenda 21 was a daring programme of action to achieve sustainable development in the twenty-first century and was one of the Earth Summit's most consequential outputs. One hundred and seventy-nine countries approved it. At the same time, a parallel meeting of non-governmental organisations created and ratified the Earth Charter. In addition to Agenda 21, the other most consequential output of the summit was the United Nations Framework Convention on Climate Change – the first written document exemplifying environmental multilateralism for climate action.

Once again in Rio, in 2012 – forty years after Stockholm 1972 and twenty years after Rio 1992 – multilateralism brought forth the Sustainable Development Goals, which became an international normative agenda. In 2022, fifty years after the Stockholm conference, environmental multilateralism is again gaining ground (Rockström et al., 2021). Stockholm+50 is not only a celebration but also an important event examining the role of environmental multilateralism. To mark the event, Stockholm+50 is anchored in the United Nations Decade of Action under the theme 'a healthy planet for the prosperity of all – our responsibility, our opportunity'.

For fifty years, environmental multilateralism has acted as a springboard to accelerate the global environmental agenda. Stockholm+50 marks the eighth year before the expiration of the Sustainable Development Goals, seven years following the Paris Agreement, and is within the period by which we have to ensure the adoption of green post-COVID-19 recovery plans. Stockholm+50 also comes at a significant historical moment where extreme weather events punctuate other global miseries: the present pandemic and ongoing violent conflicts. One could add to this mix the many decaying democracies, the rise of global multinationals, and an era of social distrust and disillusionment.

The next fifty years will most likely be troublesome for the planet and for our species. We can expect a cacophony of environmental, political, and social despair and hopelessness underlined by frequent weather extremes, violent conflicts, intense political polarisation, and the widening gap between rich and poor. However, Stockholm+50 is an opportune time for stocktaking and assessing the role of environmental multilateralism in imminent, cascading, and complex crises that mix environmental catastrophes with socio–political–economic perturbations.

Environmental multilateralism brought us environmental treaties that rebuilt the ozone layer (Biermann and Simonis, 1999). The Montreal Protocol, as it is known, is key evidence of environmental multilateralism at work. Despite its flaws, the Paris Agreement is another display of international collaboration for the commons (Bernardo et al., 2021). Multilateralism has also juxtaposed polycentrism and green pluralism (Smith, 2017; Dorsch and Flachsland, 2017). As a result of Stockholm 1972, global environmental governance has evolved into a system with several layers of players, including states, international institutions, non-governmental organisations, the scientific community, and the corporate sector.

Non-state actors are crucial players in environmental governance (Arts, 2006; Bernauer and Betzold, 2012). The 1992 Earth Summit further recognised the right of the private sector and civil society to participate as 'major groups' (Bäckstrand, 2006). Following Rio 1992, there are now ensembles of players and regimes with varying degrees of influence in global environmental governance, including climate action, as a result of the proliferation of non-state entities (Bäckstrand and Kuyper, 2017). More importantly, contemporary environmentalism is based on growing awareness of the interconnected nature of environmental issues, calling for coordination and a better understanding of the nature of our complex global system. Multilateralism, despite its imperfections, remains a potent tool for addressing the tragedies of our commons.

Environmental governance is no longer only the responsibility of governments. With the proliferation of global standard-setting transnational players, we now have private governance, public–private agreements, and non-market systems (Bäckstrand and Kuyper, 2017; Rowlands, 2001). However, this does not mean that states are reduced in their primary roles as stewards of the environment. Indeed, I argue to the contrary. Environmental nationalism is as crucial as environmental multilateralism, especially in addressing the climate emergency.

Climate change is now accelerating its impacts. Right before our eyes, we see how the world is getting hotter, is on fire, and is flooding. In the past three years alone, from 2018 to 2021, wildfires have ripped through California in the United States, British Columbia in Canada, and Victoria in Australia, to name just a few. Stronger typhoons led to flooding that caused storm surges in Kolkata in India, Visayas and Mindanao in the Philippines, and Newark and New York City in the United States, again, to name just a few. In addition, slow onset climate impacts are expected to bring additional miseries – including melting glaciers and sea level rise, among others.

It is now very crucial that we adapt to these weather extremes, as well as with slow onset impacts of the climate crises, and prepare our communities for resilience. Preparations involve making infrastructures stronger and sturdier and our social ties more resilient than ever. We must work towards making our physical defences and social capitals as anti-fragile as possible, not merely able to bounce back from previous states. While adaptation to these, most likely, cascading crises is vital in a warming world, it is also necessary to address the critical causes of anthropogenic climate change and to transform the ways and means by which we generate and use energy. Given that it is responsible for the lion's share of global emissions, a focus on the energy sector is warranted.

Environmental multilateralism is crucial in setting the tone for global cooperation to reduce emissions in the energy sector. The Paris Agreement, which strode its way from Rio de Janeiro in 1992 to Paris in 2015, is an important document showing international cooperation on climate action. However, mobilisation of the necessary policies, capital, and people power is a role that rests mainly with the state. The Paris Agreement is essential in nudging governments to work their way to climate action, but national legislation remains critical if the goals of the Agreement are to be met.

I made an argument for the role of the state in climate action in my work on accelerating sustainable energy transitions (Delina, 2016). We can look at the COVID-19 pandemic response and see how governments entered a 'state of exception', suspending the ordinary course of events and adopting extraordinary measures from lockdowns to price controls to mask mandates etc. It provides an example of the role of the state in mobilisation. To be clear, a 'state of exception' can easily be a Pandora's box, hence it must be carefully employed (Zinn, 2020).

A national project to accelerate the energy transition, however, goes beyond curtailing liberties; in fact, such a project could be used to expand freedoms. The state could lead a different kind of 'state of exception' by mobilising its power towards ensuring that emissions now and in the future are curtailed on a scale and at a speed never seen before in the history of technology and innovation. Doing this, while highlighting the transformative power of citizen-led and community-organised energy transition, underlines the critical role of the citizen in the transition (Delina, Diesendorf, and Merson, 2014; Delina, 2018, 2019).

States could lead the rapid transition to 100 per cent renewable energy to power all energy services from electricity to transport to heating and cooling (Delina, 2016; Delina and Diesendorf, 2013). Indeed, electrifying everything with renewable energy is the only way to mitigate future climate change. While we are already baked in global heating of +1.5 to 2°C relative to pre-industrial levels, depending on where you are on the planet, a rapid change move away from fossil fuel–based energy generation and use still offers an opportunity for our species to change course: from despair to hope.

The complete transition to renewables can be done in one to two decades, depending on location, state capacity, natural endowments, and, most significantly, political will. Again, this can be done by recalling nations' ability to address the ongoing COVID-19 pandemic, that is, the state functioning under a 'state of exception'. Several cities have already shown that this can be done at a governance level below that of the state. Burlington, one of my favourite cities in New England, produced enough power from renewable sources to cover all its electricity needs. We could also mention Georgetown in Texas (yes, Texas) and Aspen in Colorado as other examples.

These are real-life examples of the energy transition at work. Models and simulations have also shown us that large-scale energy transition to 100 per cent renewables is possible at national and regional levels (e.g., Lund and Mathiesen, 2009; Hansen, Mathiesen, and Skov, 2019; Deason, 2018). In unison, these projections suggest that renewable energy, with significant inputs from energy efficiency activities, can power all energy services globally using market-ready wind, water, and sunlight energy technologies. There are caveats, of course, especially regarding the technological challenges in requisite yet still underdeveloped energy technologies and systems. These presently immature infrastructures include smart grids and storage technologies; yet, research and development around these technologies has been ramping up. We are seeing innovations developing in these spaces almost weekly worldwide.

Achieving the energy transition to 100 per cent renewables globally and bringing it up to speed will not only demand radical shifts in technological systems; it also compels changes in governance, policy, institutions, financing, and capacity building to coordinate and monitor the fast deployment of renewable energy technologies (Delina, 2016). This major turnaround would need a return to planning, with governments asking for a 'state of exception' so they may act during an unprecedented period, that is, the climate emergency. A 'state of exception' is a prerequisite since these activities require expenditures on capital, labour, and other resources that exceed the norm. Fortunately, a transition to planning is not entirely unprecedented, even in capitalist regimes (Delina, 2016; Delina and Diesendorf, 2013).

The increase of Allied mobilisation during the Second World War is one lens through which this extraordinary phenomenon might be viewed. I explored this in my book *Strategies for Rapid Climate Mitigation: Wartime Mobilisation as a Model for Action?* (Delina, 2016) a few months after the introduction of the Paris Agreement. In this work, I revisited histories of wartime mobilisation to examine how governments marshalled their resources in response to a life-threatening event, a world war.

The mobilisation in the United States amounted to more than US$4 trillion in today's money. It helped guarantee that Europe and the Pacific, including the Philippines, which was then an American colony, were not lost to Axis powers. Nobody now would suggest that the decision by the United States to disburse such vast sums was unsound. As wartime mobilisation indicated, the American economy can be spun into an engine of production to ward off a threat.

History demonstrates that armaments can be rapidly made and supplied to battlefronts, that public finance is required to execute this endeavour, and that labour can be rapidly organised. This history also demonstrates that the state could mobilise its administrative agents and institutions to supervise resources, take assets, sell bonds, halt the manufacture of 'competing' products (in this instance, private automobiles and other luxuries), and assemble the necessary labour power. Similarly, an accelerated climate mitigation programme that rapidly implements sustainable energy transitions could be modelled on this history.

As a reminder, the 1972 conference in Stockholm occurred under the shadows of the Cold War. Today, as these words are written, the violent wars in Ukraine, Ethiopia, Gaza, Afghanistan, Myanmar, and elsewhere backdrop Stockholm+50. Stockholm+50 will, once again, remind us of the consequential impacts of multilateralism, cooperation, and our complex interdependence. In 1972, the dominant narratives of the East–West split and capitalism-versus-central-planning were supplanted by realistic arguments about how to harness the markets, the role of individuals and communities, and the level of state regulation of the environment.

However, a recurring storyline throughout time and environmental regimes is the issue of justice (Schlosberg, 2013). While it is true that states are essential actors in the mobilisation of climate action, they have different capacities. The

Majority World–Minority World divide in addressing environmental challenges, first brought to the fore in Stockholm in 1972, remains an elusive issue that must be handled with much clarity and will. The Majority World requires resources to facilitate their energy transitions and contribute to the global agenda of accelerated climate action. This brings us back to vaccine nationalism, discussed earlier in this chapter. The Majority World is still hoping for major increases in assistance to help fund climate action (Fonta, Ayuk, and van Huysen, 2018).

Stockholm 1972 was the first time the notion of 'additionality' was articulated (MacLeod, 1974), suggesting that industrialised nations were accountable for covering the additional development expenses associated with environmental preservation (Campbell, 1973). Similar to this concept is that of 'common but differentiated responsibilities', one of the essential texts in the United Nations Framework Convention on Climate Change. Majority World countries need energy transition resources from the Minority World since they still have to fund many other development priorities, such as education and health. Yet, the expected international aid flows from the North to the South are yet to fully materialise (Fonta, Ayuk, and van Huysen, 2018).

The Majority World remains highly sceptical about the legitimacy of global environmental governance due to the fact that the Paris Agreement's ambitions remain inadequately financed to meet the stated obligations: US$100 billion per year in total, globally, starting in 2020. In its annual report on climate funding, the Organisation for Economic Co-operation and Development (OECD, 2022) reported that rich countries provided just US$80 billion in mitigation and adaptation finance. Most of these funds were from multilateral development banks in the form of loans.

Despite their repeated commitment, rich countries are dispensing relatively little financial support to assist climate action in the Majority World. In 2019, delivered and pledged climate action funding reached only US$685 billion, paling in comparison to the US$1.54 trillion foreign direct investment flows of all kinds made during the same year, according to the OECD (2022) report. Funding commitments by rich countries are still far from the dollars needed to replace traditional cooking and heating fuels, such as wood, cow dung, kerosene, and coal, with modern energy options by 2030. This is even further away from the capitalisation needed to decarbonise Majority World countries' energy systems by replacing coal and gas combustion with wind, solar, and water energy.

Without addressing these legitimate concerns, and enabling more widespread compliance on fund flows and technology transfers, environmental multilateralism, especially for climate action, will be difficult to sustain. The focus now should be on meeting the promises of a truly just and fair international cooperation by supporting the acceleration of energy transition to renewable energy systems in the Majority World; this remains a crucial precondition for addressing our rapidly changing climate.

References

Agwu, F. A. (2021). *Foreign Policy in the Age of Globalization, Populism and Nationalism.* Cham: Springer.

Alexandroff, A., Bradford, C., & Tiberghien, Y. (2020). Toward 'effective multilateralism' in turbulent times. *Global Solutions Journal*, 5, 54–60.

Andonova, L. B., & Hoffmann, M. J. (2012). From Rio to Rio and beyond: Innovation in global environmental governance. *Journal of Environment & Development*, 21(1), 57–61.

Arts, B. (2006). Non-state actors in global environmental governance: New arrangements beyond the state. In M. Koenig-Archibugi & M. Zurn (Eds.), *New Modes of Governance in the Global System* (pp. 177–200). London: Palgrave Macmillan.

Asundi, A., O'Leary, C., & Bhadelia, N. (2021). Global COVID-19 vaccine inequity: The scope, the impact, and the challenges. *Cell Host & Microbe*, 29 (7), 1036–1039.

Bäckstrand, K. (2006). Democratizing global environmental governance? Stakeholder democracy after the World Summit on Sustainable Development. *European Journal of International Relations*, 12(4), 467–498.

Bäckstrand, K., & Kuyper, J. W. (2017). The democratic legitimacy of orchestration: The UNFCCC, non-state actors, and transnational climate governance. *Environmental Politics*, 26(4), 764–788.

Bernardo, C., Wang, L., Vasca, F., Hong, Y., Shi, G., & Altafini, C. (2021). Achieving consensus in multilateral international negotiations: The case study of the 2015 Paris Agreement on climate change. *Science Advances*, 7 (51), eabg8068.

Bernauer, T., & Betzold, C. (2012). Civil society in global environmental governance. *Journal of Environment & Development*, 21(1), 62–66.

Bernstein, S. (2002). Liberal environmentalism and global environmental governance. *Global Environmental Politics*, 2(3), 1–16.

Bhat, P., & Klein, O. (2020). Covert hate speech: White nationalists and dog whistle communication on twitter. In G. Bouvier & J. Rosenbaum (Eds.), *Twitter, the Public Sphere, and the Chaos of Online Deliberation* (pp. 151–172). Cham: Palgrave Macmillan.

Biermann, F., & Simonis, U. E. (1999). The Multilateral Ozone Fund: A case study on institutional learning. *International Journal of Social Economics*, 26, 239–273.

Bollyky, T. J., & Bown, C. P. (2020). The tragedy of vaccine nationalism: Only cooperation can end the pandemic. *Foreign Affairs*, September–October.

Burki, T. (2021). Global COVID-19 vaccine inequity. *The Lancet Infectious Diseases*, 21(7), 922–923.

Campbell, T. E. (1973). The political meaning of Stockholm: Third World participation in the environment conference process. *Stanford Journal of International Studies, 8*, 138–153.

Deason, W. (2018). Comparison of 100% renewable energy system scenarios with a focus on flexibility and cost. *Renewable and Sustainable Energy Reviews, 82*, 3168–3178.

Delina, L. L. (2016). *Strategies for Rapid Climate Mitigation: Wartime Mobilisation as a Model for Action?* Abingdon, UK: Routledge.

Delina, L. L. (2018). *Climate Actions: Transformative Mechanisms for Social Mobilisation*. London: Palgrave Macmillan.

Delina, L. L. (2019). *Emancipatory Climate Actions: Strategies from Histories*. London: Palgrave Macmillan.

Delina, L. L., & Diesendorf, M. (2013). Is wartime mobilisation a suitable policy model for rapid national climate mitigation? *Energy Policy, 58*, 371–380.

Delina, L. L., Diesendorf, M., & Merson, J. (2014). Strengthening the climate action movement: Strategies from histories. *Carbon Management, 5*(4), 397–409.

Diaz, I. I., & Mountz, A. (2020). Intensifying fissures: Geopolitics, nationalism, militarism, and the US response to the novel coronavirus. *Geopolitics, 25*(5), 1037–1044.

Dorsch, M. J., & Flachsland, C. (2017). A polycentric approach to global climate governance. *Global Environmental Politics, 17*(2), 45–64.

Eccleston-Turner, M., & Upton, H. (2021). International collaboration to ensure equitable access to vaccines for COVID-19: The ACT-Accelerator and the COVAX Facility. *Milbank Quarterly, 99*(2), 426–449.

Elias, A., Ben, J., Mansouri, F., & Paradies, Y. (2021). Racism and nationalism during and beyond the COVID-19 pandemic. *Ethnic and Racial Studies, 44*(5), 783–793.

Fehl, C., & Thimm, J. (2019). Dispensing with the indispensable nation? Multilateralism minus one in the Trump era. *Global Governance: A Review of Multilateralism and International Organizations, 25*(1), 23–46.

Fonta, W. M., Ayuk, E. T., & van Huysen, T. (2018). Africa and the Green Climate Fund: Current challenges and future opportunities. *Climate Policy, 18*(9), 1210–1225.

Gover, A. R., Harper, S. B., & Langton, L. (2020). Anti-Asian hate crime during the COVID-19 pandemic: Exploring the reproduction of inequality. *American Journal of Criminal Justice, 45*(4), 647–667.

Grenfell, R. F. Q., & Oyeyemi, O. T. (2022). Access to COVID-19 vaccines and testing in Africa: The importance of COVAX-Nigeria as a case study. *Pathogens and Global Health*, 1–15.

Guterres, A. (2018). Secretary-General's remarks at Security Council Open Debate on 'Strengthening Multilateralism and the Role of the United Nations', 9 November. www.un.org/sg/en/content/sg/statement/2018-11-09/secretary-generals-remarks-security-council-open-debate.

Hameleers, M., van der Meer, T., & Vliegenthart, R. (2021). Civilized truths, hateful lies? Incivility and hate speech in false information–evidence from fact-checked statements in the US. *Information, Communication & Society, 25*(11), 1596–1613.

Hansen, K., Mathiesen, B. V., & Skov, I. R. (2019). Full energy system transition towards 100% renewable energy in Germany in 2050. *Renewable and Sustainable Energy Reviews, 102*, 1–13.

Jotzo, F., Depledge, J., & Winkler, H. (2018). US and international climate policy under President Trump. *Climate Policy, 18*(7), 813–817.

Katz, I. T., Weintraub, R., Bekker, L. G., & Brandt, A. M. (2021). From vaccine nationalism to vaccine equity – finding a path forward. *New England Journal of Medicine, 384*(14), 1281–1283.

Lee, E. (2020). America first, immigrants last: American xenophobia then and now. *Journal of the Gilded Age and Progressive Era, 19*(1), 3–18.

Linn, J. (2017). Recent threats to multilateralism. *Global Journal of Emerging Market Economies, 9*(1–3), 86–113.

Lund, H., & Mathiesen, B. V. (2009). Energy system analysis of 100% renewable energy systems – The case of Denmark in years 2030 and 2050. *Energy, 34*(5), 524–531.

MacLeod, S. (1974). *Financing Environmental Measures in Developing Countries: The Principle of Additionality*. International Union for the Conservation of Nature.

Milner, H. V. (2021). Voting for populism in Europe: Globalization, technological change, and the extreme right. *Comparative Political Studies, 54*(13), 2286–2320.

Najam, A. (2005). Developing countries and global environmental governance: From contestation to participation to engagement. *International Environmental Agreements: Politics, Law and Economics, 5*(3), 303–321.

Nhamo, G., Chikodzi, D., Kunene, H. P., & Mashula, N. (2021). COVID-19 vaccines and treatments nationalism: Challenges for low-income countries and the attainment of the SDGs. *Global Public Health, 16*(3), 319–339.

Nourbakhsh, S. N., Ahmadi, S. A., Yazdanpanah Dero, Q., & Faraji Rad, A. (2022). Rise of the far right parties in Europe: From nationalism to Euroscepticism. *Geopolitics Quarterly, 18*(68), 47–70.

OECD. (2022). *Aggregate Trends of Climate Finance Provided and Mobilised by Developed Countries in 2013–2020*. OECD, Paris.

Paglia, E. (2021). The Swedish initiative and the 1972 Stockholm Conference: The decisive role of science diplomacy in the emergence of global environmental governance. *Humanities and Social Sciences Communications, 8*(1), 1–10.

Rockström, J., Gupta, J., Qin, D., Pedde, S., Broadgate, W., & Warszawski, L. (2021). Stockholm to Stockholm: Achieving a safe Earth requires goals that incorporate a just approach. *One Earth, 4*(9), 1209–1211.

Rowlands, I. H. (2001). Transnational corporations and global environmental politics. In D. Josselin & W. Wallace (Eds.), *Non-State Actors in World Politics* (pp. 133–149). London: Palgrave Macmillan.

Rutschman, A. S. (2021). Is there a cure for vaccine nationalism? *Current History, 120* (822), 9–14.

Schlosberg, D. (2013). Theorising environmental justice: The expanding sphere of a discourse. *Environmental Politics, 22*(1), 37–55.

Siegel, A. A., Nikitin, E., Barberá, P., Sterling, J., Pullen, B., Bonneau, R., ... & Tucker, J. (2021). Trumping hate on Twitter? Online hate speech in the 2016 US election campaign and its aftermath. *Quarterly Journal of Political Science, 16*(1), 71–104.

Smith, K. (2017). Innovating for the global commons: Multilateral collaboration in a polycentric world. *Oxford Review of Economic Policy, 33*(1), 49–65.

Wagner, C. E., Saad-Roy, C. M., Morris, S. E., Baker, R. E., Mina, M. J., Farrar, J., ... & Grenfell, B. T. (2021). Vaccine nationalism and the dynamics and control of SARS-CoV-2. *Science, 373*(6562), eabj7364.

Waisbord, S. (2018). The elective affinity between post-truth communication and populist politics. *Communication Research and Practice*, *4*(1), 17–34.

Weiss, T. G. (2018). The UN and multilateralism under siege in the 'Age of Trump'. *Global Summitry*, *4*(1), 1–17.

Yasmin, L. (2022). The growth of populism and populist publics: Globalization under the gun? In I. A. Hussain (Ed.), *Global–Local Tradeoffs, Order–Disorder Consequences* (pp. 61–88). London: Palgrave Macmillan.

Zhou, Y. R. (2022). Vaccine nationalism: Contested relationships between COVID-19 and globalization. *Globalizations*, *19*(3), 450–465.

Ziems, C., He, B., Soni, S., & Kumar, S. (2021). Racism is a virus: Anti-Asian hate and counterhate in social media during the COVID-19 crisis. *Proceedings of the 2021 IEEE/ACM International Conference on Advances in Social Networks Analysis and Mining*, Calgary.

Zinn, J. O. (2020). 'A monstrous threat': How a state of exception turns into a 'new normal'. *Journal of Risk Research*, *23*(7–8), 1083–1091.

7
Toggling the System

> *To tilt the scales in favour of a faster energy transition, significant efforts to decarbonise the economy are required. This means flipping the political and economic systems that are failing to deliver deep decarbonisation and replacing them with ones built on compassion and justice. Through a cascade of regime transitions in the energy sector, mass mobilisation, and support politics, these reforms are achievable.*

After so many wasted years of climate denial, delay, and deflection, incremental change will no longer bring us back to a safe climate. We must now cut greenhouse gas emissions by about 7 per cent per year to have a fair chance of not missing the 1.5°C increase in global heating (Christensen and Olhoff, 2019). Achieving this reduction rate requires an even quicker speed than when emissions sank in 2020 during the early months of the COVID-19 pandemic – especially given the risks of multiple and cascading tipping points (Rocha et al., 2018; Cai, Lenton, and Lontzek, 2016).

Political regime shifts are now crucial to averting systemic environmental collapse (Hughes et al., 2013; Kinzig et al., 2006). Decisive decisions are required more than ever to ensure that no fossil fuels are taken out of the ground and burned after 2030. There is no compromise between fossil fuel interests and this policy direction. Accelerating climate action is imperative (Delina, 2016); otherwise, environmental collapse could cascade, especially as planetary systems pass critical thresholds (Lenton et al., 2019).

Climate breakdown will not be sequential, orderly, or gradual (Brook et al., 2013; Bentley et al., 2014; cf., Malm, 2020). Atmospheric systems will soak up the pressures and then swing without warning. This is just how a complex system works. When subjected to stress, our complex biosphere, atmosphere, and oceans immediately seek balance. Shoved too far out of their state of equilibrium, these complex systems can hurl quickly, without warning, into another state of equilibrium. It is easier to push complex systems past their tipping points than to push them back. A tipping point is the moment at which a tiny change in a system's future state may create a shift (Lenton and Williams, 2013), such as the transition from one state of a complicated dynamic system to another (Bentley et al., 2014). In simple terms, it is the point at which the system's reaction to changing circumstances becomes non-linear or the rate of change abruptly shifts (Brook et al., 2013). Once the change has occurred, it cannot be altered.

The Atlantic Meridional Overturning Circulation, the complex ocean current system circulating heat around the world and propelling the Atlantic Gulf Stream, may have already progressed from its reasonably steady state to being on the verge of crucial change (Boers and Rypdal, 2021; Boers, 2021). Shifts in this circulation occurred in prehistory, and, when they did, northern Europe and eastern North America plunged into intolerable cold. A sluggish Atlantic Meridional Overturning Circulation might cause the Amazon rainforest to dry up and disturb the East Asian monsoon, which could accelerate Antarctic ice loss as the Southern Ocean heats up (Lenton et al., 2019). The Amazon is a crucial carbon sink, which, once collapsed, could drive a spiral of more global heating (Nobre and Borma, 2009). Earth systems are not limited or confined within their boxes. If one system shifts into a different state, that flipping could trigger shifts in other Earth systems.

Before a transition occurs, systems may first tremble (Wang et al., 2012). When irregularities start happening, complex systems fast approach their tipping points (Steffen et al., 2015). Fires, floods, and super typhoons in 2021 and the European overheating in 2022 terrifyingly suggest the most recent flickering of changes in the climate system. If this complex system tips following accelerating global heating, our only hope of avoiding collapse from climate breakdown is combining rapid decarbonisation of the global economy and the drawing down of carbon already in the atmosphere. The Paris Agreement's temperature targets are exceedingly difficult to achieve without doing both. Speed is essential here: releasing the pressure on the accelerator to destruction and stoking the engine of rapid decarbonisation and carbon drawdown.

Rapid decarbonisation is a topic I have explored in my work on accelerating the energy transition (e.g., Delina, 2016; Delina and Diesendorf, 2013). In this work, I consider a planetary project to replace fossil fuel–based energy systems with renewable energy from wind, water, and sunlight, to be accomplished in one to two decades. In a *gedankenexperiment* (thought experiment), I extracted the lessons of rapid wartime mobilisation to generate strategies for superintending the deployment of renewable energy technologies, mobilising capital, and arranging institutions for this gargantuan task (Delina, 2016; Delina and Diesendorf, 2013). The key idea is that all energy services, including electricity, heating and cooling, residential and industrial uses, and transport, can be fully electrified with renewable energy from wind, water, and sunlight.

Rapid changes in energy systems are not new. They have happened before. One example is the transition from 25 per cent of coal supply to zero in eleven years, from 2003 to 2014, in the province of Ontario, Canada (Sovacool, 2016). Ontario did this by investing in wind, hydro, solar, and nuclear, as well as in grid upgrades and energy efficiency (Sovacool, 2016). New technologies tend to self-accelerate following increased efficiencies and economies of scale. In this way, one can hope that as renewables penetrate the energy mix and approach a critical threshold, positive feedback will lead to the extinction of fossil fuel use.

Take, for example, electric mobility. Electric vehicles have become more desirable as battery performance and charging spots improve, costs decline, and car prices drop (Jung, Silva, and Han, 2018). The same can be projected with the more significant electricity infrastructure. Renewable energy from wind, water, and sunlight will become the energy generation of choice as these technologies drop in price and storage options become more efficient. Of course, these transitions are not only engineering projects; they require parallel, and strong, policy support (Delina, 2016).

Government interventions could trigger the transition, and, I argue, they must (Delina, 2016). Rapid and large-scale technological deployments necessitate policy push. As new technologies become prevalent, old systems become socially undesirable. As the prices of replacement technologies plunge, they are locked in as new systems. This new economic regime, one can expect, will spill the transition from one country to another.

Storage technologies, already introduced and used in the transport sector, can also spread into other energy systems, spurring regime transitions in, for example, the electricity grid. As solar electricity and offshore wind fall steeply in price, conventional coal and gas power plants will look like extravagant choices for energy generation. The energy transition will be locked in as fossil fuel dominoes start to fall.

While energy transition is a clear-cut direction for climate action, carbon drawdown technologies are contentious (e.g., Low and Schäfer, 2020; Delina, 2020). These are methods and technologies that extract greenhouse gases already in the atmosphere. Carbon drawdown is an excellent idea in principle but it perpetuates a belief in technofix that diminishes the need to accelerate emissions reduction now (Gunderson, Stuart, and Petersen, 2020). This portfolio of technologies painfully provides a licence to recklessly burn fossil fuels on the assumption that their emissions can, after all, be drawn down later.

The problem with carbon capture in fossil fuel–fired power stations is that it is a costly technology. Huge sums are required to install carbon scrubbers in these power stations, build pipes to transport captured carbon, and construct geologically suitable storage sites. These extra costs undermine the very motivation for burning coal, which is to generate relatively cheap electricity. Thus far, only one electric company on the planet has retrofitted carbon capture equipment in its power plant: the 824 MW Boundary Dam coal-fired power plant in Saskatchewan, Canada.

Another approach to carbon drawdown is by using forests as carbon sinks (Pan et al., 2011). By counting the amount of carbon stored in trees and soil, emissions from fossil fuels is subtracted from mitigation obligations. In essence, trees are planted, which absorb carbon dioxide in the atmosphere, thus mitigating future emissions. A future with more trees could, in effect, counter the current burning of fossil fuels. However, this approach does not result in a reliable carbon drawdown since these future 'carbon sinks' are never guaranteed (Ojha et al., 2019). Bioenergy with carbon capture and storage is another fast-emerging carbon drawdown technology (Fridahl and Lehtveer, 2018). This is done by burning 'renewable' biomass, such as crop residues and wood chips, as a replacement for coal in power plants and then capturing emissions from the power station's chimneys and storing it below ground.

But utilising forests as carbon sinks and bioenergy with carbon capture and storage are too good to be true. According to the Intergovernmental Panel on Climate Change, a 66 per cent chance of limiting temperature increase to 1.5°C requires bioenergy with carbon capture and storage technologies to remove twelve billion tonnes of carbon dioxide annually (Metz, Davidson, and De Coninck, 2005). These technologies would need to plant billions of trees and bioenergy crops to achieve this. Certainly, the Earth needs more trees. Instead of regrowing forests, however, bioenergy with carbon capture and storage technologies requires dedicated industrial-scale plantations regularly harvested for their bioenergy, not for storing carbon in forests (cf., Fleischman et al., 2020).

The carbon drawdown technologies described above have limited potential to reliably mitigate climate change. These proposals allow those in power today to eschew their responsibility and pass their accountabilities to tomorrow's generations. The proposed technologies have little likelihood of being used at scale in the future because they are not being used at scale today. A poignant metaphor is to keep on smoking, assuming that one day a cure will be found for cancer.

Relying on promised technofixes of carbon capture and storage in power plants and bioenergy only risks irreversible change. A true carbon drawdown lets the natural environment absorb the greenhouse gases we produce. This means accelerating energy transition, leaving fossil fuels in the ground, reining in industrial and livestock farming, and restoring forests and other natural carbon sinks.

How can we flip towards this true energy transition and carbon drawdown? As with the complex systems on which our lives and livelihoods depend, the social systems we have created can also be flipped quickly (Bentley et al., 2014). The COVID-19 pandemic provides a lens through which we can draw lessons on how our social structures could be destabilised if external pressures become too great to bear (cf., Pinner, Rogers, and Samandari, 2020). When we were driven past our tipping points as we scrambled to contain the pandemic, develop vaccines, and ensure economic stability our social structures also, in unison, flipped at confounding speed. With climate breakdown, our best hope, then, is to bank on and use these social tipping points to our advantage to stimulate a cascade of regime changes.

Small perturbations can trigger required transformations in energy systems (Sharpe and Lenton, 2021). Crucial in complex system dynamics is to activate one tipping point to trigger another, resulting in a snowball and proliferation – in other words, a 'domino dynamics' (Ashwin, Creaser, and Tsaneva-Atanasova, 2017). Small numbers of initial actions, in the right place at the right time, can stimulate significant changes at a planetary scale, and then flip the system to a new state. This is how COVID-19, first detected in Wuhan in late 2019, ballooned into a global pandemic by March 2020. The Wuhan incident was a city-scale shock before it spread and amplified globally. We could take the same context of domino dynamics to ignite rapid decarbonisation.

The deployment of electric vehicles provides an example. The production of electric cars is now increasing as battery performance continues to improve in tandem with the expansion of charging infrastructures and battery cost decline (Muratori et al., 2021; Nykvist and Nilsson, 2015). It is not only the technology and the economics that have moved forwards. Policy also played a crucial role in driving this change. Regulations that limit vehicle emission intensity and require car sales to be of electric vehicles have propelled the electric vehicle transition in China (Wu et al., 2021) and the European Union (Tagliapietra et al., 2019). The Norwegian electric vehicle policy provides another unique example: the use of a progressive tax system that made most electric vehicles cheaper to buy than petrol-based models (Ingeborgrud and Ryghaug, 2019). This policy made Norway a world leader in the transition to electric mobility.

Domino dynamics do not imply that decarbonisation can occur without intense opposition. The power of fossil fuel companies and their lobbying efforts are so strong that they will exert all possible means to keep their businesses afloat. We have seen this in the United States (Brulle, 2018), Australia (Hudson, 2020), and even in a seeming climate leader, Canada (Graham, Carroll, and Chen, 2020; Carroll, Daub, and Gunster, 2022). If the antiquated fossil fuel industry continues to foil decarbonisation, the transition to renewable energy – which can still happen but not within the timeline now required – will be inconsequential. By then, the planetary systems could already have been pushed past their tipping points, where much of the Earth becomes unsuitable for life.

Certainly, energy transition does not always promise heaven on Earth. Returning to the example of electric vehicles, the massive deployment of batteries could mean tearing down forests and displacing communities in order to extract the minerals and resources required in their production (Xia and Li, 2022; Bekel and Pauliuk, 2019). The ongoing transition to electric mobility in China, Europe, and elsewhere is, in fact, being built on the back of blood lithium (Kaunda, 2020; cf., Agusdinata et al., 2018; Valle and Holmes, 2013). The same can be said with rare earth elements required to manufacture solar cells. Rivers are now being polluted, while people are forced to work in near-slavery conditions in rare earth metal mines (Lee et al., 2020; Sovacool et al., 2020). Most of these mines are located in developing countries in the Majority World, echoing violence and injustices familiar during the era of Western colonisation.

An authentic and just energy transition, therefore, demands system change. Mine workers have to be treated fairly, their rights protected, and their access to the benefits of the transition guaranteed (Scott and Powells, 2020). In urban areas, the shift to electric vehicles also requires a move away from the structural arrangements built for private car use (Gössling, 2016). The transition requires setting aside road space for walking and cycling while working hard to reduce the volume of cars on the road in the long term. In short, this is not only an energy generation issue; it is also an urban design challenge (Nikšič and Sezer, 2017). Building self-sufficient communities where one can access shops, parks, schools, and workplaces without driving is transformative. Compact townships create a sense of community, improve public health, and strengthen local economies. For longer journeys, electrifying public transport should be prioritised.

To make these transitions happen, we return again to domino dynamics. We must arrive at a critical threshold where a certain number of the population decide to alter their views and move out of their status quo. Our recent history provides examples of various societal tipping points. The #MeToo movement brought front and centre the need to diminish toxic masculinity and sexual abuse (Maricourt and Burrell, 2022; Harrington, 2021). The Black Lives Matter movement highlighted the need to eradicate white supremacy and fight racism (Francis and Wright-Rigueur, 2021; Esposito and Romano, 2016). Both mobilisations offer reasons to remain optimistic (cf., Stephens, 2020).

Throughout history, tipping points have also been important drivers of large-scale social and political shifts in the histories of nations. I have examined, for example, how collectives of determined citizens and small groups of people have pushed for change. Among these examples of determined movements are the mobilisation against the abuses of Philippine dictator, Ferdinand Marcos; for the passage of the Civil Rights Act of 1964 in the United States; and for the independence of India from Great Britain (Delina, 2019; Delina, Diesendorf, and Merson, 2014). A critical lesson from these mobilisations is that when a devoted minority achieves a critical mass, the social system passes a tipping point. During those moments, activities precipitate a cascade of behaviour changes that quickly enhance the acceptability of their formerly minority viewpoint. Social tipping points, thus, matter greatly in social transformations.

How small is small? Where does the social tipping point lie? Damon Centola and colleagues from the University of Pennsylvania found that a critical threshold is achieved once the size of that small-but-committed minority reaches between 25 and 27 per cent of the population. Once that critical mass is reached, social conventions quickly change (Centola et al., 2018).

The *Fridays for Future* climate protests exemplify domino dynamics in the mobilisations for climate action (Braun and Schäfer, 2022; Wallis and Loy, 2021; Winkelmann et al., 2022). From Greta Thunberg's lone school strike for the climate outside the Swedish parliament building in August 2018, her Friday strikes snowballed into a global movement. The strikes led to historic victories for Green parties in the 2019 European Parliament election. *Fridays for Future* also produced wins for the Austrian, Belgian, and Swiss Greens that year. These bottom-up movements came close to pushing the European political system towards a critical 'state' that could have aligned European climate policy with the Paris Agreement. The pandemic, however, stood in the way. Although a tipping is yet to be achieved, *Fridays for Future* contributed significantly to attitude change. Germany, for instance, began to regard the environment as the most pressing public policy concern, ahead of migration and economic difficulties (Braun and Schäfer, 2022; Winkelmann et al., 2022).

Decarbonisation requires substantial efforts to tip the scales towards a rapid energy transition. Domino dynamics suggest we can trigger a cascade of regime shifts in the energy sector and in the politics necessary to enable these transformations. Our best hope now lies in triggering tipping points in social mobilisations, which can then trigger rapid decarbonisation of energy systems and the acceleration of just carbon drawdowns. Raising the scale of climate activism by mobilising a quarter of the world population can toggle the system.

References

Agusdinata, D. B., Liu, W., Eakin, H., & Romero, H. (2018). Socio-environmental impacts of lithium mineral extraction: Towards a research agenda. *Environmental Research Letters*, *13*(12), 123001.

Ashwin, P., Creaser, J., & Tsaneva-Atanasova, K. (2017). Fast and slow domino regimes in transient network dynamics. *Physical Review E*, *96*(5), 052309.

Bekel, K., & Pauliuk, S. (2019). Prospective cost and environmental impact assessment of battery and fuel cell electric vehicles in Germany. *International Journal of Life Cycle Assessment*, *24*(12), 2220–2237.

Bentley, R. A., Maddison, E. J., Ranner, P. H., Bissell, J., Caiado, C. C., Bhatanacharoen, P., . . . & Garnett, P. (2014). Social tipping points and Earth systems dynamics. *Frontiers in Environmental Science*, *2*, 1–7.

Boers, N. (2021). Observation-based early-warning signals for a collapse of the Atlantic Meridional Overturning Circulation. *Nature Climate Change*, *11*(8), 680–688.

Boers, N., & Rypdal, M. (2021). Critical slowing down suggests that the western Greenland ice sheet is close to a tipping point. *Proceedings of the National Academy of Sciences*, *118*(21), e2024192118.

Braun, D., & Schäfer, C. (2022). Issues that mobilize Europe: The role of key policy issues for voter turnout in the 2019 European Parliament election. *European Union Politics*, *23*(1), 120–140.

Brook, B. W., Ellis, E. C., Perring, M. P., Mackay, A. W., & Blomqvist, L. (2013). Does the terrestrial biosphere have planetary tipping points? *Trends in Ecology & Evolution*, *28*(7), 396–401.

Brulle, R. J. (2018). The climate lobby: A sectoral analysis of lobbying spending on climate change in the USA, 2000 to 2016. *Climatic Change*, *149*(3), 289–303.

Cai, Y., Lenton, T. M., & Lontzek, T. S. (2016). Risk of multiple interacting tipping points should encourage rapid CO_2 emission reduction. *Nature Climate Change*, *6*(5), 520–525.

Carroll, W. K., Daub, S., & Gunster, S. (2022). Regime of Obstruction: Fossil capitalism and the many facets of climate denial in Canada. In D. Tindall, M. Stoddart, & R. Dunlap (Eds.), *Handbook of Anti-Environmentalism* (pp. 216–233). Cheltenham, UK: Edward Elgar Publishing.

Centola, D., Becker, J., Brackbill, D., & Baronchelli, A. (2018). Experimental evidence for tipping points in social convention. *Science*, *360*(6393), 1116–1119.

Christensen, J. M., & Olhoff, A. (2019). *The Emissions Gap Report 2019*. United Nations Environment Programme.

Delina, L. L. (2016). *Strategies for Rapid Climate Mitigation: Wartime Mobilisation as a Model for Action?* Abingdon, UK: Routledge.

Delina, L. L. (2019). *Emancipatory Climate Actions: Strategies from Histories*. London: Palgrave Macmillan.

Delina, L. L. (2020). Potentials and critiques of building a Southeast Asian interdisciplinary knowledge community on critical geoengineering studies. *Climatic Change*, *163*(2), 973–987.

Delina, L. L., & Diesendorf, M. (2013). Is wartime mobilisation a suitable policy model for rapid national climate mitigation? *Energy Policy*, *58*, 371–380.

Delina, L. L., Diesendorf, M., & Merson, J. (2014). Strengthening the climate action movement: Strategies from histories. *Carbon Management*, *5*(4), 397–409.

Esposito, L., & Romano, V. (2016). Benevolent racism and the co-optation of the Black Lives Matter movement. *Western Journal of Black Studies, 40*(3), 161–173.

Fleischman, F., Basant, S., Chhatre, A., Coleman, E. A., Fischer, H. W., Gupta, D., ... & Veldman, J. W. (2020). Pitfalls of tree planting show why we need people-centered natural climate solutions. *BioScience, 70*(11), 947–950.

Francis, M. M., & Wright-Rigueur, L. (2021). Black Lives Matter in historical perspective. *Annual Review of Law and Social Science, 17*, 441–458.

Fridahl, M., & Lehtveer, M. (2018). Bioenergy with carbon capture and storage (BECCS): Global potential, investment preferences, and deployment barriers. *Energy Research & Social Science, 42*, 155–165.

Gössling, S. (2016). Urban transport justice. *Journal of Transport Geography, 54*, 1–9.

Graham, N., Carroll, W. K., & Chen, D. (2020). Carbon capital's political reach: A network analysis of federal lobbying by the fossil fuel industry from Harper to Trudeau. *Canadian Political Science Review, 14*(1), 1–31.

Gunderson, R., Stuart, D., & Petersen, B. (2020). The fossil fuel industry's framing of carbon capture and storage: Faith in innovation, value instrumentalization, and status quo maintenance. *Journal of Cleaner Production, 252*, 119767.

Harrington, C. (2021). What is 'toxic masculinity' and why does it matter? *Men and Masculinities, 24*(2), 345–352.

Hudson, M. (2020). Enacted inertia: Australian fossil fuel incumbents' strategies to undermine challengers. In G. Wood & K. Baker (Eds.), *The Palgrave Handbook of Managing Fossil Fuels and Energy Transitions* (pp. 195–222). Cham: Palgrave Macmillan.

Hughes, T. P., Carpenter, S., Rockström, J., Scheffer, M., & Walker, B. (2013). Multiscale regime shifts and planetary boundaries. *Trends in Ecology & Evolution, 28*(7), 389–395.

Ingeborgrud, L., & Ryghaug, M. (2019). The role of practical, cognitive and symbolic factors in the successful implementation of battery electric vehicles in Norway. *Transportation Research Part A: Policy and Practice, 130*, 507–516.

Jung, H., Silva, R., & Han, M. (2018). Scaling trends of electric vehicle performance: Driving range, fuel economy, peak power output, and temperature effect. *World Electric Vehicle Journal, 9*(4), 46.

Kaunda, R. B. (2020). Potential environmental impacts of lithium mining. *Journal of Energy & Natural Resources Law, 38*(3), 237–244.

Kinzig, A. P., Ryan, P., Etienne, M., Allison, H., Elmqvist, T., & Walker, B. H. (2006). Resilience and regime shifts: Assessing cascading effects. *Ecology and Society, 11*(1), Art. 20.

Lee, J., Bazilian, M., Sovacool, B., & Greene, S. (2020). Responsible or reckless? A critical review of the environmental and climate assessments of mineral supply chains. *Environmental Research Letters, 15*(10), 103009.

Lenton, T. M., & Williams, H. T. (2013). On the origin of planetary-scale tipping points. *Trends in Ecology & Evolution, 28*(7), 380–382.

Lenton, T. M., Rockström, J., Gaffney, O., Rahmstorf, S., Richardson, K., Steffen, W., & Schellnhuber, H. J. (2019). Climate tipping points – too risky to bet against. *Nature, 575*, 592–595.

Low, S., & Schäfer, S. (2020). Is bio-energy carbon capture and storage (BECCS) feasible? The contested authority of integrated assessment modeling. *Energy Research & Social Science, 60*, 101326.

Malm, A. (2020). *Corona, Climate, Chronic Emergency: War Communism in the Twenty-First Century*. London: Verso Books.

Maricourt, C. D., & Burrell, S. R. (2022). #MeToo or #MenToo? Expressions of backlash and masculinity politics in the #MeToo era. *Journal of Men's Studies*, *30*(1), 49–69.

Metz, B., Davidson, O., and De Coninck, H. (Eds.). (2005). *Carbon Dioxide Capture and Storage: Special Report of the Intergovernmental Panel on Climate Change*. New York: Cambridge University Press.

Muratori, M., Alexander, M., Arent, D., Bazilian, M., Cazzola, P., Dede, E. M., ... & Ward, J. (2021). The rise of electric vehicles – 2020 status and future expectations. *Progress in Energy*, *3*(2), 022002.

Nikšič, M., & Sezer, C. (2017). Public space and urban justice. *Built Environment*, *43*(2), 165–172.

Nobre, C. A., & Borma, L. D. S. (2009). 'Tipping points' for the Amazon forest. *Current Opinion in Environmental Sustainability*, *1*(1), 28–36.

Nykvist, B., & Nilsson, M. (2015). Rapidly falling costs of battery packs for electric vehicles. *Nature Climate Change*, *5*(4), 329–332.

Ojha, H., Maraseni, T., Nightingale, A., & Bhattarai, B. (2019). Rescuing forests from the carbon trap. *Forest Policy and Economics*, *101*, 15–18.

Pan, Y., Birdsey, R. A., Fang, J., Houghton, R., Kauppi, P. E., Kurz, W. A., ... & Hayes, D. (2011). A large and persistent carbon sink in the world's forests. *Science*, *333*(6045), 988–993.

Pinner, D., Rogers, M., & Samandari, H. (2020). Addressing climate change in a post-pandemic world. *McKinsey Quarterly*, April.

Rocha, J. C., Peterson, G., Bodin, Ö., & Levin, S. (2018). Cascading regime shifts within and across scales. *Science*, *362*(6421), 1379–1383.

Scott, M., & Powells, G. (2020). Towards a new social science research agenda for hydrogen transitions: Social practices, energy justice, and place attachment. *Energy Research & Social Science*, *61*, 101346.

Sharpe, S., & Lenton, T. M. (2021). Upward-scaling tipping cascades to meet climate goals: Plausible grounds for hope. *Climate Policy*, *21*(4), 421–433.

Sovacool, B. K. (2016). How long will it take? Conceptualizing the temporal dynamics of energy transitions. *Energy Research & Social Science*, *13*, 202–215.

Sovacool, B. K., Ali, S. H., Bazilian, M., Radley, B., Nemery, B., Okatz, J., & Mulvaney, D. (2020). Sustainable minerals and metals for a low-carbon future. *Science*, *367*(6473), 30–33.

Steffen, W., Richardson, K., Rockström, J., Cornell, S. E., Fetzer, I., Bennett, E. M., ... & Sörlin, S. (2015). Planetary boundaries: Guiding human development on a changing planet. *Science*, *347*(6223), 1259855.

Stephens, J. C. (2020). *Diversifying Power: Why We Need Antiracist, Feminist Leadership on Climate and Energy*. Washington, DC: Island Press.

Tagliapietra, S., Zachmann, G., Edenhofer, O., Glachant, J. M., Linares, P., & Loeschel, A. (2019). The European union energy transition: Key priorities for the next five years. *Energy Policy*, *132*, 950–954.

Valle, V. M., & Holmes, H. C. (2013). Bolivia's energy and mineral resources trade and investments with China: Potential socioeconomic and environmental effects of lithium extraction. *Latin American Policy*, *4*(1), 93–122.

Wallis, H., & Loy, L. S. (2021). What drives pro-environmental activism of young people? A survey study on the Fridays For Future movement. *Journal of Environmental Psychology, 74*, 101581.

Wang, R., Dearing, J. A., Langdon, P. G., Zhang, E., Yang, X., Dakos, V., & Scheffer, M. (2012). Flickering gives early warning signals of a critical transition to a eutrophic lake state. *Nature, 492*(7429), 419–422.

Winkelmann, R., Donges, J. F., Smith, E. K., Milkoreit, M., Eder, C., Heitzig, J., ... & Lenton, T. M. (2022). Social tipping processes towards climate action: A conceptual framework. *Ecological Economics, 192*, 107242.

Wu, Y. A., Ng, A. W., Yu, Z., Huang, J., Meng, K., & Dong, Z. Y. (2021). A review of evolutionary policy incentives for sustainable development of electric vehicles in China: Strategic implications. *Energy Policy, 148*, 111983.

Xia, X., & Li, P. (2022). A review of the life cycle assessment of electric vehicles: Considering the influence of batteries. *Science of The Total Environment, 814*, 152870.

8
Decluttering Consumption

> *We need better economic ideas that encourage moderation in our consumption while tackling the underlying constraints of neo-liberal economics in sustaining life on Earth and solving the global inequality crisis. Minimalism and self-sufficiency declutter consumption practices and respect the limits of the living planet.*

As the COVID-19 pandemic drew attention to jarring inequities globally (Deaton, 2021), the inadequacy of mainstream neo-liberal economic thought – hinged on the philosophy of perpetual growth and unfettered consumption – to articulate what matters most has become abundantly clear. If there is one thing we should have learned during the pandemic, it is how to differentiate between things that matter and those that do not. Let us also not forget that the onset of the pandemic coincided with a moment when we were already in the throes of multiple global challenges, such as catastrophic climate change (Urban, 2015), blatant human rights abuses (Schmid, 2021), rising income disparity (Hing et al., 2019), the deterioration of democracies (Merkel, 2018), and maladies of both poverty and affluence (Iceland, 2019). Once the pandemic has ended, we will need to go back to dealing with these crises. This requires us to make significant adjustments, not only to how we interact with one another as human beings and with the rest of nature, but also to how we use and consume resources.

Excessive consumption and affluence, when allowed to run unchecked, may lead to production methods and behaviours that are unsustainable and unequal for all (Thøgersen, 2014). The destruction of forests, the mining of lands, the damming of rivers, and the conversion of vast swaths of land into industrial meat or monocultural crop production are all necessary steps in the quest for unfettered affluent lifestyles. In addition to causing irreparable harm to the environment, these activities result in the uprooting of hundreds of thousands, if not millions, of people from the houses and lands they have called home (cf., Calzadilla, 2021; Timmons Roberts and Parks, 2007).

Most of the 'products' manufactured for prosperous lifestyles are referred to as non-essentials by their end users (Pereira Heath and Chatzidakis, 2012). These are now more accessible and affordable than they were ten to twenty years ago, creating an illusion of plentiful supply (Dobers and Strannegård, 2005). This perceived abundance was created by uncontrolled globalisation of trade and finance and the expansionist principle systemic in neo-liberal capitalism. The proliferation of kitchen and food shows on television, Netflix, and other internet streaming providers is one example of this illusion of plenty (Buerkle, 2019). But, the things that the 'affluent' class desire are only accessible in limited amounts, and we are quickly running out of materials to produce consumer goods.

The great majority of the goods we use and consume are, in some way, derived from fossil fuels (Pirani, 2018). This may be directly as in the case of plastics (Stanton et al., 2021) or indirectly, in the transport or energy required to make consumer goods. When, for example, we discard mobile phones that are still fully functional so that we may upgrade to the newest model, we not only contribute to destructive mining operations in the Congo or elsewhere but also to the climate crisis. People who can purchase goods and services from anywhere on Earth leave an ecological and social imprint far larger than any of us are ever able to notice.

The prevailing neo-liberal ideology and practices, governed by powerful financial–military–industrial complexes, favours greed-based accumulation rather than need-based consumption (Robinson, 2020). Fixing this means radically transforming how our economy is managed and who governs it. In the guise of 'progress', neo-liberalism justifies the ever-increasing acquisition of products, known as consumerism. Neo-liberal capitalism conceals the reality that such unnecessary expansion bears a relation to reducing poverty and hardship (Donnelly, 2019). Neo-liberal capitalism may, in fact, increase deprivation and suffering by destroying nature-based livelihoods (Fletcher, Dressler, and Büscher, 2015). We need a transition to everyday practices of what exactly is required to live as a human as opposed to what a human being wants.

However, understanding and recognising this difference between needs and wants, the essentials and the non-essentials is not as simple as it may seem. There are several goods that the vast majority of people would probably agree can simply be placed in the 'non-essentials' category. For many, luxury automobiles, yachts, and private planes are considered non-essentials – but for a very few, they are. Some things that were formerly considered luxuries have now been elevated to essentials. Examples are electricity, mobile phones, washing machines, refrigerators, and personal motorised vehicles.

During the pandemic lockdowns, we were shown that it is possible to differentiate 'essentials' from 'non-essentials'. Such differentiations were not wholly based on personal preferences. As we chose to put a premium on what matters, that is, our essential needs, we were also decluttering. Decluttering and minimalism was already having its moment before the pandemic, especially in the Minority World. Marie Kondo's lifestyle books became bestsellers. And the cultural moment of minimalism was brought to new heights when people were locked inside their homes (Sandlin and Wallin, 2022; Iran et al., 2022; Eike et al., 2021). YouTube channels, podcasts, books, and documentaries on 'focusing on what brings one joy', simplicity, tiny houses, and digital nomadism provided clues of this cultural turn.

While minimalism and decluttering continue to circulate on both traditional and social media, it remains challenging to understand what they truly mean since they are, inarguably, being co-opted by consumer culture (Rodriguez, 2018). After all, the so-called and self-proclaimed minimalist gurus are monetising their YouTube videos, selling books, and offering speaking tours while proclaiming to maintain simple and focused lifestyles. Regardless of these vanities, the modern minimalism movement – if it can be called such – has committed to decluttering 'things' and thus addresses exacerbating waste management pressures and the relationship of its practitioners with consumption (Eike et al., 2021).

Minimalism, as it emerged as a cultural phenomenon in the Minority World, is already practised in many places in the Majority World, although it is not described as such. It is a way of life. In this context, minimalism is about living simply without wanting luxurious commodities and goods. Under pandemic lockdown in 2020 and 2021, I re-experienced how it is to live this way. Because of the raging virus, I was confined in a roughly 2,000 square metre compound in my village in Southern Philippines, along with my parents, my younger brother's family, and my three nieces; we were concerned but not to the point that we worried for our survival and sustenance. We raised hogs and chickens in our backyard and grew vegetables in our small space. We were self-sufficient. We rode the pandemic for more than a year. We thrived because it is the way we live.

Self-sufficiency is not about depriving oneself of things. It is about consciously choosing what matters most and what is necessary. Self-sufficiency is very common in many agricultural societies, where crops are left in the field for months before they can be harvested (Bishwajit et al., 2013). While waiting for the crops to ripen, farmers would content themselves by living their lives with what was available. As a son of rice farmers, I am used to the idea that only during harvest time – and this occurs only twice a year, almost five months apart – can we have some luxuries. These include the opportunity to buy new clothes and, if the harvest is abundant, new shoes.

Living a simple life underlined by consuming only what is necessary is also part of many philosophies. One example is the ancient Indian philosophy of *aparigraha*, which emphasises the necessity of practising non-possession, non-attachment, and non-greed (Singh, 2016; Pawar, 2021). *Aparigraha*, one of the tenets of the *Bhagavad Gita*, is a form of self-control that avoids coveting and envying material gains that hurt other beings, including nature.

In Thailand, a number of groups adopt and practise the moderation society philosophy (which is specific to Thailand but has a broad and global application), following Rama IX's development concept of self-sufficiency (Delina, 2020, 2022). This philosophy is manifested in several rural development projects scattered around Thailand to spur sustainable development in the countryside. While there are criticisms surrounding the political economy of the moderation society philosophy and its application to rural Thailand (which is the entrenchment of what can be called modern feudalism), these development projects are able to close some development gaps.

I observed this translation of philosophy to development first hand during my visit to one of these rural communities during my fieldwork in 2017 (Delina, 2020, 2022). The Pa Deng moderation society network is a group of more than 100 households inside the Kaeng Krachan National Park. Network members subscribed to the moderation society philosophy to devise mechanisms to provide families inside the Park, who do not have electricity grid access, with the opportunity to obtain modern and clean forms of energy. Members would contribute an amount monthly to a mutual fund. The amounts were then pooled to support small-scale biogas digesters for producing cooking gas or solar home systems for lighting and powering small appliances. Recipients would then pay back the principal amounts in amortisations plus minimal interest to the mutual fund so that other members could also benefit.

In this example, minimalism extends beyond access to essentials – energy, food, and clothes (Delina, 2020, 2022). The network members' practice of self-sufficiency also meets several of society's non-material needs. Among these co-benefits include enhanced intangible capacities and assets such as people's social relationships and connections to the rest of the natural world. Network members also gain access to new opportunities for intellectual development by learning skills related to the operations and maintenance of renewable energy systems. These portable skills allow members to diversify their livelihoods.

Perhaps the most crucial benefit of this practice is the ability of community members to participate in group dynamics, where they can take lessons from and add value to each other. The group practised deliberative meetings to ensure everyone gets involved in decision-making (Delina, 2020, 2022). Gender considerations were also incorporated into other aspects of life in the

Pa Deng network. Gender empowerment occurred in terms of women members participating in leadership roles and working together on cottage industry projects such as soap and winemaking (Delina, 2020, 2022).

Decluttering, living simply, self-sufficiency, and minimalism have been thrust into our minds as a result of the COVID-19 pandemic (Sandlin and Wallin, 2022). As the climate crisis intensifies its impact, situations in which people endure series, if not parallel, adversities can profit from the stories of living simply during pandemic lockdowns (Mishra and Rath, 2020). For all the deaths and suffering the pandemic brought us, this global misery also provided an alternative picture of how societies could thrive in the future.

During the pandemic, people have, all of a sudden, been exposed to cleaner air as industrial activities and fossil fuel–powered mobility were reduced (Corlett et al., 2020). People have been required, or given the opportunity, to reconnect with their families, as I did (Prime, Wade, and Browne, 2020; Cassinat et al., 2021). Many will also recall the pandemic as an opportunity to revive relationships with their pets and neighbours as they experienced lockdown conditions together (Morgan et al., 2020). Most of all, the pandemic gave many people the opportunity to reflect on what it means to be alive.

Thus, the pandemic lockdowns also revealed the harsh fact that most people could not even satisfy their most fundamental needs for food, water, and clean air (Bottan, Hoffmann, and Vera-Cossio, 2020). As a result of economic inequality skyrocketing to unfathomable heights over the past few decades, and becoming more glaring during the pandemic, growth-centred development has ripped away subsistence supplies like land and water. Neo-liberalism has privatised fundamental human rights like well-being, schooling, and housing (Mansfield, 2009). Right-wing governance has whittled down democratic spaces (Rapeli and Saikkonen, 2020). Billions of people have found accessing their material and non-material needs a challenge. The pandemic brought this inequality front and centre to many.

Modern inequality is a continuation of ancient forms of inequality, such as caste discrimination, racism, sexism, and similar practices (cf., Singh, 2018). We must face social inequalities and poverty head-on to address global problems, not just the pandemic but also other crises, including the climate emergency. Solutions driven mainly by technology or the market will simply be insufficient. The Minority World does not need further growth (Eisenmenger et al., 2020). Instead, we require a progressive redistribution of wealth and power from those in whom it is consolidated to those who have little or nothing. In short, we need to rethink the political economy of our modernity.

Mahatma Gandhi's ideas are more important than ever in today's world. One is *satyagraha*, which means speaking truth to power and having the right to protest peacefully (Kool and Agrawal, 2018; Rai and Tiwary, 2021). This idea is now required, more than ever, to push for new economic thinking that curtails excessive consumption, especially by the rich. Two further ideas of Gandhi are relevant today – *swaraj*, which means that personal and collective liberties are premised on obligation towards the freedoms of everyone (Kakati, 2021; Jain, 2022), and *sarvodaya*, which implies the upliftment of all and the awareness that we exist together in one world (Bose, 2021; Kakoty, 2022). What is bad for the bee is terrible for the hive. Hence, we must strive towards a future in which economic institutions function on the basis of the 'welfare of all' and preserve the 'right of all', starting with the most disenfranchised, vulnerable, and marginalised members of society.

Instead of looking for consumption-based development, capital investment, and profit-seeking as we have with the neo-liberal economic model, we need a new economic system based on moderation, self-sufficiency, and guaranteed freedoms for all. The ideas of social and climate justice should drive this system. The nurturing of inherent human values of empathy and altruism, especially as peoples in the Majority World bear the worst impacts of the climate emergency, should also be a critical part of this system. The protection of the natural environment, the basis of our very survival, is also an imperative component of this new economic system. Beyond economics, these changes must be reflected in politics. We should also be moving away from a political system in which a few individuals hold the majority of power and rule over the rest of the population towards a system in which power is more evenly distributed among all.

Most of us have been significantly inconvenienced by the effects of the COVID-19 pandemic. There is no denying that fact. However, this also raises the question of what the term 'convenient' means. Because of increasing isolation, individualism, and materialism associated with neo-liberalism and excessive consumption, we now consider any kind of physical labour to be 'inconvenient'. This paves the way for companies to provide 'convenience' while outsourcing physical work to machines or labour sources that are less expensive.

Outsourcing has made us careless of the reality that someone, somewhere, is paying the cost of our convenience. Outsourcing involves an immense cost to the environment (Zhang and Huang, 2012). Workers in the Majority World are also in danger of their dignity and the resources necessary for their survival being robbed by outsourcing practices. This happens when the rights of outsourced workers are not protected (Suppa and Bureš, 2020). It also occurs when resources are extracted from natural environments held by people and their communities for centuries, if not millennia, without due process.

Despite rapid global heating, we can still restructure our economy to better sustain life on Earth. Governments should lead in this restructuring to create new forms of employment. More importantly, only those industries that can assist in ensuring the continued existence of human beings and the rest of the living world should get government support. Oil, airline, and car companies should not be bailed out in these restructuring efforts. Governments should buy out these polluting businesses and refocus them towards developing clean technologies (cf., Newell, 2021).

The pandemic has offered us a second and most important opportunity to address global misery brought about by cascading crises. The first opportunity, which occurred during the economic recession of 2008, was frivolously thrown away (González Hernando, 2019; Peters et al., 2012). While enormous sums of public money were spent on reconfiguring the sleazy old economy through so-called economic stimuli, these programmes ensured that wealth would continue to be held by those who were already wealthy, instead of rallying sustainable efforts. It is worrisome that several governments are still intent on repeating these disastrous blunders.

As we think about the present economic system and envisage a just system, it is crucial to note that the so-called free market was always the result of government policy decisions. If anti-trust regulations are lax, only a few enormous corporations will thrive, while the rest will fail (Hope and Limberg, 2022). We see this with tax systems that favour big corporations and the super-rich. By contrast, businesses that promote environmental sustainability have had their chances of thriving reduced.

The degree to which big businesses depend on public policy, especially in capitalist countries, is at its highest point in recent history. We now see several industries wholly dependent on the state for their continued existence (e.g., Gaddi, Garbellini, and Garibaldo, 2021). One example is the oil industry, which, for decades, received and enjoyed subsidies and tax breaks provided by many governments (Erickson et al., 2017; Skovgaard and van Asselt, 2019). Most governments also provide a similar level of support to the coal and gas sectors (Touchette, 2015).

It was worrying, therefore, when governments bailed out the oil industry in 2020, when millions of barrels of oil were unsaleable (Ma, Xiong, and Bao, 2021). Yet again, governments simply repeated what they did with the banking sector when it was in the same position in 2008. Governments failed to utilise their power to eliminate the socially damaging behaviours prevalent in the oil sector and to reconstruct it based on the need to sustain life on Earth. In 2020, the opportunity to curtail the oil sector was lost – and oil prices continue to surge to new heights as these words are written, in July 2022. The increasing price of oil secured windfalls for oil barons and their shareholders. To add insult to injury, environmental protections are now being dismantled, as in the case of a June 2022 United States Supreme Court ruling that favoured polluters when it decided that the US Environmental Protection Agency does not have the authority to regulate carbon dioxide emissions.

To close this chapter: the COVID-19 pandemic gives us a peek at how much work is ahead of us if we are to reverse the dreadful climate emergency. While necessary, the significant changes many people are making in their lives in terms of questioning excessive consumption and pursuing a decluttered lifestyle during this global misery will probably only result in a measly reduction in global carbon dioxide emissions. To have a fair chance of averting an increase in global temperature of 1.5°C or higher, we need to reduce our emissions more than we can from minimalism and decluttering combined. This rapid decarbonisation entails making fundamental adjustments to accomplish the required reduction. It necessitates formulating and implementing an altogether new political and economic system that pays attention to the capacity of the planet to sustain life while also addressing and reducing inequality.

References

Bishwajit, G., Sarker, S., Kpoghomou, M. A., Gao, H., Jun, L., Yin, D., & Ghosh, S. (2013). Self-sufficiency in rice and food security: A South Asian perspective. *Agriculture & Food Security*, *2*(1), 1–6.

Bose, N. K. (2021). The theory and practice of sarvodaya. In P. Power (Ed.), *The Meanings of Gandhi* (pp. 79–90). Honolulu: University of Hawaii Press.

Bottan, N., Hoffmann, B., & Vera-Cossio, D. (2020). The unequal impact of the coronavirus pandemic: Evidence from seventeen developing countries. *PLoS One*, *15*(10), e0239797.

Buerkle, C. W. (2019). Kitchen porn: Of consumerist fantasies and desires. In M. Meyers (Ed.), *Neoliberalism and the Media* (pp. 147–162). Abingdon, UK: Routledge.

Calzadilla, P. V. (2021). The Sustainable Development Goals, climate crisis and sustained injustices. *Oñati Socio-Legal Series*, *11*(1), 285–314.

Cassinat, J. R., Whiteman, S. D., Serang, S., Dotterer, A. M., Mustillo, S. A., Maggs, J. L., & Kelly, B. C. (2021). Changes in family chaos and family relationships during the COVID-19 pandemic: Evidence from a longitudinal study. *Developmental Psychology*, *57*(10), 1597–1610.

Corlett, R. T., Primack, R. B., Devictor, V., Maas, B., Goswami, V. R., Bates, A. E., ... & Roth, R. (2020). Impacts of the coronavirus pandemic on biodiversity conservation. *Biological Conservation*, *246*, 108571.

Deaton, A. (2021). *COVID-19 and Global Income Inequality* (No. w28392). National Bureau of Economic Research, Cambridge, MA.

Delina, L. L. (2020). A rural energy collaboratory: Co-production in Thailand's community energy experiments. *Journal of Environmental Studies and Sciences*, *10*(1), 83–90.

Delina, L. L. (2022). Co-producing just energy transition in everyday practices: Sociotechnical innovation and sustainable development in the Thailand–Myanmar border. *Local Environment*, *27*(1), 16–31.

Dobers, P., & Strannegård, L. (2005). Design, lifestyles and sustainability. Aesthetic consumption in a world of abundance. *Business Strategy and the Environment*, *14*(5), 324–336.

Donnelly, S. (2019). *The Lie of Global Prosperity: How Neoliberals Distort Data to Mask Poverty and Exploitation*. New York: New York University Press.

Eike, R. J., Burton, M., Hustvedt, G., & Cho, S. (2021). The 'joy of letting go': Decluttering and apparel. *Fashion Practice*, *14*(2), 225–241.

Eisenmenger, N., Pichler, M., Krenmayr, N., Noll, D., Plank, B., Schalmann, E., ... & Gingrich, S. (2020). The Sustainable Development Goals prioritize economic growth over sustainable resource use: A critical reflection on the SDGs from a socio-ecological perspective. *Sustainability Science*, *15*(4), 1101–1110.

Erickson, P., Down, A., Lazarus, M., & Koplow, D. (2017). Effect of subsidies to fossil fuel companies on United States crude oil production. *Nature Energy*, *2*(11), 891–898.

Fletcher, R., Dressler, W., & Büscher, B. (2015). NatureTM Inc.: Nature as neoliberal capitalist imaginary. In R. Bryant (Ed.), *The International Handbook of Political Ecology*. Cheltenham, UK: Edward Elgar.

Gaddi, M., Garbellini, N., & Garibaldo, F. (2021). The growing inequalities in Italy – North/South – and the increasing dependency of the successful North upon German and French industries. *European Planning Studies*, *29*(9), 1637–1655.

González Hernando, M. (2019). *British Think Tanks After the 2008 Global Financial Crisis*. Cham: Palgrave Macmillan.

Hing, L. S. S., Wilson, A. E., Gourevitch, P., English, J., & Sin, P. (2019). Failure to respond to rising income inequality: Processes that legitimize growing disparities. *Daedalus*, *148*(3), 105–135.

Hope, D., & Limberg, J. (2022). The economic consequences of major tax cuts for the rich. *Socio-Economic Review*, *20*, 539–559.

Iceland, J. (2019). Racial and ethnic inequality in poverty and affluence, 1959–2015. *Population Research and Policy Review*, *38*(5), 615–654.

Iran, S., Joyner Martinez, C. M., Vladimirova, K., Wallaschkowski, S., Diddi, S., Henninger, C. E., ... & Tiedke, L. (2022). When mortality knocks: Pandemic-inspired attitude shifts towards sustainable clothing consumption in six countries. *International Journal of Sustainable Fashion & Textiles*, *1*(1), 9–39.

Jain, S. K. (2022). On the normative structure of Gandhian thought: With special reference to Hind Swaraj. In R. Bhargava (Ed.), *Politics, Ethics and the Self* (pp. 110–118). New Delhi: Routledge.

Kakati, B. K. (2021). Gram swaraj: The sustainable model for rural industrialisation and employment. *International Journal of Community and Social Development*, *3*(3), 274–289.

Kakoty, S. (2022). Time to globalize sarvodaya? In S. Mukherjee & L. Zsolnai (Eds.), *Global Perspectives on Indian Spirituality and Management* (pp. 123–131). Singapore: Springer.

Kool, V. K., & Agrawal, R. (2018). Gandhian philosophy for living in the modern world: Lessons from the psychology of satyagraha. In D. Fernando & R. Moodley (Eds.), *Global Psychologies* (pp. 229–243). London: Palgrave Macmillan.

Ma, R. R., Xiong, T., & Bao, Y. (2021). The Russia–Saudi Arabia oil price war during the COVID-19 pandemic. *Energy Economics*, *102*, 105517.

Mansfield, B. (Ed.). (2009). *Privatization: Property and the Remaking of Nature–Society Relations*. John Wiley & Sons.

Merkel, W. (2018). Challenge or crisis of democracy. In W. Merkel & S. Kneip (Eds.), *Democracy and Crisis* (pp. 1–28). Cham: Springer.

Mishra, C., & Rath, N. (2020). Social solidarity during a pandemic: Through and beyond Durkheimian lens. *Social Sciences & Humanities Open, 2*(1), 100079.

Morgan, L., Protopopova, A., Birkler, R. I. D., Itin-Shwartz, B., Sutton, G. A., Gamliel, A., ... & Raz, T. (2020). Human–dog relationships during the COVID-19 pandemic: Booming dog adoption during social isolation. *Humanities and Social Sciences Communications, 7*(1), 1–11.

Newell, P. (2021). Towards a fossil fuel treaty. In S. Bohm & S. Sullivan (Eds.), *Negotiating Climate Change in Crisis* (pp. 209–216). Cambridge: Open Book Publishers.

Pawar, S. S. (2021). Mahatma Gandhi's economic thoughts on agriculture. *Turkish Journal of Computer and Mathematics Education, 12*(9), 2144–2148.

Pereira Heath, M. T., & Chatzidakis, A. (2012). 'Blame it on marketing': Consumers' views on unsustainable consumption. *International Journal of Consumer Studies, 36*(6), 656–667.

Peters, G. P., Marland, G., Le Quéré, C., Boden, T., Canadell, J. G., & Raupach, M. R. (2012). Rapid growth in CO_2 emissions after the 2008–2009 global financial crisis. *Nature Climate Change, 2*(1), 2–4.

Pirani, S. (2018). *Burning Up: A Global History of Fossil Fuel Consumption*. London: Pluto Press.

Prime, H., Wade, M., & Browne, D. T. (2020). Risk and resilience in family well-being during the COVID-19 pandemic. *American Psychologist, 75*(5), 631–643.

Rai, D., & Tiwary, R. M. (2021). Gandhi and satyagraha: A quest for global transformation. *Social Change, 51*(1), 121–133.

Rapeli, L., & Saikkonen, I. (2020). How will the COVID-19 pandemic affect democracy? *Democratic Theory, 7*(2), 25–32.

Robinson, W. I. (2020). Global capitalism post-pandemic. *Race & Class, 62*(2), 3–13.

Rodriguez, J. (2018). The US minimalist movement: Radical political practice? *Review of Radical Political Economics, 50*(2), 286–296.

Sandlin, J. A., & Wallin, J. J. (2022). Decluttering the pandemic: Marie Kondo, minimalism, and the 'joy' of waste. *Cultural Studies ↔ Critical Methodologies, 22*(1), 96–102.

Schmid, L. (2021). Deportation, harms, and human rights. *Ethics & Global Politics, 14*(2), 98–109.

Singh, P. (2016). Significance of Gandhian contemplation about self-sufficient village economy of India after economic reform. *Quest – The Journal of UGC-HRDC Nainital, 10*(2), 151–156.

Singh, V. (2018). Myths of meritocracy: Caste, karma and the new racism, a comparative study. *Ethnic and Racial Studies, 41*(15), 2693–2710.

Skovgaard, J., & van Asselt, H. (2019). The politics of fossil fuel subsidies and their reform: Implications for climate change mitigation. *Wiley Interdisciplinary Reviews: Climate Change, 10*(4), e581.

Stanton, T., Kay, P., Johnson, M., Chan, F. K. S., Gomes, R. L., Hughes, J., ... & Xu, Y. (2021). It's the product not the polymer: Rethinking plastic pollution. *Wiley Interdisciplinary Reviews: Water, 8*(1), e1490.

Suppa, A., & Bureš, P. (2020). Can multinational corporations be responsible for human rights violation of its outsourcee company? Response of national or international law? *International & Comparative Law Review, 20*(1), 153–179.

Thøgersen, J. (2014). Unsustainable consumption: Basic causes and implications for policy. *European Psychologist, 19*(2), 84–95.

Timmons Roberts, J., & Parks, B. C. (2007). Fueling injustice: Globalization, ecologically unequal exchange and climate change. *Globalizations, 4*(2), 193–210.

Touchette, Y. (2015). *G20 Subsidies to Oil, Gas and Coal Production.* International Institute for Sustainable Development.

Urban, M. C. (2015). Accelerating extinction risk from climate change. *Science, 348*(6234), 571–573.

Zhang, A., & Huang, G. Q. (2012). Impacts of business environment changes on global manufacturing outsourcing in China. *Supply Chain Management: An International Journal, 17*, 138–51.

9
Confronting Neo-Liberalism

We need an alternative economic system founded on the physical constraints of the living Earth rather than on economic abstractions. To confront the neo-liberal paradigm at its core, we must build a society in which individual sufficiency coexists with public luxury, rather than one based on the paradigm of infinite growth.

Six out of ten people in more than 100 countries suggest that local businesses announcing changes to make their activities sustainable is one of the crucial signs of post-pandemic economic recovery (Ipsos, 2021). The public's appreciation of low-carbon recovery suggests, in part, that carbon-based economic activities are the ways of the past. It also signals that perpetual growth based on unsustainable practices will be entirely disastrous – including for the climate and all species living on the planet. There is no way to make the quest for perpetual growth more environmentally friendly. To correct this, we require a new economic paradigm. Everyone must work hard to convince their governments to act in this best interest, rather than in the interest of companies seeking to maintain and sustain overconsumption and fossil fuel combustion. Breaking the ties that bind politicians to these industries, which they ought to be regulating or, in this instance, shutting down, is an ongoing struggle.

The goal of perpetual economic growth is to allow those with lower incomes to enjoy the same standard of living as those with higher incomes. However, we have already reached the point where we are beyond the physical boundaries of the Earth. We are close to overshooting tipping points as the climate system changes at speed (Ritchie et al., 2021). In addition to the disruption of the climate system, the extinction of ecosystems and species, the depletion of soil, and the accumulation of plastic in the ocean have all been caused by unfettered consumerism (cf., Murphy et al., 2021). It is impossible to satisfy the demand of individual affluence for all people since there is insufficient room for this, either physically and ecologically (Wiedmann et al., 2020).

The corollary promise is that we will be able to balance unending economic expansion and the preservation of our ecosystems by engaging in environmentally responsible consumption. However, there is no discernible difference in the carbon impact left by individuals concerned about their footprints and those who do not (Tabi, 2013; Ivanova et al., 2016). People who are more environmentally aware often have more money and therefore use more energy and consume more than those who are less aware. This is because those who are more financially secure often have a greater understanding of environmental issues. It is not our mindset that determines how much influence we have on the planet but, instead, our money (Ivanova et al., 2016). Despite our good intentions, our planetary footprint expands as our wealth increases. The wealthiest 1 per cent of the world's population produces around 175 times as much carbon as the lowest 10 per cent (Gore, 2020).

This does not mean we should stop working to lessen the negative impacts of our actions, but we should be mindful of the constraints imposed by our consumption practices. Our efforts cannot alter the results produced by our economic and production systems; it is necessary to make adjustments to the system itself. But is it possible?

Decoupling growth from sustainability has been advocated as a response (Ward et al., 2016). Our era of unfettered consumption tells us we can do anything we set our minds to. We can get any electronic device that we are capable of imagining, as well as a good number of those that we are not. Decoupling suggests we can live like kings without sacrificing the planet's ability to provide for our needs and our luxuries. The promise that comes with the further development of economies is that they will become more resource-efficient over time, making all of this a reality. Even the ideals of sustainable development may be traced back to the core assumption of decoupling. It is at the centre of all conferences on climate change, including at the Conferences of Parties (COPs) to the United Nations Framework Convention on Climate Change (UNFCCC) and other conferences that address environmental concerns. But, it seems to lack any basis in reality (Fletcher and Rammelt, 2017).

Decoupling economic growth from material resource use cannot be achieved over the long run because there are physical limitations to the efficiency of production (Næss and Høyer, 2009). Despite the possibility that materials used in growing the economy can be decreased, the overall amount of resources used will continue to increase because growth will continue to exceed efficiency. In this perpetual growth paradigm, the goal is always to ensure that the economy doubles, then doubles once again, and then continues multiplying forever. The problem is that the eternal quest for economic expansion is impossible on a planet that is not expanding. This is a crucial reason why environmental catastrophes – including climate change – are progressing at such a rapid pace.

Defenders of the perpetual economic growth paradigm defend the system on the assumption that economic development is necessary to address poverty. However, the extra income created by an increase in the economy – measured in terms of gross domestic product – is received by less than 10 per cent of the world's poorest populations (cf., Stiglitz, 2018). If the perpetual economic growth paradigm continues, it will take 200 years to reach the goal of providing a decent living for everyone. The quest for eternal growth is never a tool for alleviating poverty (Castree, 2010); rather, it is a recipe for ruining the planet and life on Earth.

In addition, decoupling is an irrationality. It is calculated in this way. To find what is known as 'domestic material consumption', one must begin with the raw materials extracted in one's own country, then add those raw materials to the items imported from other nations, and then deduct those items that are exported. However, because only the finished goods that are traded from one country to another are taken into account, and not the raw materials that are used in their production, the overall amount of resources used by wealthy nations is grossly underestimated by this method.

For instance, if copper is to be mined and processed in South Cotabato in the southern Philippines (my home province), which is said to hold Asia's largest copper deposits, these raw materials, as well as the equipment and infrastructure necessary to create the finished metal (including energy resources most likely from combusted coal), are included in the domestic material consumption figures. This is the case regardless of whether South Cotabato's copper is exported or not. However, only the weight of that copper is considered when we import a completed product from another country. Since copper mining has moved from developed nations, such as Australia and the United States, to developing nations, like the Philippines, it would seem that developed nations are utilising fewer resources.

Rather than using 'domestic material consumption' in measuring decoupling, 'material footprint' is a more appropriate measurement. Material footprint accounts for all of the economy's use of raw materials regardless of where those commodities were obtained. To return to the example of a material footprint scenario, Australia and the United States will factor into their calculations the copper they extracted from my home province that is used to make products. When these imported raw materials are considered, the advantages of efficiency in Australia and the United States that were seen before effectively vanish. There is, therefore, a gross underestimation of the raw materials used.

The big paradox of unfettered consumption and environmental conservation is that governments encourage us to increase our consumption *and* our level of conservation simultaneously. The amount of fossil fuel we use has to be reduced, yet we need to get more fossil fuel from the ground to ensure more and more economic activities. We should simultaneously grow, trash, and replace the number of things that come into our homes while reducing, reusing, and recycling them. It would be better for the living world if we ate less meat, but it would also benefit the agricultural sector if we ate more meat. The same can be said with energy transition. We need to deploy renewable energy systems extensively and at a quick speed. The price we pay for this, among others, is the mining of rare elements and metals that, if not done with social and environmental safeguards, pose detriments to communities and the natural environments from which these resources are extracted.

The fact that we do not confront the consumption–conservation paradox is not the only problem. Very few people even acknowledge its existence. It seems as if the problem is just too complex and terrifying to even consider. It would seem that we are unwilling to recognise the reality that our 'paradise' is also our 'nightmare' and that the processes of creation and destruction appear to be two sides of the same coin.

If decoupling is not the way forward, what is?

The Green New Deal that many had advocated for long before the COVID-19 pandemic occurred is one strategy for a green post-pandemic recovery (e.g., Le Billon et al., 2021). These packages recognise the limits of the living planet while working towards the recovery of the economy and revitalisation of the social aspects of life (Pettifor, 2020). While many call them stimulus packages, Green New Deal packages should not be described thus. They are unlike the stimulus packages of the economic recession of 2008, which were designed to stimulate industries that burn fossil fuels and companies that stoke unfettered consumption (Akerlof et al., 2014; Mastini, Kallis, and Hickel, 2021).

Because, over the last century, countries in the Minority World have encouraged consumerism and burned fossil fuels wantonly, we now face a climate emergency. The impacts of this crisis are felt and experienced worst by those in the Majority World, whose historical consumption and greenhouse gas emissions are far less compared to those in the Minority World. The Green New Deals in climate vulnerable countries are thus survival packages (cf., Selwyn, 2021). They are to avert disasters, create jobs, and redistribute wealth.

The Green New Deals also contain strategies and mechanisms to address inequality in terms of income and wealth (Pettifor, 2020). Within these frameworks, affluent people should pay a far higher percentage of their income in taxes. They also call for a maximum limit on wages or incomes. Measures that seek radical redistribution of wealth will do far more than raise economic growth rates, and will do so without contributing to the ecological damages entailed in the perpetual economic growth paradigm.

Alongside Green New Deals, we must also re-establish our place in nature, acknowledging that we are only one of an infinite number of kinds of life. This means recognising that the world was created for all life forms, not just humans. The Indigenous perspective of stewardship – not domination – is an apt concept in the making of this recognition (Falkner and Buzan, 2019; Bennett et al., 2018). Stewardship starts by acknowledging we do not own the world; instead, we are a part of it. Stewardship further suggests we have been entrusted with treating the world as a legacy for succeeding generations (Bennett et al., 2018).

Changes in culture and mentality of substantial magnitude are essential to stewardship. Neo-liberalism and unfettered consumerism, with male privilege as a base, thrive on ego, privatising almost all sectors of life – in fact, life itself, as we see in the patenting of flora and fauna (e.g., Bhattacharya, 2014; Tyfield, 2010). Ego, male privilege, and masculinity are the foundations upon which neo-liberalism and corporatism are built (Hearn, 2017). The transition from patriarchy in mindset and culture also necessitates an appreciation of the concept that freedoms cannot be presumed without commensurate obligations. Within the framework of the climate emergency, obligations and responsibility become essential points that may direct our activities as people, groups, and organisations.

Together with ongoing global challenges, the massive crisis of survival caused by the pandemic, with the accompanying lockdowns and significant decline in economic activities, also necessitates us to re-evaluate the rationale behind rapid urbanisation. Frequently pushed as purposeful policy in many countries in the Majority World such as in China (Wang et al., 2015) and Africa (Collier, 2017), the expansion of urban spaces is detrimental to the environment (Nathaniel, Nwulu, and Bekun, 2021). The need to de-urbanise is now undeniable – including in order to reduce the risks of future zoonotic diseases (Eskew and Olival, 2018). This can be accomplished by establishing self-sufficient, resilient, and socially just rural livelihoods (cf., Munya, Hussain, and Njuguna, 2015; Hussain and Byrd, 2016).

However, de-urbanisation – despite its appeal – has a second face. Without plans for sustainable rural livelihoods, de-urbanisation programmes can be disastrous. The *Balik Probinsya* (Return to the Province) programme provides an example. *Balik Probinsya* is an attempt by the Philippine government at balanced regional development in response to interregional disparities and the economic dominance of Metro Manila. While the programme's objectives are crucial for improving the quality of life outside the country's capital, the government has limited capacity to provide the necessary conditions for making *Balik Probinsya* work. Decent waged work remains contentious and sparse, and investment opportunities outside Metro Manila are constrained (Corpuz, 2020).

In addition to creating sustainable livelihoods, encouraging livelihoods in the countryside should also be based on the protection of housing and land tenure (Chigbu et al., 2017; Chigbu, Alemayehu, and Dachaga, 2019) and a responsibility to preserve natural resources. There is also the imperative of returning public places and products, such as land, air, water, forests, and other ecologies, as well as knowledge, technology, and culture, back to the commons (e.g., Toyoda, 2018). Revitalising the commons is essential in reimagining a society that functions for the benefit of all.

If we do this, we can ensure that the millions who continue to rely on rural economies for their means of subsistence will have a secure future (cf., Li, Westlund and Liu, 2019). Such economies can innovate to improve livelihoods in rural economies such as agriculture, fishing, forestry, and artisanal labour (Koopmans et al., 2018). Additionally, community-led tourism – if there is potential – may be used to ensure livelihoods in such economies (Romanenko et al., 2020). Because of this, would-be urban migrants would not be forced into choosing to live dangerous and unpredictable lives in hostile metropolitan regions.

Even in the most mechanised and industrialised societies, such as those in Australia, Europe, and North America, and among younger generations, there is a rising longing to go back to the land, lead simple lives, and once again produce things by hand (e.g., Benessaiah and Eakin, 2021; Halfacree, 2001). The most challenging aspect of this endeavour is ensuring that 'going-back-to-the-land' does not become merely a pastime for the young and wealthy. Instead, 'going-back-to-the-land' should acknowledge and respect the abilities and expertise of those who have inhabited their place for generations, including those who have traditionally worked with their hands.

'Going-back-to-the-land' also entails restoring a sense of pride in such labour and requiring those who are currently privileged to approach it with a sense of modesty and a desire to learn from those with more experience in these skills (Dawkins, 2011). This can be achieved by reshaping the school system. Craftspeople, food producers, and other artisans should be recruited as teachers. Children and young people should be provided with opportunities to engage with their minds, hands, and hearts. The revitalisation of rural life and the culture of handmaking may result in the production of new generations able to find joy in the straightforwardness of life rather than in the aimless pursuit of luxury and wealth inessential to survival.

The global organisation of industry propagates dependent ties, and this meant that workers in the Majority World were particularly vulnerable during the COVID-19 pandemic. The intensification of globalisation since the 1970s, accompanied by an increase in efficiency, has featured restrictive power dynamics and profound risks for those already vulnerable. While many countries in the

Majority World were able to transition towards manufacturing, this kind of production is still associated with relatively cheap and low-tech labour.

As the pandemic raged, we saw factory employees losing their jobs due to the cancellation of orders from multinational businesses. A universal basic income has become an essential social safety net to alleviate lost income for these employees and protect them in crises to come (Nettle et al., 2021; Johnson et al., 2020). However, universal basic income avoids addressing the fundamental issue of how the structure of global production is formed in the first place. While a basic income can offer some short-term relief to jump-start economic recovery, we still need to get creative about how we can facilitate the rebalancing of production. Such rebalancing will make it possible for businesses in the Majority World to become more self-sufficient, secure, and focused on meeting the requirements of their own rather than other countries.

However, countries in the Majority World are susceptible to the financial cycles that the Minority World produces. As with any crisis, the COVID-19 pandemic brought a turnaround in capital movements as investors flocked to their so-called safe assets. Several nations in the Majority World have also had their currencies decline. As other economic disturbances occur in the future alongside the climate emergency, we must confront the reality that these external forces restrict the fiscal space that the Majority World desperately needs. Addressing these constraints requires debt moratoria, relief, and forgiveness.

References

Akerlof, G. A., Blanchard, O., Romer, D., & Stiglitz, J. E. (Eds.). (2014). *What Have We Learned? Macroeconomic Policy After the Crisis*. Cambridge, MA: MIT Press.

Benessaiah, K., & Eakin, H. (2021). Crisis, transformation, and agency: Why are people going back-to-the-land in Greece? *Sustainability Science, 16*(6), 1841–1858.

Bennett, N. J., Whitty, T. S., Finkbeiner, E., Pittman, J., Bassett, H., Gelcich, S., & Allison, E. H. (2018). Environmental stewardship: A conceptual review and analytical framework. *Environmental Management, 61*(4), 597–614.

Bhattacharya, S. (2014). Bioprospecting, biopiracy and food security in India: The emerging sides of neoliberalism. *International Letters of Social and Humanistic Sciences*, (12), 49–56.

Castree, N. (2010). Crisis, continuity and change: Neoliberalism, the left and the future of capitalism. *Antipode, 41*, 185–213.

Chigbu, U. E., Schopf, A., de Vries, W. T., Masum, F., Mabikke, S., Antonio, D., & Espinoza, J. (2017). Combining land-use planning and tenure security: A tenure responsive land-use planning approach for developing countries. *Journal of Environmental Planning and Management, 60*(9), 1622–1639.

Chigbu, U., Alemayehu, Z., & Dachaga, W. (2019). Uncovering land tenure insecurities: Tips for tenure responsive land-use planning in Ethiopia. *Development in Practice, 29*(3), 371–383.

Collier, P. (2017). African urbanization: An analytic policy guide. *Oxford Review of Economic Policy, 33*(3), 405–437.

Corpuz, A. G. (2020). The specious logic, planning implications, and opportunities of the 'Balik Probinsya, Bagong Pag-Asa' program. *Philippine Sociological Review, 68*, 111–120.

Dawkins, N. (2011). Do-it-yourself: The precarious work and postfeminist politics of handmaking (in) Detroit. *Utopian Studies, 22*(2), 261–284.

Eskew, E. A., & Olival, K. J. (2018). De-urbanization and zoonotic disease risk. *Ecohealth, 15*(4), 707–712.

Falkner, R., & Buzan, B. (2019). The emergence of environmental stewardship as a primary institution of global international society. *European Journal of International Relations, 25*(1), 131–155.

Fletcher, R., & Rammelt, C. (2017). Decoupling: A key fantasy of the post-2015 sustainable development agenda. *Globalizations, 14*(3), 450–467.

Gore, T. (2020). *Confronting Carbon Inequality.* Oxfam and Stockholm Environment Institute.

Halfacree, K. (2001). Going 'back-to-the-land' again: Extending the scope of counterurbanisation. *Espace Populations Sociétés, 19*(1), 161–170.

Hearn, J. (2017). Men around the world: Global and transnational masculinities. In J. M. Armengol, M. B. Villarrubias, A. Carabi, & T. Requena (Eds.), *Masculinities and Literary Studies* (pp. 39–55). Abingdon, UK: Routledge.

Hussain, N. H. M., & Byrd, H. (2016). 'Balik Kampong': Is Malaysia facing the trends of de-urbanization? *International Journal of the Malay World and Civilisation (Iman), 4*(2016), 35–43.

Ipsos. (2021). Citizens don't expect national economies to recover anytime soon. *Ipsos News*, 5 August 2021.

Ivanova, D., Stadler, K., Steen-Olsen, K., Wood, R., Vita, G., Tukker, A., & Hertwich, E. G. (2016). Environmental impact assessment of household consumption. *Journal of Industrial Ecology, 20*(3), 526–536.

Johnson, M. T., Johnson, E. A., Webber, L., & Nettle, D. (2020). Mitigating social and economic sources of trauma: The need for universal basic income during the coronavirus pandemic. *Psychological Trauma: Theory, Research, Practice, and Policy, 12*(S1), S191.

Koopmans, M. E., Rogge, E., Mettepenningen, E., Knickel, K., & Šūmane, S. (2018). The role of multi-actor governance in aligning farm modernization and sustainable rural development. *Journal of Rural Studies, 59*, 252–262.

Le Billon, P., Lujala, P., Singh, D., Culbert, V., & Kristoffersen, B. (2021). Fossil fuels, climate change, and the COVID-19 crisis: Pathways for a just and green post-pandemic recovery. *Climate Policy, 21*(10), 1347–1356.

Li, Y., Westlund, H., & Liu, Y. (2019). Why some rural areas decline while some others not: An overview of rural evolution in the world. *Journal of Rural Studies, 68*, 135–143.

Mastini, R., Kallis, G., & Hickel, J. (2021). A Green New Deal without growth? *Ecological Economics, 179*, 106832.

Munya, A., Hussain, N. H. M., & Njuguna, M. B. (2015). Can devolution and rural capacity trigger de-urbanization? Case studies in Kenya and Malaysia respectively. *GeoJournal, 80*(3), 427–443.

Murphy Jr, T. W., Murphy, D. J., Love, T. F., LeHew, M. L. A., & McCall, B. J. (2021). Modernity is incompatible with planetary limits: Developing a PLAN for the future. *Energy Research & Social Science, 81*, 102239.

Næss, P., & Høyer, K. G. (2009). The emperor's green clothes: Growth, decoupling, and capitalism. *Capitalism Nature Socialism, 20*(3), 74–95.

Nathaniel, S. P., Nwulu, N., & Bekun, F. (2021). Natural resource, globalization, urbanization, human capital, and environmental degradation in Latin American and Caribbean countries. *Environmental Science and Pollution Research, 28*(5), 6207–6221.

Nettle, D., Johnson, E., Johnson, M., & Saxe, R. (2021). Why has the COVID-19 pandemic increased support for universal basic income? *Humanities and Social Sciences Communications, 8*(1), 1–12.

Pettifor, A. (2020). *The Case for the Green New Deal*. London: Verso Books.

Ritchie, P. D., Clarke, J. J., Cox, P. M., & Huntingford, C. (2021). Overshooting tipping point thresholds in a changing climate. *Nature, 592*(7855), 517–23.

Romanenko, Y. O., Boiko, V. O., Shevchuk, S. M., Barabanova, V. V., & Karpinska, N. V. (2020). Rural development by stimulating agro-tourism activities. *International Journal of Management, 11*(4), 605–613.

Selwyn, B. (2021). A Green New Deal for agriculture: For, within, or against capitalism? *Journal of Peasant Studies, 48*(4), 778–806.

Stiglitz, J. E. (2018). Globalism's discontents. In D. B. Grusky & S. Szelenyi (Eds.), *The Inequality Reader* (pp. 672–680). Abingdon, UK: Routledge.

Tabi, A. (2013). Does pro-environmental behaviour affect carbon emissions? *Energy Policy, 63*, 972–981.

Toyoda, M. (2018). Revitalizing local commons: A democratic approach to collective management. In R. Rozzi, R. H. May Jr, F. S. Chapin III, F. Massardo, M. C. Gavin, J. Klaver, ... & D. Simberloff (Eds.), *From Biocultural Homogenization to Biocultural Conservation* (pp. 443–457). Cham: Springer.

Tyfield, D. (2010). Neoliberalism, intellectual property and the global knowledge economy. In K. Birch & V. Mykhnenko (Eds.), *The Rise and Fall of Neoliberalism: The Collapse of an Economic Order* (pp. 60–76). London: Zed Books.

Wang, X. R., Hui, E. C. M., Choguill, C., & Jia, S. H. (2015). The new urbanization policy in China: Which way forward? *Habitat International, 47*, 279–284.

Ward, J. D., Sutton, P. C., Werner, A. D., Costanza, R., Mohr, S. H., & Simmons, C. T. (2016). Is decoupling GDP growth from environmental impact possible? *PLoS One, 11*(10), e0164733.

Wiedmann, T., Lenzen, M., Keyßer, L. T., & Steinberger, J. K. (2020). Scientists' warning on affluence. *Nature Communications, 11*(1), 1–10.

10
Ceasing Arrogance

Humans assume they are superior to nature. There is no better place to see this arrogance than in the affluent societies of the Minority World. The COVID-19 pandemic ignored arbitrarily defined geographical borders and the fantasy of fake prosperity was shattered as the coronavirus raged. Never again will we resort to this myth created on the backs of people in the Majority World and propped up by environmental plunder. The arrogance of control and superiority have to cease.

I come from a family of rice farmers. Growing up in a village in the southern Philippines surrounded by rice fields, I know the distinct smell of rice paddies. With weather extremes, typhoons, and droughts, how will my family grow rice? Rice is only one of the many crops that sustain us. The same can be said of corn, wheat, and potatoes. How will we feed ourselves given erratic and extreme weather, expanding desertification, and a shifting climate? During the COVID-19 pandemic, some people fought over toilet paper. It was really ugly. Will we fight over food?

Accumulated evidence reveals how the climate crisis is likely to damage our food systems (Fanzo et al., 2018; Clapp, Newell, and Brent, 2018). Rice farming in my village and in other parts of the world is already being hit by droughts and floods (e.g., Manalo, van de Fliert, and Fielding, 2020; Khan et al., 2021; Ojo and Baiyegunhi, 2020). Other pressures compound rice farming risks, including social and economic factors, as shown, for example, by young people migrating to cities and even overseas in search of greener pastures (Nguyen and Sean, 2021; Bhandari and Mishra, 2018). Other crops are also affected by global heating. Fires burn fields in central Chile (Castillo, Plaza, and Garfias, 2020); locusts swarm in East Africa (Salih et al., 2020). Farmers may need to prepare for sudden pest invasions as insects and other creatures move into new territories, ravaging crops along the way (Trebicki and Finlay, 2019; Deutsch et al., 2018). With a zoonotic disease triggering the COVID-19 pandemic (Mishra, Mishra, and Arora, 2021), hazards of biblical proportions are indeed upon us.

Every extra degree of global heating is disastrous for our food systems (Vermeulen, Campbell, and Ingram, 2012; Fanzo et al., 2018). Warming between 3 and 4°C above pre-industrial levels could push these systems into a death spiral. As heatwaves and other climate impacts pile on top of each other, temperatures could become so hot that living outdoors may be insufferable for human beings (Kornhuber et al., 2019; Miller et al., 2021). My rice farming family will carry an extreme burden when that happens, making their livelihood almost impossible. Rice paddies can turn to dust. Heat stress will also kill livestock (Smoyer-Tomic, Kuhn, and Hudson, 2003). Multiple breadbasket failures (Gaupp et al., 2020) – something beyond the experience of contemporary human societies – are now fast becoming highly likely on a planetary scale (Tigchelaar et al., 2018; Deutsch et al., 2018).

A United Nations report suggests that by mid-twenty-first century we need to expand irrigation water use by 20 per cent, relative to the present, in order to feed our species (UNESCO, 2016). But with 3 to 4°C global heating, this much-needed irrigation water may be lost through evaporation and by using, storing, and hoarding water for survival. At the same time, soil may be denuded, leaving ground infertile. Pollinators may also be decimated by the loss of plants and flowers (Giannini, 2017).). Water will also be scarce since we will have already used water in our aquifers and rivers (Gleeson et al., 2012). Even the Himalayan glaciers supplying water to South Asian populations are rapidly retreating (King et al., 2019; Nie et al., 2021), opening up new possibilities for conflict between countries and peoples in that region (Klare, 2020). Precipitation during the dry season is also likely to be reduced, severely impacting production capacity on farms (Nkemelang, New, and Zaroug, 2018).

With these changes in food and water availability as well as growth in resource use and population, many people could be pushed into famine (Balasubramanian, 2018). With food insecurity, billions could suffer or die from hunger. Yet, this will not be everybody's burden. While the Minority World may survive food scarcity, those in the Majority World stand to suffer from structural food shortages.

This inequality has always been present. Although there has been a global overabundance of food for some time now – think of food waste in the Minority World (Alexander et al., 2017; Stuart, 2009), millions of people remain either undernourished or malnourished (Koning et al., 2008). Access to and distribution of food is unequally tilted in favour of affluent societies in the Minority World. We can expect that as the world heats up to between 3 and 4°C, food and water availability will become a serious issue; hoarding will happen. The COVID-19 pandemic has shown us how richer countries stockpile supplies, including food and vaccines, to the detriment of the world's poor people (Tse et al., 2022; Bollyky and Bown, 2020). In an intensely warm world, people with power and material wealth will easily elect to grab food from the mouths of the poor in order to thrive.

This future could well happen. Even if all nations keep their promises to contribute to climate mitigation under the Paris Agreement – which seems unlikely (Taylor and Vink, 2021) – the Earth will still warm up by between 3 and 4°C. In any case, food insecurity is now close to being almost a certainty (Hasegawa et al., 2018), given that the decline in food production remains a foretold catastrophe that is not being anticipated. Planning for this future remains nil. The success of our industrialisation has puffed us up so that we are deceived by this veneer of security. We do almost nothing to plan for these existential risks.

Human societies believe they are above the natural world. And there is no place that better encapsulates this than affluent communities in the Minority World. The economic gains they have accumulated, the resources wantonly extracted over decades of colonialism and imperialism, have made them gloss over what is real. They are living an illusion: a mirage of fake prosperity at the expense of poor people in the Majority World. They have convinced themselves that they are immune from the hazards of the natural and biological worlds.

But biology charged. The pandemic did not respect artificially drawn territorial boundaries. As COVID-19 raged, the fantasy of fake prosperity was breached. People found themselves exposed and unguarded. As their bubbles burst, the allure is for affluent societies to invent another illusion when the pandemic passes. However, future human societies should not yield to that new fantasy. Those who deny facts should never again be allowed a voice in the public sphere. What this means is we should accept the harsh facts of life that we have rejected for a long time – wake up from our smugness.

The Earth has compounding and cascading morbidities (Franzke et al., 2022). Some of these maladies, however, make the COVID-19 pandemic, by contrast, seemingly easy to cure. The decline in food production due to global heating is foremost among these infirmities. The soil crisis, which threatens the loss of our fertile lands because of erosion and contamination is another (Koch et al., 2013). Phosphate, a crucial mineral in agriculture, is also contracting in supply (Blackwell, Darch, and Haslam, 2019; Geissler, Mew, and Steiner, 2019; Langton, 2019; cf., Ji, Liu, and Shi, 2020). Rock phosphate is a finite resource found primarily in politically unstable countries, such as Syria, making it a contentious resource in future food systems, especially since this supply may be exhausted by 2040 (Blackwell, Darch, and Haslam, 2019).

Intensive food production is further ripping the biosphere apart. The surface of the planet has evolved from being laced with intricate wild ecosystems to one characterised as a dumbed-down human food production and consumption system (Clay, 2013). Complexity has been erased in favour of oversimplification. Monocropping and factory farming have become the norm. As a result, emissions from agriculture and land use have surged. Rivers, lakes, and streams have become polluted. On the seas, industrial fishing has plundered our ocean resources (McCauley et al., 2018). To put it bluntly, we have chased resources over every inch of the planet.

Everything we put in our mouths now carries an indefensible cost to the environment. The avocado we spread over toast or mix with our salad requires an enormous environmental and social cost to produce (De la Vega-Rivera and Merino-Pérez, 2021). Cows and other farm animals contribute 14 per cent of our total greenhouse gas emissions (Grossi et al., 2019). Methane from their burps and manure has a major impact on global heating. This is because methane is more potent than carbon dioxide as it remains in the atmosphere for much longer. Rice, which my family has planted for generations using flooding methods, also releases large amounts of methane.

Food production needs rethinking. New technologies for producing food outside the confines of conventional farms offer possibilities to reverse our looming food insecurity. These technologies could end most deforestation, animal exploitation, pesticide and fertiliser use, and trawling. Meat will still be meat, but it will be produced not from the bodies of animals but in confined and climate-controlled spaces (Srutee and Uday, 2021; Ben-Arye and Levenberg, 2019). Countries without farmland could produce stable and reliable food using these technologies.

It might seem odd that this solution has a patina of technofix, but nowhere on Earth can we find farm policies that pay attention to truly sustainable farming. This is particularly the case given that subsidies remain the largest for industrial agriculture; no government is spending to increase a healthier food supply for people and the planet (Laborde et al., 2021).

The trade-offs are apparent. The shift towards these new food production systems will hit millions of people working in farming and food processing, including my rice farming family. Many will also eventually lose jobs. Instead of extending lifelines to environmentally destructive industries, governments should provide relief funds to those who will lose their livelihoods because of the transition to healthier food systems that are respectful of our planetary limits.

There is also a hazard in concentrating the new food industry through patenting crucial technologies. These patents should be vigorously opposed to ensure a wide diffusion of ownership. The vaccine access imbalance between rich and developing countries during the COVID-19 pandemic is illustrative here. Countries in the Majority World were left in the lurch when richer nations utilised their market strength to acquire vaccination rights in advance (Zhou, 2022; Lagman, 2021). Despite COVAX's efforts to address this issue, its market influence is far inferior to that of the United States, the European Union, Canada, and other countries in the Minority World. The capacity of nations in the Majority World to create food utilising non-agricultural approaches should be encouraged, not constrained by the influence of private multinational corporations or political power.

Food production using non-farm approaches means emission avoidance and rewilding, if done correctly. Rewilding helps to restore ecosystems and tackle climate change at the same time (Perino et al., 2019). Reintroducing large herbivores, such as elephants, reinvigorates landscapes, turning them into bushes or forests that act as carbon sinks (Cromsigt et al., 2018). Rewilding also has adaptation benefits, especially in terms of curtailing wildfires (García-Ruiz et al., 2020; Johnson et al., 2018). For instance, white rhinos, reintroduced in one of South Africa's national parks, have been thought to help suppress fire because they graze on tall grasses, which enable fires to spread between trees (Waldram, Bond, and Stock, 2008).

Although non-farm food production technologies offer us some hope, we cannot afford to wait passively for this technology to save us. We must temporarily shift towards a plant-based diet which has the lowest possible impacts (Cleveland and Gee, 2017; Van Vliet, Kronberg, and Provenza, 2020). This also means eating avocados or off-season tomatoes sparingly. Plant-based diets can help us buy time until the world has an abundant and cheap food supply without devouring every inch of the planet.

The COVID-19 pandemic has been a moment when we have begun to see ourselves, once more, as a species governed by biology that thrives in communities. Never again should we return to the fantasy of prosperity built on the backs of people in the Majority World and juxtaposed with the pillage of the natural environment.

References

Alexander, P., Brown, C., Arneth, A., Finnigan, J., Moran, D., & Rounsevell, M. D. (2017). Losses, inefficiencies and waste in the global food system. *Agricultural Systems*, *153*, 190–200.

Balasubramanian, M. (2018). Climate change, famine, and low-income communities challenge Sustainable Development Goals. *The Lancet Planetary Health*, *2*(10), e421–422.

Ben-Arye, T., & Levenberg, S. (2019). Tissue engineering for clean meat production. *Frontiers in Sustainable Food Systems, 3*, Art. 46.

Bhandari, H., & Mishra, A. K. (2018). Impact of demographic transformation on future rice farming in Asia. *Outlook on Agriculture, 47*(2), 125–132.

Blackwell, M. S. A., Darch, T., & Haslam, R. P. (2019). Phosphorus use efficiency and fertilizers: Future opportunities for improvements. *Frontiers of Agricultural Science and Engineering, 6*(4), 332–340.

Bollyky, T. J., & Bown, C. P. (2020). The tragedy of vaccine nationalism: Only cooperation can end the pandemic. *Foreign Affairs*, September–October.

Castillo, M., Plaza, Á., & Garfias, R. (2020). A recent review of fire behavior and fire effects on native vegetation in Central Chile. *Global Ecology and Conservation, 24*, e01210.

Clapp, J., Newell, P., & Brent, Z. W. (2018). The global political economy of climate change, agriculture and food systems. *Journal of Peasant Studies, 45*(1), 80–88.

Clay, J. (2013). *World Agriculture and the Environment: A Commodity-by-Commodity Guide to Impacts and Practices*. Washington, DC: Island Press.

Cleveland, D. A., & Gee, Q. (2017). Plant-based diets for mitigating climate change. In F. Mariotti (Ed.), *Vegetarian and Plant-Based Diets in Health and Disease Prevention* (pp. 135–156). London: Academic Press.

Cromsigt, J. P., Kemp, Y. J., Rodriguez, E., & Kivit, H. (2018). Rewilding Europe's large grazer community: How functionally diverse are the diets of European bison, cattle, and horses? *Restoration Ecology, 26*(5), 891–899.

De la Vega-Rivera, A., & Merino-Pérez, L. (2021). Socio-environmental impacts of the avocado boom in the Meseta Purepecha, Michoacan, Mexico. *Sustainability, 13*(13), 7247.

Deutsch, C. A., Tewksbury, J. J., Tigchelaar, M., Battisti, D. S., Merrill, S. C., Huey, R. B., & Naylor, R. L. (2018). Increase in crop losses to insect pests in a warming climate. *Science, 361*(6405), 916–919.

Fanzo, J., Davis, C., McLaren, R., & Choufani, J. (2018). The effect of climate change across food systems: Implications for nutrition outcomes. *Global Food Security, 18*, 12–19.

Franzke, C. L., Ciullo, A., Gilmore, E. A., Matias, D. M., Nagabhatla, N., Orlov, A., ... & Sillmann, J. (2022). Perspectives on tipping points in integrated models of the natural and human Earth system: Cascading effects and telecoupling. *Environmental Research Letters, 17*(1), 015004.

García-Ruiz, J. M., Lasanta, T., Nadal-Romero, E., Lana-Renault, N., & Álvarez-Farizo, B. (2020). Rewilding and restoring cultural landscapes in Mediterranean mountains: Opportunities and challenges. *Land Use Policy, 99*, 104850.

Gaupp, F., Hall, J., Hochrainer-Stigler, S., & Dadson, S. (2020). Changing risks of simultaneous global breadbasket failure. *Nature Climate Change, 10*(1), 54–57.

Geissler, B., Mew, M. C., & Steiner, G. (2019). Phosphate supply security for importing countries: Developments and the current situation. *Science of the Total Environment, 677*, 511–523.

Giannini, T. C., Costa, W. F., Cordeiro, G. D., Imperatriz-Fonseca, V. L., Saraiva, A. M., Biesmeijer, J., & Garibaldi, L. A. (2017). Projected climate change threatens pollinators and crop production in Brazil. *PLoS One, 12*(8), e0182274.

Gleeson, T., Wada, Y., Bierkens, M. F., & Van Beek, L. P. (2012). Water balance of global aquifers revealed by groundwater footprint. *Nature, 488*(7410), 197–200.

Gómez-González, S., González, M. E., Paula, S., Díaz-Hormazábal, I., Lara, A., & Delgado-Baquerizo, M. (2019). Temperature and agriculture are largely associated with fire activity in Central Chile across different temporal periods. *Forest Ecology and Management*, *433*, 535–543.

Grossi, G., Goglio, P., Vitali, A., & Williams, A. G. (2019). Livestock and climate change: Impact of livestock on climate and mitigation strategies. *Animal Frontiers*, *9*(1), 69–76.

Hasegawa, T., Fujimori, S., Havlík, P., Valin, H., Bodirsky, B. L., Doelman, J. C., ... & Witzke, P. (2018). Risk of increased food insecurity under stringent global climate change mitigation policy. *Nature Climate Change*, *8*(8), 699–703.

Ji, Y., Liu, H., & Shi, Y. (2020). Will China's fertilizer use continue to decline? Evidence from LMDI analysis based on crops, regions and fertilizer types. *PLoS One*, *15*(8), e0237234.

Johnson, C. N., Prior, L. D., Archibald, S., Poulos, H. M., Barton, A. M., Williamson, G. J., & Bowman, D. M. (2018). Can trophic rewilding reduce the impact of fire in a more flammable world? *Philosophical Transactions of the Royal Society B: Biological Sciences*, *373*(1761), 20170443.

Khan, N. A., Gao, Q., Abid, M., & Shah, A. A. (2021). Mapping farmers' vulnerability to climate change and its induced hazards: Evidence from the rice-growing zones of Punjab, Pakistan. *Environmental Science and Pollution Research*, *28*(4), 4229–4244.

King, O., Bhattacharya, A., Bhambri, R., & Bolch, T. (2019). Glacial lakes exacerbate Himalayan glacier mass loss. *Scientific Reports*, *9*(1), 1–9.

Klare, M. T. (2020). Climate change, water scarcity, and the potential for interstate conflict in South Asia. *Journal of Strategic Security*, *13*(4), 109–122.

Koch, A., McBratney, A., Adams, M., Field, D., Hill, R., Crawford, J., ... & Zimmermann, M. (2013). Soil security: Solving the global soil crisis. *Global Policy*, *4*(4), 434–441.

Koning, N. B. J., Van Ittersum, M. K., Becx, G. A., Van Boekel, M. A. J. S., Brandenburg, W. A., Van Den Broek, J. A., ... & Smies, M. (2008). Long-term global availability of food: Continued abundance or new scarcity? *NJAS: Wageningen Journal of Life Sciences*, *55*(3), 229–292.

Kornhuber, K., Osprey, S., Coumou, D., Petri, S., Petoukhov, V., Rahmstorf, S., & Gray, L. (2019). Extreme weather events in early summer 2018 connected by a recurrent hemispheric wave-7 pattern. *Environmental Research Letters*, *14*(5), 054002.

Laborde, D., Mamun, A., Martin, W., Piñeiro, V., & Vos, R. (2021). Agricultural subsidies and global greenhouse gas emissions. *Nature Communications*, *12*(1), 1–9.

Lagman, J. D. N. (2021). Vaccine nationalism: A predicament in ending the COVID-19 pandemic. *Journal of Public Health*, *43*(2), e375–376.

Langton, T. G. (2019). The fertilizer industry. In C. E. Beige & A. Hero (Eds.), *Natural Resources in US–Canadian Relations* (pp. 93–122). Abingdon, UK: Routledge.

Manalo IV, J. A., van de Fliert, E., & Fielding, K. (2020). Rice farmers adapting to drought in the Philippines. *International Journal of Agricultural Sustainability*, *18*(6), 594–605.

McCauley, D. J., Jablonicky, C., Allison, E. H., Golden, C. D., Joyce, F. H., Mayorga, J., & Kroodsma, D. (2018). Wealthy countries dominate industrial fishing. *Science Advances*, *4*(8), eaau2161.

Miller, S., Chua, K., Coggins, J., & Mohtadi, H. (2021). Heat waves, climate change, and economic output. *Journal of the European Economic Association*, *19*(5), 2658–2694.

Mishra, J., Mishra, P., & Arora, N. K. (2021). Linkages between environmental issues and zoonotic diseases: With reference to COVID-19 pandemic. *Environmental Sustainability*, *4*(3), 455–467.

Nguyen, T. P. L., & Sean, C. (2021). Do climate uncertainties trigger farmers' out-migration in the Lower Mekong Region? *Current Research in Environmental Sustainability*, *3*, 100087.

Nie, Y., Pritchard, H. D., Liu, Q., Hennig, T., Wang, W., Wang, X., ... & Chen, X. (2021). Glacial change and hydrological implications in the Himalaya and Karakoram. *Nature Reviews: Earth & Environment*, *2*(2), 91–106.

Nkemelang, T., New, M., & Zaroug, M. (2018). Temperature and precipitation extremes under current, 1.5°C and 2.0°C global warming above pre-industrial levels over Botswana, and implications for climate change vulnerability. *Environmental Research Letters*, *13*(6), 065016.

Ojo, T. O., & Baiyegunhi, L. J. S. (2020). Determinants of climate change adaptation strategies and its impact on the net farm income of rice farmers in south-west Nigeria. *Land Use Policy*, *95*, 103946.

Perino, A., Pereira, H. M., Navarro, L. M., Fernández, N., Bullock, J. M., Ceaușu, S., ... & Wheeler, H. C. (2019). Rewilding complex ecosystems. *Science*, *364* (6438), eaav5570.

Salih, A. A., Baraibar, M., Mwangi, K. K., & Artan, G. (2020). Climate change and locust outbreak in East Africa. *Nature Climate Change*, *10*(7), 584–585.

Smoyer-Tomic, K. E., Kuhn, R., & Hudson, A. (2003). Heat wave hazards: An overview of heat wave impacts in Canada. *Natural Hazards*, *28*(2), 465–486.

Srutee, R. R. S. S., & Uday S. A. (2021). Clean meat: Techniques for meat production and its upcoming challenges. *Animal Biotechnology*, 1–9.

Stuart, T. (2009). *Waste: Uncovering the Global Food Scandal*. New York: W. W. Norton & Company.

Taylor, G., & Vink, S. (2021). Managing the risks of missing international climate targets. *Climate Risk Management*, *34*, 100379.

Tigchelaar, M., Battisti, D. S., Naylor, R. L., & Ray, D. K. (2018). Future warming increases probability of globally synchronized maize production shocks. *Proceedings of the National Academy of Sciences*, *115*(26), 6644–6649.

Trebicki, P., & Finlay, K. (2019). Pests and Diseases under Climate Change: Its Threat to Food Security. In S. S. Yadav, R. J. Redden, J. L. Hatfield, A. W. Ebert, & D. Hunter (Eds.), *Food Security and Climate Change* (pp. 229–249). Hoboken, NJ: John Wiley & Sons.

Tse, D. C., Lau, V. W., Hong, Y. Y., Bligh, M. C., & Kakarika, M. (2022). Prosociality and hoarding amid the COVID-19 pandemic: A tale of four countries. *Journal of Community & Applied Social Psychology*, *32*(3), 507–520.

UNESCO. (2016). *World Water Development Report 2016*.

Van Vliet, S., Kronberg, S. L., & Provenza, F. D. (2020). Plant-based meats, human health, and climate change. *Frontiers in Sustainable Food Systems*, Art. 128.

Vermeulen, S. J., Campbell, B. M., & Ingram, J. S. (2012). Climate change and food systems. *Annual Review of Environment and Resources*, *37*(1), 195–222.

Waldram, M. S., Bond, W. J., & Stock, W. D. (2008). Ecological engineering by a mega-grazer: White rhino impacts on a South African savanna. *Ecosystems*, *11*(1), 101–112.

Zhou, Y. R. (2022). Vaccine nationalism: Contested relationships between COVID-19 and globalization. *Globalizations*, *19*(3), 450–465.

11
Making Amends

Countries in the Minority World that have made the most substantial contributions to the climate emergency must accept that they should also make the most significant contributions to its solutions. It is reasonable and right that governments in the Minority World should assume responsibility for their actions and make amends. Indeed, it is only fair and decent that they do so after centuries of robbing the Majority World.

The Philippines 'celebrated' the quincentennial of the arrival of Catholicism in the country in 2021. The 500th anniversary of Catholic presence in the Philippines could have been joyfully celebrated if it had not been for the COVID-19 pandemic. Yet, one should not forget that this event also marked the country's history as a colonised nation. For centuries, the Spanish Empire pillaged lands and resources in the Philippines and other colonies, the effects of which are still harshly felt by formerly colonised peoples. The quincentennial occurred at the same time that COVID-19 was wreaking havoc, and the effects of accelerating climate change were continuing to devastate lives and livelihoods. Indeed, in 2021, powerful typhoons severely impacted many areas of the Philippines. Even though former colonies are typically the least to blame for the climate emergency, they often experience the worst of its effects: devastating droughts, rampaging floods, and poor harvests.

About half a millennium's worth of world history can be summed up in one narrative: that of pillaging and plundering (cf., Perrotta, 2020). European nations, which were masters in both brutality and naval power, used these abilities to their advantage to conquer the land, labour, and resources of other people's nations. The Philippines, a country I call home, where I was born and raised, were colonised by Spain for 333 years. My country served as Spain's outpost in Asia. The nations that colonised my country, and others, constantly vied for control over it. The British reigned over the Philippines for twenty months in the mid-1700s before Spain retook possession of it. At the turn of the twentieth century, Spain sold the Philippines to the United States.

Other colonised nations changed hands from one colonial master to another. Wars broke out between these colonising nations over competition for control of other peoples' lands and resources. European colonisers would claim that it was their moral duty to 'save' other peoples – including mine – from our 'degeneracy', 'primitiveness', and 'savageness', which was their justification for acts of violence (Watson, 2009; Barta, 2010). Such an intention to 'save' frequently resulted in the wholesale slaughter of peoples and the destruction of their cultures (Wolfe, 2006). Indeed, Spain, the coloniser of the Philippines coloniser, was also responsible for acts of genocide and looting against Indigenous Peoples in many parts of the Americas (Moses, 2008). The industrial revolutions launched by European colonisers during centuries of hegemony were fuelled in large part by the looting of goods, as well as by slave labour and lands stolen from colonised peoples and nations.

As a result of never-ending conflicts among colonisers themselves and the uprisings led by the people they colonised, European countries were forced to withdraw from the territories they had occupied. However, the process by which these peoples organised themselves into independent countries frequently resulted in imperfect forms of self-rule. The wealthy nations continued their plunder, but this time they used new methods of dominance and control. One of their crafty instruments has been the establishment of proxy governments and the subsequent arming of those governments. Another tool is to burden formerly colonised nations with international debt (Gardner, 2017; Hodge, 2011).

As industrial revolutions occurred in Europe utilising resources from the colonies, detritus was discharged onto the land and into the water and atmosphere. At first, European countries polluted their own air, land, and rivers. Later, they relocated their polluting industries to areas they had not previously damaged, leaving those in poverty to bear the burden of the damage caused by their pollution (Hodge, 2011). Much later, industrialised and wealthy nations stumbled upon a ground-breaking realisation: they did not need to pollute their own countries; instead, they could move their polluting smokestacks to other nations (Agbonifo, 2002; Yates, 1996). This contemporary form of colonialism left scars on the surface of the planet and contributed to the build-up of invisible pollutants in the air.

Decades of dumping pollutants have led to concentrated carbon dioxide and other gases in the atmosphere. The effects of this pollution are now being strongly felt in places that were formerly colonies. Indeed, previously dependent colonies have emerged as nations at the global epicentre of rapid climate change in recent years.

The Philippines is one of many former colonised nations that are most susceptible to the impacts of the climate crisis. The former territories of colonial powers in Latin America and sub-Saharan Africa are also in danger. Those in the Majority World who saw the fewest positive effects of the industrial revolutions in Europe, America, and Australia are bearing the brunt of their global heating impacts.

Countries in the Minority World, with their saviour complexes, have committed to helping their former colonies adapt to the changing climate and adjust to the mayhem they have caused. At the Conference of the Parties to the United Nations Framework Convention on Climate Change in Copenhagen, in 2009, rich countries committed to providing annual climate finance of US$100 billion to developing countries.

Ten years after that pledge was made, countries in the Minority World contributed only US$80 billion. Of this amount, only US$20 billion was designated for climate adaptation funding; that is, only a quarter of the money was earmarked to assist people in adapting to the climate pandemonium imposed on them. A meagre 7 per cent went to countries with the highest poverty rates. If you compare these handouts to the subsidies that wealthy countries give to the fossil fuel industries in their own countries – which totalled US$3.3 trillion in 2015 – you might find yourself biting your tongue out of anger (cf., Kumar, 2015; Zhang et al., 2017).

As the climate emergency unleashes catastrophes, wealthy nations have expended resources to ensure that people fleeing from weather extremes are prevented from entering their territories (Feng, Krueger, and Oppenheimer, 2010). Their borders have effectively been effectively closed off (McLeman, 2019). The wealthy nations of the world have fortified themselves with climate walls, thus isolating themselves from the victims of centuries of plundering.

Present climate finance arrangements directed at countries in the Majority World are preposterous. Most of these resources are in the form of loans, meaning this money must be repaid – that is, the principal amounts plus interest. Countries in the Majority World, many of which are already in debt, now face increased pressures to bear an additional debt to finance their efforts to adapt to climate catastrophes. It is beyond comprehension how unfair and unjust this situation is.

Wealthy nations portray their climate pittance, also known as loans, as a favour rather than a form of compensation for the losses and damages that countries in the Majority World are experiencing from climate impacts. Countries that have been the most responsible for causing the climate emergency are now positioning themselves as liberators of the world, hiding their true colonial colours. However, the victims of plundering and the wanton combustion of fossil fuels in the process of Minority World industrialisation have no need for saviours and no interest in their altruism.

The countries of the Majority World, which are home to the vast majority of the world's population, require restorative justice. Restorative climate justice holds that those who are most responsible for the climate crisis, that is, countries in the Minority World, have an ethical obligation to compensate those who are least responsible –countries in the Majority World. This is the moral responsibility that restorative justice imposes (Robinson and Carlson, 2021). Wealthy countries do not owe the countries of the Majority World climate loans or climate aid; instead, they owe the Majority World climate damages.

The emergency brought about by climate change is a form of injustice that must also be addressed through legislation and policy. This is the crux of the matter when it comes to climate reparations (Burkett, 2009; Chapman and Ahmed, 2021; Fruh, 2021). These policies should include the means to make amends for decisions that the Minority World has made and continues to make that have led to climate-related suffering, trauma, and harm, both past and present. Climate reparations are also about admitting that people in poor and formerly colonised countries have made minimal contribution to the climate crisis yet carry the majority of climate miseries. Formerly colonised countries should be paid back by governments in the Minority World.

Climate reparations are thus about the necessity of recognising and allocating responsibility for the loss of land and culture caused by the climate crisis. Indeed, acknowledging the climate damages caused by countries in the Minority World and taking responsibility for those actions are both essential components of climate reparations (cf., James et al., 2014; Boyd et al., 2017). Accountability is what separates climate reparations from loans, aid, or alms.

Climate reparation payments could be disbursed through an international body, which would collect fees from Minority World countries and the multinational corporations responsible for the climate crisis, such as fossil fuels firms. It would then receive claims from climate-vulnerable countries and disburse money to them for climate insurance, adaptation, and mitigation. Individuals awarded this compensation should have complete discretion over how the funds are used.

The discussion of climate finance and the concept of 'loss and damage' is thus extremely important in the discourse of restorative climate justice. The term 'climate finance' refers to investments made by countries in the Minority World to Majority World countries to hasten their transition to low-carbon economies and ensure their adaptation to the impacts of climate change, which can no longer be avoided. The concept of 'loss and damage' refers to the fact that the inevitable repercussions of the climate emergency will not otherwise be endured (James et al., 2014; Boyd et al., 2017). People will lose their lives and livelihoods and, at the same time, vital infrastructure will be obliterated. Those in the Minority World, the wealthy world, have done this to people in the Majority World.

Reparations pertaining to the impacts of the climate emergency have the potential to act as a launch pad to reorient our world towards climate justice. By raising the topic of restorative climate justice, we draw attention to the larger injustices caused by colonialism, neocolonialism, and neo-liberal capitalism. We cannot have a conversation about compensations and reparations until we have first discussed past and present climate injustices and how the neo-liberal market economy marginalises and kills peoples and communities. Reparations for climate change can provide immediate assistance to people harmed by the oppressive systems of neocolonialism and capitalism and those whom the climate emergency has most impacted (Perry, 2021). Reparations for the effects of climate change are not quick fixes; instead, they are components of a larger framework of just policies aimed at achieving climate justice. Beyond reparations, other mechanisms of restorative climate justice include the cancellation of sovereign debts and the funding of a rapid transition to more environmentally friendly forms of energy.

The demand for climate reparations must be accompanied by an offer of debt cancellation if there is to be any hope of realising fair and equal climate justice for all (e.g., Cárdenas et al., 2021; Rambarran, 2018). The goals of restorative climate justice cannot be achieved without first making significant changes to the economic conditions that keep countries in the Majority World in a state of structural debt to the Minority World. If we want to get rid of debt, countries in the Minority World have to take into account all of their obligations, not just the ones that are related to climate change but also their histories of colonialism.

Because the major emitters in the Minority World were responsible for the present climate crisis, these nations should be the ones paying those who are not responsible for it in the first place. At this time, however, the majority of the funding from the Minority World to the Majority World in the form of assistance for climate action is in the form of long-term loans. When countries in the Majority World take out loans, they are responsible for paying interest, which results in additional financial outlays and adds an additional burden to public budgets that are already under pressure.

Entrenched debts further solidify the global divide between the Minority World and the Majority World. Financial compensation for the effects of climate change should thus come in the form of untied grants and technology transfer, not loans (Ghosh and Woods, 2009; Khan et al., 2020). A climate finance system based on the distribution of grants and renewable energy technologies would help prevent further entanglement of countries in the Majority World with these profoundly unjust structures of global debt.

Nations that have contributed excessively to the present climate emergency should set a positive example. Setting goals is a critical first step in the battle against the climate crisis. Headway should be made on plans that will be implemented to accomplish these objectives.

Many people believe that since China is the largest emitter on the planet at the moment, the government in Beijing is solely to blame for the problem. However, China did not begin its industrialisation until recent decades, in contrast to the rich countries in the Minority World. After taking into account China's accumulated emissions over time and adjusting the results the size of population, one can see a vast difference between China and Minority World countries in general. The cumulative emissions produced by the people of the United Kingdom, for example, are more than five times higher than those produced by the population of China (Ritchie, Roser, and Rosado, 2020).

The countries of the Minority World have been responsible for a disproportionate amount of the damage to the climate system, and they are still doing so today. Although nations worldwide need to step up their efforts to combat climate change and cut emissions, Minority World countries have been the primary contributors to the current climate emergency. Wealthy countries thus have a moral obligation to make a financial contribution to a global just energy transition that acknowledges their historical responsibility for the climate crisis.

A national perspective on the climate crisis is insufficient when considered within the framework of globalised capitalism, which produces inequality both within and between nations. While many countries in the Majority World are still dealing with the after-effects of colonialism, many nations in the Minority World have moved their production facilities to the Majority World, which has resulted in the Minority World emitting more greenhouse gases, albeit not in their own countries.

It is also essential to remember that most of those responsible for the majority of emissions are not countries but multinational corporations. Twenty fossil fuel companies have been responsible for 35 per cent of all energy-related emissions globally since 1965 (cf., Gunderson and Fyock, 2021). Many of these corporations have spent years working to subvert the scientific consensus on climate change and to play down the dangers of the climate crisis.

The growing severity of the climate emergency can be traced back, more than anything, to extreme global inequality, as well as the unchecked power of corporations, which have become multinational and even bigger than many economies in the Majority World (cf., Timmons Roberts, 2001). As a direct result, steps must be taken, simultaneously, to reduce emissions and ensure that economic justice is achieved.

If we wait for corporations to take the lead in addressing the climate emergency, all that will happen is that we will continue to muddle along the same emission pathways that we have followed until this point. Instead, the solutions should be implemented 'upstream' or at the level where our monetary and financial systems are situated. This strategy requires the implementation of structural reforms that will result in a reduced carbon footprint for everyone, regardless of whether or not corporations are prepared to carry out or invest in reforms. Because of the scope of the much-needed energy transition that needs to take place and the urgency with which it must be accomplished, change needs to be directed by states and coordinated at the international level.

This shift requires a fundamental transformation of energy systems, transportation, and agricultural industries and restructuring economies' production, distribution, and consumption patterns. It necessitates employing every tool that is available, including but not limited to regulations, legislation, taxes, subsidies, renationalisation, and fiscal policy, to achieve the desired results. In addition, it is necessary to coordinate the allocation of resources on a scale that has not been witnessed since the conclusion of the Second World War.

In sum, countries in the Minority World must make significant financial climate reparations to countries in the Majority World so they can also process their transitions. However, rather than placing additional financial strain on developing nations already drowning in debt, these reparations should take the form of unconditional grants, the cancellation of existing debt, and the transfer of technological know-how. Debt cancellation should be done on the condition that the total amount of forgiven debt is reinvested in decentralised renewable energy generation and other climate action technologies and practices.

References

Agbonifo, J. (2002). The colonial origin and perpetuation of environmental pollution in the postcolonial Nigerian state. *Critique*, (Fall), 1–17.

Barta, T. (2010). Genocide and colonialism from new and old perspectives. *Borderlands*, 9(1).

Boyd, E., James, R. A., Jones, R. G., Young, H. R., & Otto, F. E. (2017). A typology of loss and damage perspectives. *Nature Climate Change*, 7(10), 723–729.

Burkett, M. (2009). Climate reparations. *Melbourne Journal of International Law*, 10(2), 509–542.

Cárdenas, J. C., Jaramillo, F., León, D., López-Uribe, M. D. P., Rodriguez, M., & Zuleta, H. (2021). *With a Little Help from My Friends: Debt Renegotiation and Climate Change*. Universidad del Rosario, Colombia.

Chapman, A. R., & Ahmed, A. K. (2021). Climate justice, humans rights, and the case for reparations. *Health and Human Rights*, *23*(2), 81–94.

Feng, S., Krueger, A. B., & Oppenheimer, M. (2010). Linkages among climate change, crop yields and Mexico–US cross-border migration. *Proceedings of the National Academy of Sciences*, *107*(32), 14257–14262.

Fruh, K. (2021). Climate change driven displacement and justice: The role of reparations. *Essays in Philosophy*, *22*(1/2), 102–121.

Gardner, L. (2017). Colonialism or supersanctions: Sovereignty and debt in West Africa, 1871–1914. *European Review of Economic History*, *21*(2), 236–257.

Ghosh, A., & Woods, N. (2009). Developing country concerns about climate finance proposals. In R. Stewart, B. Kingsbury, & B. Rudyck (Eds.), *Climate Finance* (pp. 157–164). New York: New York University Press.

Gunderson, R., & Fyock, C. (2021). Are fossil fuel CEOs responsible for climate change? Social structure and criminal law approaches to climate litigation. *Journal of Environmental Studies and Sciences*, *12*, 378–385.

Hodge, J. M. (2011). Colonial experts, developmental and environmental doctrines, and the legacies of late British colonialism. In C. F. Ax, N. Brimnes, N. T. Jensen, & K. Oslund (Eds.), *Cultivating the Colonies: Colonial States and their Environmental Legacies* (pp. 300–326). Columbus: Ohio University Press.

James, R., Otto, F., Parker, H., Boyd, E., Cornforth, R., Mitchell, D., & Allen, M. (2014). Characterizing loss and damage from climate change. *Nature Climate Change*, *4*(11), 938–939.

Khan, M., Robinson, S. A., Weikmans, R., Ciplet, D., & Roberts, J. T. (2020). Twenty-five years of adaptation finance through a climate justice lens. *Climatic Change*, *161*(2), 251–269.

Kumar, S. (2015). Green Climate Fund faces slew of criticism. *Nature*, *527*(7579), 419–420.

McLeman, R. (2019). International migration and climate adaptation in an era of hardening borders. *Nature Climate Change*, *9*(12), 911–918.

Moses, A. D. (Ed.). (2008). *Empire, Colony, Genocide: Conquest, Occupation, and Subaltern Resistance in World History*. New York: Berghahn Books.

Perrotta, C. (2020). *Is Capitalism Still Progressive?* Cham: Palgrave Pivot.

Perry, K. K. (2021). The new 'Bond-age', climate crisis and the case for climate reparations: Unpicking old/new colonialities of finance for development within the SDGs. *Geoforum*, *126*, 361–371.

Rambarran, J. (2018). Debt for climate swaps: Lessons for Caribbean SIDS from the Seychelles' Experience. *Social and Economic Studies*, *67*(2–3), 261–291.

Ritchie, H., Roser, M., & Rosado, P. (2020). CO_2 and greenhouse gas emissions. *Our World in Data*.

Robinson, S. A., & Carlson, D. A. (2021). A just alternative to litigation: Applying restorative justice to climate-related loss and damage. *Third World Quarterly*, *42*(6), 1384–1395.

Timmons Roberts, J. (2001). Global inequality and climate change. *Society & Natural Resources*, *14*(6), 501–509.

Watson, I. (2009). Aboriginality and the violence of colonialism. *Borderlands*, *8*(1), 1–8.

Wolfe, P. (2006). Settler colonialism and the elimination of the native. *Journal of Genocide Research*, *8*(4), 387–409.

Yates, D. A. (1996). *The Rentier State in Africa: Oil Rent Dependency and Neocolonialism in the Republic of Gabon*. Trenton, NJ: Africa World Press.

Zhang, H. B., Dai, H. C., Lai, H. X., & Wang, W. T. (2017). US withdrawal from the Paris Agreement: Reasons, impacts, and China's response. *Advances in Climate Change Research*, *8*(4), 220–225.

12

Collective Solidarities

Collective solidarity emphasises the significance of communities. When governments fail to help their people, collective solidarity appears, especially given that top-down, externally determined risk management systems are often inadequate.

'Give according to your means, take according to your need' reads a cardboard poster in one of the makeshift community pantries that sprouted up all over the Philippines from April 2020. These tables and makeshift cupboards bestowed free items, including the Filipino staple, rice, alongside canned goods, eggs, fruits, and vegetables, made available to millions. Food banks are not new, but the Philippine community pantries portrayed much more. On the one hand, it was a display of compassion and benevolence; on the other, it was a demonstration of public frustration against the Philippine state. It was an symbol of Filipino solidarity as people strove to endure the misery of the COVID-19 pandemic.

The years 2020 and 2021 saw the Philippines lock down its national borders and its city, as well as provincial and regional borderlines; this turned into the world's longest and most stringent lockdowns. I was stranded in my home, unable to move beyond the confines of my town. The community pantries, started by local entrepreneur Ana Patricia Non for her community in Barangay Maginhawa in Quezon City, made a big difference to many Filipinos. Farmers, local vegetable vendors, and ordinary citizens donated what little cash or groceries they could. Beyond these acts of generosity, people displayed respect for others, lining up for hours to take just enough for their families, conscious of those behind them who were also in need.

Community food banks not only display giving, but also respect and regard for others. Filipino sociologist Randy David would characterise these actions as anonymous giving and discrete receiving. The Filipino community pantries also conveyed the strong political message of a Filipino public frustrated with their government's sheer ineptitude in taking care of its people. While financial *ayuda* (help) was made available to some eighteen million low-income Filipinos, this was never enough to meet even their day-to-day needs. Many replicated Non's community pantry in Maginhawa so that hundreds more mushroomed all over the country in a matter of only two weeks after the Maginhawa pantry opened. This became a silent revolution exposing the deficiencies of the Philippine government's response to the pandemic.

When Non's community pantry started to multiply in numbers, the national police blatantly linked it to the communist party, accusing her private initiative of being a recruitment front. Under Rodrigo Duterte's regime, once a person is labelled a communist (or 'red-tagged' in Filipino vernacular), he or she often ends up dead. Non was compelled to shut her food pantry in fear for her life. This provoked public indignation, precipitating more donations to community pantries. Duterte and his government's threats backfired.

The Filipino community pantries are important illustrations of how solidarity arises in times of crisis (cf., Libal and Kashwan, 2020). In the face of emergencies, including disasters, we are concerned about people panicking and our social infrastructures breaking down. Panic exhibits as self-interest and individualistic behaviours when people are subjected to acute and severe danger, and, as these fears cascade with further worries, so that other individuals also register panic, social connections disintegrate. Agitated individuals would then be expected to enter a state of chaos, carrying out actions to preserve their lives. However, there is scarce evidence that panic, as described in this way, emerges in a disaster situation. Instead of individuals atomising themselves and social cohesion disintegrating, people cooperate in solidarity; this happened during the COVID-19 pandemic (Elcheroth and Drury, 2020; Lalot et al., 2022).

This is not, however, to suggest that people are not fearful during moments of crises or disasters. Instead, it highlights major conclusions from empirical work suggesting that people in distress prop up their bonds, banding together despite their collective fear and misery (Spade, 2020; Yin and Wu, 2022). For instance, survivors of super typhoon Haiyan that ravaged the central Philippines in 2013 collaborated with fellow survivors (Bartolucci and Magni, 2017). Haiyan was one of the strongest typhoons to make landfall on record. Over sixteen hours, this super typhoon swept through six provinces creating a humanitarian crisis. About fourteen million people were affected, with more than four million displaced. More than 6,000 people were killed, and nearly 2,000 were missing. More than one million houses were ruined, and six million people needed relief. The connections that many survivors of the super typhoon forged with their fellow survivors worked in two ways: as seekers of assistance and as sources of help (Robles and Ichinose, 2016). The same level of solidarity was even extended to total strangers, who were similarly distressed by the event (Bartolucci and Magni, 2017).

Thus, public hysteria at times of crisis is a fallacy (cf., Bagus, Peña-Ramos, and Sánchez-Bayon, 2021). The media often use the term 'panic' to illustrate how a confused public reacts during emergencies (Clarke, 2002). Laypeople also adopt the terminology, so that the word is reduced to mean something trivial, empty of substance. Panic is used to describe a situation when people are confused. The term has been misused to connote a problem whereby people simply look for more information. Panic is associated with people's emotional state of being fearful or with people running away – even at times when escaping is the most rational response available to them.

During the pandemic, people were urged to replenish their supplies and prepare for lockdowns. When they did prepare for it and supplies, such as toilet paper, could not meet demand, people were labelled as a panicked public (Taylor, 2021). Authorities even withheld facts or, worse, stalled action on the grounds that people would panic. Empirical work, however, is unambiguous in its findings. During crises, the public can deal with unpleasant information, including bad news, and they can be relied on to react aptly, as long as substantiated facts are communicated to them (Glick, 2007; cf., Xie et al., 2020).

Behaviours during disasters are profoundly collaborative. People under stress do not panic, loot, or engage in mass hysteria (Quarantelli, 2008; Tierney, Bevc, and Kuligowski, 2006). People carry out rescue efforts and participate in recovery efforts (Heide, 2004; Tierney, Bevc, and Kuligowski, 2006). People volunteer and donate. People, without prompting, form groups to assist disaster survivors. Groups and organisations without prior disaster work adjust to recovery and rebuilding efforts. People mobilise locally and nationally. These happen because even the most thought-out disaster response strategies inevitably disintegrate and fail to deliver.

The community pantries that mushroomed in the Philippines during the COVID-19 pandemic provide an illustrative example (Gozum et al., 2022). As the Filipino public faced inadequate support from their government, these pantries embodied cooperation and solidarity among exhausted Filipinos looking for reassurance by lending a hand to each other (Cordero, 2021). As with other relief work, these pantries may, in time, wither away without sustained community action. But they established that people under stress during crises, disasters, and misery are capable of articulating benevolence, mobilising activism, and conjuring solidarity – bringing out the best in people even in inauspicious times.

This, certainly, does not mean that disasters, crises, and misery evoke only the positive. It is important to acknowledge that collective solidarities can also produce adverse consequences. For instance, cooperation and collaboration may also lead to a collective opinion of recreancy (Freudenburg, 1993). Recreancy grows when people stop having confidence in their leaders, who they counted on to shield them from harm. During the pandemic, recreancy emerged when people criticised their governments, as happened in Brazil (Storopoli, da Silva Neto, and Mesch, 2020). Some politicians even attacked international agencies, such the World Health Organization, for their belated pandemic response. Scientists have also become victims of public animosity (Kapucu and Moynihan, 2021).

Other disturbing effects of collective solidarity include 'othering' processes (e.g., Triandafyllidou, 2022). This practice of scapegoating transpires when one group regards and treats another group as if something with it is amiss. The COVID-19 pandemic, for instance, unleashed detestation towards Chinese people, Chinese diaspora, and the Chinese government itself, seen as responsible for the global misery (Li and Nicholson, 2021). People of Asian descent were also targets of hatred. Asians faced discrimination, isolation, and racist encounters both online and offline (Chou and Gaysynsky, 2021). The pandemic and this process of othering and blaming surfaced at a time when global politics is marked by expanding inequalities and racial discrimination both in the Minority World and the Majority World. These racist incidents are not isolated but are suggestive of concealed negative attitudes towards people from groups that the public and leaders connect with the pandemic (Starks, 2021).

Othering and scapegoating exacerbate prevailing frictions, tensions, and prejudice between and within groups and peoples. Crises can activate extant xenophobic attitudes towards marginalised groups. Suppose that othering can be taken as an indication of what can happen when people of different colours and ethnicity start to migrate as climate change impacts intensify. In this instance, one can imagine how isolation, divisions, and stigmatisation can occur along racial lines (Dionne and Turkmen, 2020; Onoma, 2021).

The 2020 crisis at the US–Mexico border as Central American migrants tried to enter the United States provides an example. At that time, nearly 200,000 people attempted to cross, the highest number in two decades. Two back-to-back hurricanes hit the countries from which most of these people came: Honduras, El Salvador, and Guatemala. The storms displaced people and destroyed their crops. These weather extremes, among other drivers, pushed people to try to cross borders. While climate change was not the primary reason for this forced migration, climate-related disasters could force people to move from place to place. Forced migration due to intensifying climate impacts will become more likely as land becomes less productive and access to clean water, food, and livelihoods becomes increasingly difficult.

Despite its two cutting edges, collective solidarity highlights the importance of communities. On the one hand, it underlines the pivotal role of social connectedness in responding to uncertainty, especially at times of misery. Collective solidarity is a wisdom that can emerge when governments fail to support their people, especially given that top-down, externally defined risk management approaches are often inadequate (Hunt and Benford, 2004).

References

Bagus, P., Peña-Ramos, J. A., & Sánchez-Bayón, A. (2021). COVID-19 and the political economy of mass hysteria. *International Journal of Environmental Research and Public Health*, *18*(4), 1376.

Bartolucci, A., & Magni, M. (2017). Survivors' solidarity and attachment in the immediate aftermath of the typhoon Haiyan (Philippines). *PLoS Currents*, *9*.

Chou, W. Y., & Gaysynsky, A. (2021). Racism and xenophobia in a pandemic: Interactions of online and offline worlds. *American Journal of Public Health*, *111*(5), 773–775.

Clarke, L. (2002). Panic: Myth or reality? *Contexts*, *1*(3), 21–26.

Cordero Jr, D. A. (2021). Virtue of solidarity or vice of laziness: Understanding the existence of Philippine community pantries during the COVID-19 pandemic. *Journal of Public Health*, *43*(3), e561–562.

Dionne, K. Y., & Turkmen, F. F. (2020). The politics of pandemic othering: Putting COVID-19 in global and historical context. *International Organization*, *74*(S1), e213–230.

Elcheroth, G., & Drury, J. (2020). Collective resilience in times of crisis: Lessons from the literature for socially effective responses to the pandemic. *British Journal of Social Psychology*, *59*(3), 703–713.

Freudenburg, W. R. (1993). Risk and recreancy: Weber, the division of labour, and the rationality of risk perceptions. *Social Forces*, *71*(4), 909–932.

Glik, D. C. (2007). Risk communication for public health emergencies. *Annual Review of Public Health*, *28*, 33–54.

Gozum, I. E. A., Capulong, H. G. M., Gopez, J. M. W., & Galang, J. R. F. (2022). Philippine community pantries as a way of helping the marginalized during the COVID-19 pandemic. *Journal of Public Health*, *44*(2), e264–265.

Heide, E. A. (2004). Common misconceptions about disasters: Panic, the disaster syndrome, and looting. In M. O'Leary (Ed.), *The First 72 hours: A Community Approach to Disaster Preparedness*. Lincoln, NE: iUniverse.

Hunt, S. A., & Benford, R. D. (2004). Collective identity, solidarity, and commitment. In D. A. Snow, S. Soule & H. Kriese (Eds.), *The Blackwell Companion to Social Movements* (pp. 433–458). Oxford: Blackwell Publishing.

Kapucu, N., & Moynihan, D. (2021). Trump's (mis)management of the COVID-19 pandemic in the US. *Policy Studies*, *42*(5–6), 592–610.

Lalot, F., Abrams, D., Broadwood, J., Davies Hayon, K., & Platts-Dunn, I. (2022). The social cohesion investment: Communities that invested in integration programmes are showing greater social cohesion in the midst of the COVID-19 pandemic. *Journal of Community & Applied Social Psychology, 32*(3), 536–554.

Li, Y., & Nicholson Jr, H. L. (2021). When 'model minorities' become 'yellow peril' – Othering and the racialization of Asian Americans in the COVID-19 pandemic. *Sociology Compass, 15*(2), e12849.

Libal, K., & Kashwan, P. (2020). Solidarity in times of crisis. *Journal of Human Rights, 19*(5), 537–546.

Onoma, A. K. (2021). The allure of scapegoating return migrants during a pandemic. *Medical Anthropology, 40*(7), 653–666.

Quarantelli, E. L. (2008). Conventional beliefs and counterintuitive realities. *Social Research: An International Quarterly, 75*(3), 873–904.

Robles, L. R., & Ichinose, T. (2016). Connections, trust and social capital in disaster: A study on the 2013 Typhoon Haiyan affected residents in Leyte, Philippines. *Journal of Environmental Information Science, 44*, 79–86.

Spade, D. (2020). *Mutual Aid: Building Solidarity during This Crisis (and the Next)*. London: Verso Books.

Starks, B. (2021). The double pandemic: COVID-19 and white supremacy. *Qualitative Social Work, 20*(1–2), 222–224.

Storopoli, J., da Silva Neto, W. L. B., & Mesch, G. S. (2020). Confidence in social institutions, perceived vulnerability and the adoption of recommended protective behaviors in Brazil during the COVID-19 pandemic. *Social Science & Medicine, 265*, 113477.

Taylor, S. (2021). Understanding and managing pandemic-related panic buying. *Journal of Anxiety Disorders, 78*, 102364.

Tierney, K., Bevc, C., & Kuligowski, E. (2006). Metaphors matter: Disaster myths, media frames, and their consequences in Hurricane Katrina. *Annals of the American Academy of Political and Social Science, 604*(1), 57–81.

Triandafyllidou, A. (2022). Spaces of solidarity and spaces of exception: Migration and membership during pandemic times. In A. Triandafyllidou (Ed.), *Migration and Pandemics* (pp. 3–21). Cham: Springer.

Xie, B., He, D., Mercer, T., Wang, Y., Wu, D., Fleischmann, K. R., ... & Lee, M. K. (2020). Global health crises are also information crises: A call to action. *Journal of the Association for Information Science and Technology, 71*(12), 1419–1423.

Yin, L., & Wu, Y. C. J. (2022). Fight alone or together? The influence of risk perception on helping behavior. *Journal of Risk and Financial Management, 15*(2), 1–15.

13
Decolonising from Within

The failure of stewardship by many colonialists is so profound that their blunder and neglect essentially mirror the same political and market forces that drive the climate crisis. Decolonising climate action thus requires the recognition, acknowledgement, and closure of histories of racism and greed.

The climate crisis is built on the foundation of colonialism that left deep scars on the colonised (cf., Sultana, 2022). Indigenous societies, most significantly, experience these colonial impacts directly through the natural world where, for millennia, they have based their survival (Porter et al., 2020; Leal Filho et al., 2021; Lynn et al., 2013). The effects of the climate emergency burden Indigenous Peoples differently from other societies (Nursey-Bray et al., 2019; Figueroa, 2011). Only by acknowledging that colonial or post-colonial frames cannot address these impacts can we address them sustainably (Sultana, 2022). The assumption that state-defined courses of action – often produced and directed by colonists or settlers – will sufficiently address the adaptation needs of Indigenous Peoples has to be confronted and challenged.

Decolonising climate action requires the recognition, acknowledgement, and closure of histories of racism and greed (e.g., Bordner, Ferguson, and Ortolano, 2020; Watkinson-Schutten, 2023). This starts with a concession that state-produced climate action processes and policies may be insufficient to acknowledge, recognise, and address the complex realities of Indigenous life. Even well-intentioned climate action can reinforce new risks and exacerbate extant vulnerabilities for Indigenous Peoples.

Without proper recognition, possible solutions to the climate crisis in Indigenous places are virtually impossible. Only through countering colonial denial can a sincere engagement and genuine interconnection be fostered. Colonialism should be recognised not only as a relic of the past; it has to be acknowledged for its structural legacies that continue to thwart the capacities of the colonised to this day. Squaring off the residues of colonialism can assist in confronting differences and engendering dialogues. These legacies need to be deliberated carefully.

Acknowledgement is crucial, especially when the dismissal of identities, human rights, connectedness, and climate change persists. Recognising the rights of Indigenous Peoples and the accelerating shifts in the natural world across spaces, scales, and species is a first step in the reflexive process of discovery, cooperation, and thriving in a world under pressure (cf., Deranger et al., 2022; Sultana, 2022).

The risks of cascading crises, including climate change, are often suggested to be higher among Indigenous populations (e.g., Shaffril et al., 2020). They are either categorised as precariously in peril or as intrinsically supple and able to adapt to these risks. While both these descriptions may contain some truth, neither is entirely accurate. The exposure to hazards and the adaptive capacities of Indigenous Peoples have to be interpreted vis-à-vis the peculiarities and complexities of the heterogeneous contexts in which they live, survive, and thrive (Ford et al., 2020).

Introducing climate action in Indigenous places has to start by recognising these peoples' diverse knowledge and varied experiences and then engaging them. Engaging Indigenous Peoples must take account of their distinct histories, particular geographies, and the peculiar impacts and consequences of colonisation (e.g., Nursey-Bray et al., 2019). More importantly, engagement should focus on what Indigenous Peoples regard as their risk landscapes, not what outsiders perceive these risks to be. This should be followed by integrating climate action into the broader project of decolonisation. Such integration can be done only through a respectful reshaping of relationships damaged by centuries of colonisation. The relationships that need to be refashioned include those among people as well as people's relationships with their natural and even spiritual worlds.

Between fourteen and seventeen million Indigenous Peoples make up 110 ethnolinguistic groupings in the Philippines. Their fight for governmental acknowledgement of their ancestral territories and their different appreciation of human relationships with the natural world are integral to the complex history of a nation colonised by one Asian and two Western nations. The right to use and power over the natural world and the resources therein, such as land and forests and those categorised under Indigenous intellectual property rights, are focal to these battles (Molintas, 2004). These conflicts are consistent with the notions of self-determination, cultural identity, and acknowledgement of the Indigenous legal systems maintained by associated Indigenous Peoples (Candelaria, 2018). Thus, laws that protect Indigenous Peoples' rights contradict laws that support extractions since Indigenous territories overlap with forests and mineral sites, including water resources, that are used or plundered by extractive industries such as mining (Molintas, 2004; Delina, 2020).

One of the most glaring examples of decades-old contentions in the struggle for Indigenous recognition in the Philippines is related to water extraction (Delina, 2020): the case of the hydro resource–rich Cordillera illustrates. Cordillera is a landlocked and mountainous region in Luzon, the Philippines' largest island. This area is regarded as the most ethnolinguistically diverse in the nation. Cordillera is home to 33 per cent of Indigenous Peoples in the Philippines, and where at least ten languages are spoken by thirty-eight ethnic groups. The Philippine government views the Cordillera as a vital resource base for the development of mining, timber, and energy sectors. Being the watershed cradle of Luzon, the region has the biggest hydroelectric and irrigation potential.

Because of this, the Philippine state has always sought ways to tap Cordillera's rich hydro resources (Delina, 2020). This quest is driven by the need to generate new electricity sources and increase the irrigation capacity not just of Cordillera itself but also its neighbouring provinces and Metro Manila. This extractivist agenda is evident in the region's development plans, where hydropower development is given high priority. More than half of Luzon's energy needs is currently met by the rivers of the Cordillera via three huge hydroelectric projects.

Hydropower projects, however, both existing and planned, have long been objects of contention among Cordillera's Indigenous Peoples (Delina, 2020). The 1960s to the 1980s were the most intense three decades of mobilisation by Indigenous Peoples of the Cordillera. Resistance to plans during this period to dam one of their major rivers, the Chico River, was based on the knowledge that this project would submerge their sacred lands. Dissent intensified significantly in the late 1970s when dictator Ferdinand Marcos instructed the commencement of survey work on the Chico River.

Indigenous dissent against the damming of the Chico and its consequence – the submergence of villages – was primarily based on cultural reasons (Delina, 2020). Among them is ancestor worship, in which deceased ancestors are thought to be eternally present in a place. Thus, protecting the landscape was essential for these Indigenous Peoples. The proposed project would also obliterate tribal relations among different groups, which, for decades, had formed their system of law. This dissent shows how Indigenous Peoples are strongly connected with their landscapes and the importance they place on protecting people–place relationships. In registering their dissent, Indigenous women went to the surveyors' campsites, where they performed the *lusay* – an act of disrobing and displaying tattooed torsos and limbs to bring bad luck to male observers (Delina, 2020). Resistance grew as Indigenous Peoples received support from the Catholic and Protestant churches, lawyers, academics, and Manila-based civil society groups.

Marcos, however, was unperturbed. With the Philippines under martial law, he militarised the Cordillera, particularly the area where the proposed dams were to be built. Dissenting locals were arrested without warrants. The sites were also declared 'free fire zones', indicating that the military might shoot any intruders at will. Under the protection of Marcos' martial law, forces of the state assassinated a prominent Indigenous leader and dam dissenter, Macli-ing Dulag, and his neighbour, Pedro Dungoc, in April 1980. Instead of silencing dissent, however, the Indigenous Peoples of Cordillera intensified their protests. For the first time in the histories of these culturally and linguistically diverse peoples, the Indigenous Peoples of Cordillera developed a strong sense of solidarity and cemented their Igorot identity. As a result, they established a united Cordillera front, which became essential in their subsequent mobilisations against the damming of the Chico. Marcos eventually withdrew his proposal (Delina, 2020).

While the Cordillera Indigenous Peoples were successful in the 1980s in protecting their ancestral domains, others were not. In some parts of the world, particularly in South America, large hydro projects have displaced Indigenous Peoples in Panama (Finley-Brook and Thomas, 2010), Guatemala, Ecuador, Peru, and Honduras (Hernández-Gutiérrez, Peña-Ramos, and Espinosa, 2022). As Indigenous Peoples uncouple from their ancestral communities, they fragment, disintegrate, and disappear. Along with these peoples, their cultures, traditions, and knowledge, produced over millennia, have consequentially been erased.

The scars of colonialism run deep. Settlers and colonisers have different conceptions of Indigenous places. Their understanding of environmental change always conflicts with that of Indigenous Peoples. Rarely is this deep appreciation of people–place relationships recognised by the systems and processes that colonisers impose on a seized landscape. In a system dominated by the logic of capital and accumulation, the natural environment has become a monetised resource to be exploited. In the process, Indigenous Peoples are removed from their ancestral domains, their livelihoods lost, and they become annihilated, or, if not, driven further into marginal and interior lands (cf., Veltmeyer, 2013; Wouters, 2020). Wealth is created as settlers and colonialists turn these landscapes and the resources therein into money. However, this wealth creation comes at a price: the exhaustion of ecosystems and the obliteration of peoples, identities, and cultures.

Colonialism and capital are always intertwined (e.g., Camba, 2016; Wouters, 2020). The economic models orchestrating colonialism are set in motion without acknowledging the interconnections and relationships they imperil and without realising that atrocities could be unchained. The economics of colonialism is built on the contention that capital can perpetually grow and that the growth-without-end dictum is achievable and, therefore, should be desired. With the logic of accumulation built into colonialism, economic growth is pursued by all means, consuming and depleting the resources of other peoples and other places. Boundaries have been crossed. Indigenous Peoples have been conquered and pushed out.

The gospel of economic growth-without-end allowed for wealth accumulation among colonialists, impoverishing local people and depleting their natural resources, livelihoods, and landscapes (Radcliffe, 2020). The degradation of the natural environment was allowed since this is considered an externality. A denuded landscape is of no value in the logic of wealth accumulation. Nature is an object to be subjugated by the colonisers, a bounty for them to take. Conquest became the rationale for coveting Indigenous People's places and their resources.

Subjugation happens by ignoring the essential fact that Indigenous places and resources are products of these peoples' prudent management of their landscapes and of generations of nurturing by their cultures (Merino, 2020). The notion that these landscapes are the result of Indigenous People's relationships with each other, their communities, the place itself, and their intangible cosmos is also disregarded. These civilisations reflect millennia of human experience, knowledge production, and adaptation to changing circumstances in a long chain of customs, traditions, and values. Their cultures provide profound illustrations of stewardship and what it means to belong and be connected to a place, which is consequential when considering the climate crisis (Koot, Hitchcock, and Gressier, 2019).

The failure of stewardship by many colonialists is so profound that their blunder and neglect essentially mirror the same political and market forces that drive the climate crisis. The greed of global businesses simply replaced the covetousness of imperial and colonial looters. The incredible wealth generated by oligarchs, from Bezos to Gates to Musk, including, most significantly, during the global COVID-19 pandemic that began in 2020, when their riches continued to skyrocket (Ahmed et al., 2022), stands in stark contrast with the perils imposed on and the misery experienced by Indigenous Peoples.

The climate crisis affects extraordinarily contemporary landscapes of risk. But the topography of risk that Indigenous Peoples have to navigate and negotiate is more intense in that these risks include their fundamental right to survive, exist, and cherish their culture and place. The capacity of Indigenous Peoples to adapt to the dangers of the climate crisis begins, in earnest, with the acknowledgement that their climate risk landscapes stand adjacent to their structural vulnerabilities. Responding to and adapting to the climate crisis in

Indigenous places is thus not only a function of technical programmes but also of social and cultural efforts that seek to address their experiences of injustice. As risks emerge and cascade, these peoples' experiences are tied deeply into their places. In these locations, the climate emergency unfurls as a crisis of connection between peoples and their places. Their survival depends on whether this relationship can continue.

References

Ahmed, N., Marriott, A., Dabi, N., Lowthers, M., Lawson, M., & Mugehera, L. (2022). *Inequality Kills*. Oxford: Oxfam International.

Bordner, A. S., Ferguson, C. E., & Ortolano, L. (2020). Colonial dynamics limit climate adaptation in Oceania: Perspectives from the Marshall Islands. *Global Environmental Change*, *61*, 102054.

Camba, A. A. (2016). Philippine mining capitalism: The changing terrains of struggle in the neoliberal mining regime. *Austrian Journal of South-East Asian Studies*, *9*(1), 69–86.

Candelaria, S. M. (2018). The plight of indigenous peoples within the context of conflict mediation, peace talks and human rights in Mindanao, the Philippines. *Thesis Eleven*, *145*(1), 28–37.

Delina, L. L. (2020). Indigenous environmental defenders and the legacy of Macli-ing Dulag: Anti-dam dissent, assassinations, and protests in the making of Philippine energyscape. *Energy Research & Social Science*, *65*, 101463.

Deranger, E. T., Sinclair, R., Gray, B., McGregor, D., & Gobby, J. (2022). Decolonizing climate research and policy: Making space to tell our own stories, in our own ways. *Community Development Journal*, *57*(1), 52–73.

Figueroa, R. M. (2011). Indigenous peoples and cultural losses. In J. Dryzek, R. Norgaard, & D. Schlosberg (Eds.), *The Oxford Handbook of Climate Change and Society* (pp. 232–249). New York: Oxford University Press.

Finley-Brook, M., & Thomas, C. (2010). Treatment of displaced indigenous populations in two large hydro projects in Panama. *Water Alternatives*, *3*(2), 269–290.

Ford, J. D., King, N., Galappaththi, E. K., Pearce, T., McDowell, G., & Harper, S. L. (2020). The resilience of indigenous peoples to environmental change. *One Earth*, *2* (6), 532–543.

Hernández-Gutiérrez, J. C., Peña-Ramos, J. A., & Espinosa, V. I. (2022). Hydro power plants as disputed infrastructures in Latin America. *Water*, *14*(3), 277.

Koot, S., Hitchcock, R., & Gressier, C. (2019). Belonging, indigeneity, land and nature in Southern Africa under neoliberal capitalism: An overview. *Journal of Southern African Studies*, *45*(2), 341–355.

Leal Filho, W., Matandirotya, N. R., Lütz, J. M., Alemu, E. A., Brearley, F. Q., Baidoo, A. A., ... & Mbih, R. A. (2021). Impacts of climate change to African indigenous communities and examples of adaptation responses. *Nature Communications*, *12*(1), 1–4.

Lynn, K., Daigle, J., Hoffman, J., Lake, F., Michelle, N., Ranco, D., ... & Williams, P. (2013). The impacts of climate change on tribal traditional foods. *Climatic Change*, 120, 545–556.

Merino, R. (2020). The cynical state: Forging extractivism, neoliberalism and development in governmental spaces. *Third World Quarterly*, 41(1), 58–76.

Molintas, J. M. (2004). The Philippine indigenous peoples' struggle for land and life: Challenging legal texts. *Arizona Journal of International & Comparative Law*, 21(1), 269–306.

Nursey-Bray, M., Palmer, R., Smith, T. F., & Rist, P. (2019). Old ways for new days: Australian indigenous peoples and climate change. *Local Environment*, 24(5), 473–486.

Pictou, S. (2020). Decolonizing decolonization: An indigenous feminist perspective on the recognition and rights framework. *South Atlantic Quarterly*, 119(2), 371–391.

Porter, L., Rickards, L., Verlie, B., Bosomworth, K., Moloney, S., Lay, B., ... & Pellow, D. (2020). Climate justice in a climate changed world. *Planning Theory & Practice*, 21(2), 293–321.

Radcliffe, S. A. (2020). Geography and indigeneity III: Co-articulation of colonialism and capitalism in indigeneity's economies. *Progress in Human Geography*, 44(2), 374–388.

Shaffril, H. A. M., Ahmad, N., Samsuddin, S. F., Samah, A. A., & Hamdan, M. E. (2020). Systematic literature review on adaptation towards climate change impacts among indigenous people in the Asia Pacific regions. *Journal of Cleaner Production*, 258, 120595.

Sultana, F. (2022). The unbearable heaviness of climate coloniality. *Political Geography*, 102638.

Veltmeyer, H. (2013). The political economy of natural resource extraction: A new model or extractive imperialism? *Canadian Journal of Development Studies*, 34(1), 79–95.

Watkinson-Schutten, M. (2023). Decolonizing climate adaptation by reacquiring fractionated tribal lands. In M. Walter, E. Kukutai, A. A. Gonzales, & R. Henry (Eds.), *The Oxford Handbook of Indigenous Sociology*. New York: Oxford University Press.

Wouters, J. J. (2020). Neoliberal capitalism and ethno-territoriality in highland Northeast India: Resource-extraction, capitalist desires and ethnic closure. *Geopolitics*, 1–23.

14
Indigenous Epistemology

> *Indigenous epistemology reimagines climate risk narratives as a plethora of disconnected local narratives rather than a linear one. A change in emphasis – from global to Indigenous – is critical because it clarifies the threats to peoples and to communities.*

The climate crisis is a global emergency occurring on a planetary scale. At this scale, it is a crisis of survival. It is not surprising, therefore, to see academic and political discourses dominated by a risk framing that suggests the climate crisis is singularly global (e.g., Warner and Boas, 2019; Benzie and Persson, 2019). These narratives sketch the landscape of climate risk as embedded in a unique planetary system whose intricacies need specialists and experts to be privileged in knowledge production and decision-making. The politics of climate negotiations, which asserts the domination of nation-states in finding climate solutions, aptly manifests this globality. However, the notion that the world is a single place is debatable.

When we look at the dynamics of international climate negotiations through a simple lens of a top-down hierarchy, we are in danger of reducing climate action to a global–local hierarchy, where policies emanate from the top, via international climate treaties, to the bottom, where national and local governments enact and translate this approach into practice. In this arrangement, one can see how the global subordinates the local. This arrangement thus mirrors a paternalistic and colonising framework, in which the international climate system simply fails to advocate for Indigenous-self-determination (cf., Brugnach, Craps, and Dewulf, 2017). Furthermore, it justifies the case for continuing colonisation, where colonial patterns and techniques of cynicism and lack of unaccountability persist (cf., Sultana, 2022). It also extends extant structures and logics of accumulation and maldistribution of wealth, power, and resources.

There should be no debate about the political, economic, and climatic characteristics of the climate emergency. The fact that there is a climate emergency is clear. What we have missed in these narratives, however, are the elements that produce people–place relationships (Devine-Wright, 2013). Often, these elements are connected to the local – people and their communities, as well as those with whom they share the place, that is, nonhumans and the cosmos. These peoples confront their risks, defined within the constraints and boundaries of their space–time experiences. Conceiving and framing these very local and time–place-specific risks as 'global' carries the risk of them being detached from their bounded sociality.

Human survival is elaborately entangled, yet dependent, on people–place relationships. These relationships are approaching thresholds as ecosystems collapse due to the climate crisis. This emergent risk landscape, punctuated by irreversible change at the global scale, propounds a glimpse of an apocalyptic world. In this shrinking time horizon, avant-garde technologies are being floated and promoted to address the climate crisis. Among these proposals are geoengineering techniques aimed at reflecting solar radiation into space by bombarding the atmosphere with aerosols (Sovacool, 2021). This planetary scale approach to addressing the climate emergency assumes the singularity of the human species, imagining that all *Homo sapiens* have one and the same experience.

This narrative of globality, as a result, conceals, if not annuls, the differences and complexities of people's lived experiences. Rendered the most invisible are Indigenous Peoples, whose cultures and knowledge were destroyed by colonial conquests. The genocide of many of these peoples became unsolved crimes, and the ensuing ecocide of their landscapes has remained hidden. The logic of accumulation and profit produced this genocide and ecocide, atrocities that continue to this day.

A week before International Human Rights Day, at noon on 3 December 2017, an Indigenous leader of the T'boli-Manobo peoples of Lake Sebu in the southern Philippines, Datu Victor Dayan, was killed by agents of the Philippine state (Delina, 2021). Also murdered that day were two of his sons and four other Indigenous persons. Dayan's land is a community of one-story wooden homes, cornfields, and a small dirt square where Indigenous children play basketball next to a water buffalo pen. Datu Victor was murdered because he was tagged a communist rebel. The communist rebellion in the Philippines is Asia's longest-running insurgency and the world's longest communist rebellion. Families of the dead and several groups, including communist rebels themselves, issued a statement saying the dead Indigenous Peoples were not insurrectionists (Delina, 2021). A fact-finding mission by civil society groups found no physical evidence to support the states claim (Delina, 2021).

The massacre of Datu Victor Dayan and others resulted from the militarisation of Dayan's land, which holds the Philippines' largest coal deposits (Delina, 2021).

The land, part of the Daguma Mountain Range, is a watershed source of the Ala and Kabulnan Rivers, two of Mindanao's most extensive river systems. The mountain range is home to various Indigenous Peoples, including the T'bolis and the Dulangan Manobos. The vast majority of this landscape is a protected forest area and a habitat of the Philippine Eagle, a giant raptor, considered one of the most powerful eagles in the world, and averaging about a metre in length with a wingspan of around two metres. When Dayan's land was opened to coal exploitation (Delina, 2021), big companies, including the Philippine conglomerate San Miguel Corporation, rushed in with plans to conquer this frontier, collect the spoils, accumulate capital, and profit from minerals that are driving the climate crisis (Delina, 2021).

The narratives of collapse resulting from climate disasters reveal truths of great importance. At the same time, however, Indigenous Peoples experience several other landscapes of risk that may appear quotidian to many. These include poverty, food insecurity, violence, marginalisation, and disease (Hilhorst et al., 2015). The COVID-19 pandemic – that appears to have started at a local wet market in Wuhan in 2019 and spiralled into a global contagion – provides an indication of these risks. It offers an illustration on how local and mundane everyday risks can infringe on international affairs.

The landscapes of risk are always contingent on the place and they are sequenced not only spatially – that is, the local to the global – but also temporally. Local and mundane everyday risks are often formulated in shorter time horizons. In the context of Datu Dayan's people, their time horizon is about how to survive a day – and, if they are lucky, a week (Delina, 2021). Indigenous Peoples perform their adaptive capacity in these everyday risk landscapes.

The plethora of violence to which many Indigenous Peoples have been subjected, not only in my home province in South Cotabato but also in many places around the world, suggests the capability of Indigenous communities to thrive and flourish in challenging circumstances. Their ability to adapt to change and survive cruelty challenges the colonial discourse of their inferior culture, irrelevant experiences, and inconsequential knowledge. This celebration of persistence and endurance should not devalue the risks Indigenous Peoples continue to experience and their will to survive, nor should the legacies of genocide and ecocide be wiped out.

As the climate crisis compounds its impacts and cascades with other risks, Indigenous survival needs to be recognised and reckoned with (Ford et al., 2020; Cochran et al., 2013). These stories of unremitting resilience champion the narratives of survival and thriving in an age of cascading crises. An Indigenous assessment of adaptation and resilience counters the dominance of technical experts and recalcitrant state actors, who often dismiss the nuances of local tacit knowledge and experience. Indigenous epistemology brings front and centre these forms of knowing and doing, providing crucial supplements to addressing the climate crisis (e.g., Mugambiwa, 2021).

It is critical to note that Indigenous epistemology does not equate with 'localness'; rather, it vocalises the relationships, linkages, and associations that produce the globality of the crisis (cf., Middleton, 2015). It does this by demanding responsibility from the economic and political systems that have driven the climate emergency: the logic of overaccumulation at the expense of peoples and places. Indigenous epistemology thus addresses the difficulties leading discourses – such as the Anthropocene – face in conceptualising climate solutions. Indigenous epistemology also counters the idea that only those with global expertise should be empowered to act decisively; instead, it counts on the wisdom of Indigenous survival and resilience.

By doing so, Indigenous epistemology reconceptualises climate risk narratives not as linear but as an abundance of detached local narratives. Nonetheless, an Indigenously led narrative of climate action should not be taken as a panacea for confronting the onerous conversations of emergency, crisis, and catastrophe and the means to adapt to and survive these situations. A shift in focus – from the global to the Indigenous – is crucial because it helps clarify the risks to peoples and communities while veering away from global climate governance (cf., Chao and Enari, 2021). The latter, of course, remains essential, but it is critical that understanding risks and deliberating solutions at the local scale are also amplified.

By switching how we think about the scale on which we embed risk, we can recognise that risks are concurrent products of our culture (the people) and natural environments (the place). Acknowledging that risks are a function of people–place relationships results in an interrogation of risks not in relation to indicators and points of reference but connected to people–place relationships. This switch in scale also requires a transition in how we consider time to comprise intergenerational misery (as experienced by the colonised) and a sense of restorative justice (as a responsibility of the coloniser).

The trauma that Indigenous Peoples have experienced and their adaptation to their catastrophic miseries provide a mirror by which we can see how to confront an apocalyptic world beleaguered by unforeseen risks and weather extremes (e.g., Nyong, Adesina, and Osman Elasha, 2007). Bringing Indigenous epistemologies front and centre in new discourses of climate survival and resilience in the Anthropocene addresses the historical marginalisation and structural silencing of these knowledge systems. Although many of these epistemologies have withstood sweeping disruptions and challenges over time, their roles in crisis adaptation could not emerge without challenging the frames that define, constrain, or erase their rights and agency.

Contesting this history requires paying attention to issues of justice. Recognising the silencing of Indigenous epistemologies and the structural marginalisation of Indigenous Peoples is one way (McGregor, Whitaker, and Sritharan, 2020). Restoring the dignity of Indigenous Peoples through processes that put a premium on care and repair is another. New thinking about the landscapes of climate risk must include respectful deliberations that examine various modes of belonging and relationships.

Embedding the tenets of justice in the processes of building climate resilience requires a reframing of the scale and temporalities of climate risks. Framing climate change as a planetary emergency in short time frames restricts our ability to better understand climate risks and prioritise climate action. Reframing climate change to the scale of communities and intergenerational care and repair, while attending to Indigenous epistemology, focuses the narratives of climate action on crucial issues of Indigenously produced mechanisms for survival, coping, and resilience.

Indigenously led climate actions and modes of surviving in a world of misery highlight the need to pursue belongingness and community. These climate actions should recognise the enduring presence of Indigenous relationships with landscapes, histories, and futures. They also involve reconfigurations of people-to-people and people-to-place relationships. In addition, governments and businesses should also be persuaded to reduce the strain humans are placing on the natural environment, including the climate.

References

Benzie, M., & Persson, Å. (2019). Governing borderless climate risks: Moving beyond the territorial framing of adaptation. *International Environmental Agreements: Politics, Law and Economics*, *19*(4), 369–393.

Brugnach, M., Craps, M., & Dewulf, A. R. P. J. (2017). Including indigenous peoples in climate change mitigation: Addressing issues of scale, knowledge and power. *Climatic Change*, *140*(1), 19–32.

Chao, S., & Enari, D. (2021). Decolonising climate change: A call for beyond-human imaginaries and knowledge generation. *eTropic: Electronic Journal of Studies in the Tropics*, *20*(2), 32–54.

Cochran, P., Huntington, O. H., Pungowiyi, C., Tom, S., Chapin, F. S., Huntington, H. P., ... & Trainor, S. F. (2013). Indigenous frameworks for observing and responding to climate change in Alaska. In J. K. Maldonado, B. Colombi, & R. Pandya (Eds.), *Climate Change and Indigenous Peoples in the United States* (pp. 49–59). Cham: Springer.

Delina, L. L. (2021). Topographies of coal mining dissent: Power, politics, and protests in southern Philippines. *World Development*, *137*, 105194.

Devine-Wright, P. (2013). Think global, act local? The relevance of place attachments and place identities in a climate changed world. *Global Environmental Change*, *23*(1), 61–69.

Ford, J. D., King, N., Galappaththi, E. K., Pearce, T., McDowell, G., & Harper, S. L. (2020). The resilience of indigenous peoples to environmental change. *One Earth, 2*(6), 532–543.

Hilhorst, D., Baart, J., van der Haar, G., & Leeftink, F. M. (2015). Is disaster 'normal' for indigenous people? Indigenous knowledge and coping practices. *Disaster Prevention and Management, 24*(4), 506–522.

McGregor, D., Whitaker, S., & Sritharan, M. (2020). Indigenous environmental justice and sustainability. *Current Opinion in Environmental Sustainability, 43*, 35–40.

Middleton, B. R. (2015). Jahát Jat'totòdom: Toward an indigenous political ecology. In R. L. Bryant (Ed.), *The International Handbook of Political Ecology* (pp. 561–576). Cheltenham, UK: Edward Elgar Publishing.

Mugambiwa, S. S. (2021). Evoking the epistemology of climate governance through indigenous knowledge systems for sustainable development in rural Zimbabwe. *Jàmbá: Journal of Disaster Risk Studies, 13*(1), 1–10.

Nyong, A., Adesina, F., & Osman Elasha, B. (2007). The value of indigenous knowledge in climate change mitigation and adaptation strategies in the African Sahel. *Mitigation and Adaptation Strategies for Global Change, 12*(5), 787–797.

Sovacool, B. K. (2021). Reckless or righteous? Reviewing the sociotechnical benefits and risks of climate change geoengineering. *Energy Strategy Reviews, 35*, 100656.

Sultana, F. (2022). The unbearable heaviness of climate coloniality. *Political Geography, 99*, 102638.

Warner, J., & Boas, I. (2019). Securitization of climate change: How invoking global dangers for instrumental ends can backfire. *Environment and Planning C: Politics and Space, 37*(8), 1471–1488.

15
Communicating Risks

It is crucial to communicate the hazards of climate change and our power to act on them, believing and acting with 'constructive optimism'. The COVID-19 pandemic has taught us the significance of effective risk communication. Transparent and credible oversight of risk management strategies by reputable authorities is vital.

Eight to nine typhoons, on average, make landfall every year in my home country, the Philippines. Although I live on the southern tip of the, where intense storms do not usually strike, the most recent typhoons have been stronger. In December 2021, Typhoon Rai hit the northern part of my home island, Mindanao, causing catastrophic damage before moving across the southern Visayas through Palawan. Rai killed more than 400 people while damaging nearly US$1 billion of crops, infrastructure, and properties.

The coastal orientation of my country means that our communities tend to settle near the waters. Indeed, we build our cities on the coasts. With strong typhoons, these coastal communities have been at risk of extreme hazards, including strong winds and sea surges. But weather extremes, such as super typhoons, are not the only hazard we Filipinos face. As a country in the Pacific Ring of Fire, active volcanoes dot our archipelago. These erupt from time to time, producing pyroclastic flows that affect lives and livelihoods. Seismic activities, including strong earthquakes, are also common phenomena. The 2019 earthquakes in Cotabato, my home region, and in Davao del Sur and Batanes were destructive.

Already burdened with seismic and volcanic hazards, the vulnerabilities of many Filipinos will exacerbate as climate change intensifies its impacts. Hydrometeorological threats, including extreme weather events like super typhoons and prolonged droughts, will increase the likelihood of misery among Filipinos. Farmers and fisherfolks, particularly, are at high risk.

Preparing for disasters has thus become de facto public policy in the Philippines. The country has robust guidelines, frameworks, and plans for disaster risk reduction. Disaster warnings and risk communications have long been the focus of the national government and, most significantly, many local governments. The corpus on disaster warnings, not only in the Philippines but globally, often tackles how to sensibly advise and alert those at risk so that they can shield and protect themselves before, during, and after disastrous events (Sylves, 2019; Islam et al., 2016; Whelchel et al., 2018).

Communicating risks is vital as climate change exacerbate its impacts and weather extremes become more frequent and more potent than previously experienced (National Academy of Sciences, 2018; Millet et al., 2020; Rabinovich and Morton, 2012; MacIntyre et al., 2019). The extant literature suggests the following criteria for risk communication and action to be effective. First, people and communities at risk should obtain and understand the warning. Second, they should comprehend that the guidance applies to them personally. Third, they should be convinced that they are at risk. Fourth, they should be aware of what they must do to cushion themselves from the risks and when to act. Fifth, they should be able to do what has been recommended. Sixth, and finally, they should be able to recognise when the threat is over. These steps must be successfully and swiftly carried out sequentially (National Academy of Sciences, 2018).

Our COVID-19 pandemic experiences best demonstrate the appropriateness of communicating risks (Paulik, Keenan, and Durda, 2020). This global misery provided lessons on the importance of appropriate risk communication. The transparent and credible superintending of the steps mentioned above by trustworthy authorities is paramount (Crick, 2021). When decision-makers meet these qualifications – transparency, credibility, trustworthiness – the public put their faith in the risk warning advice provided to them (Paulik, Keenan, and Durda, 2020; cf., Leavitt, 2003).

In the absence of these qualities, the public turn to the so-called normalcy bias. This cognitive bias leads people to minimise, even disbelieve, warnings of risks even when they are already experiencing real danger (Chang et al., 2021; Cato et al., 2021). With normalcy bias, people at risk may not follow the guidance provided. And even if they decide to take flight or evacuate, they may do so belatedly, incurring significant damages, including the possible loss of many lives and the decimation of livelihoods.

Normalcy bias is very predominant in our present understanding of the climate crisis (Deotto, 2021). Most of us believe that things will continue to function in the future as they always have in the past. This bias leads people to undervalue the probability of disasters-upon-disasters eventuating and the potency of their effects. Normalcy bias causes people to deny the need to make plans or respond to risks, crises, or miseries they have never experienced before.

The hellish summer of 2020 in the northern hemisphere was accentuated by one climate disaster hitting after another: wildfires in California and bush fires in Australia. In 2021, heavy rains flooded New York, Germany, and China. As the year ended, Typhoon Rai, mentioned earlier, heralded a sad Christmas Eve for thousands of Filipinos who lost their homes. In the summer of 2022, as these words are written, Europe is burning with heatwaves. These events are not even previews of what the future could look like. These are not the new normal. In the end, we might find these stories much kinder and gentler compared to our experiences. Despite the preponderance of evidence that climate misery will most likely distinguish our future, most of us still think the future will be OK. The collective trauma we experienced during the pandemic should discredit our normalcy bias.

We will not be getting a second free pass with the climate crisis. The next global emergency, most likely punctuated by not one, not two, but cascading climate-related events, should not be labelled 'unprecedented'. We have already seen the fragility of our international system when faced with an intractable crisis. We cannot blame others but only ourselves the next time science tells us that our overly consumerist lifestyles and wanton emissions are unsustainable. We deserve the consequences if we do not take the climate emergency seriously.

Don't Look Up, a comedy that addresses climate change, was one of the most popular offers on Netflix in early 2022. The film has an all-star ensemble, including Leonardo DiCaprio, Jennifer Lawrence, and Meryl Streep, and recounts the tale of two scientists who discover an Earth-bound comet. We see their unsuccessful efforts to convince governments and society to respond to the existential danger posed by the hurling heavenly body. The storytelling is so powerful it drove increased attention to climate change. While *Don't Look Up* became popular, it does not necessarily mean that it will change the mindsets of those not alarmed by the severe impacts of the climate crisis. Those who are already worried about the climate catastrophe are more likely to watch it, but those the movie seeks to mock are less likely to do so. However, those who are aware of or worried about climate change, but who are not yet frightened, will find *Don't Look Up* to be of great import (Delina, 2022).

What we can observe from this film is that carrying out the order of risk communication from a warning to protecting oneself posits some serious issues. These are essential lessons for communicating the risks of the climate crisis. The COVID-19 pandemic made these issues obvious. Within the general population, for instance, some groups source their information from doubtful references and dubious informants (Rocha et al., 2021; Dang, 2021). Social media became a platform for sowing misinformation about the coronavirus.

False conspiracy theories were shared on social media, for example, that the 5G cellular network had caused the virus (Ahmed et al., 2020), and fake remedies such as injecting yourself with bleach (Litman et al., 2021) or taking ivermectin (originally prescribed for horses) (Di Giorgio, 2022) were spread. Political elites, such as Donald Trump and Jair Bolsonaro, also peddled fake news, falsely claiming, for instance, that hydroxychloroquine is an antiviral agent (Casarões and Magalhães, 2021). The film *Don't Look Up* illustrates how falsehoods are invented, broadcast, and, finally, accepted by many.

The challenges of effective risk communication further extend to the personality and capacity of the receiver of the warning. While some people may tolerate any risk, others are risk-averse. During the pandemic, some may have wanted to heed the warnings, but because they were designated as 'essential' workers, they had no choice but to expose themselves and their households to risk because they needed to work. Many people were also forced to remain locked in crowded homes, where, in comparison to the economically well-off, they could not practice social distancing.

In February 2022, a Hong Kong construction worker, who tested positive for COVID-19, along with his wife, who also tested positive, decided to camp on the rooftop of their tenement building in Sham Shui Po for more than two weeks, braving the biting winter. They did it out of fear that they would infect their five-year-old daughter and two-year-old son, as well as the construction worker's sixty-six-year-old father, brother, sister-in-law, and five-year-old niece. This extended family of eight live in a less than 20 m^2 unit (Sun, 2022).

This story struck a chord with me as someone who grew up deprived of even the bare essentials. Survival was always the first order of the day for my parents. How can then one bear the additional burden of contemplating another layer of misery? Following the impacts of the pandemic on people's livelihoods, encountering another looming distress, that of the climate crisis, can only lead to melancholia. After all, *Don't Look Up*'s dark ending is scary, if not numbing.

Communicating climate change using fear appeals or narratives of hope remains a topic of significant debate. A single message will not necessarily change people's behaviour or attitudes. Disaster researchers have argued that the sources of information must be seen as credible and objective (Seppänen and Virrantaus, 2015). Bearers of this information must also be trustworthy and evince genuine concern for the public's general well-being. Consistency in messaging also matters. Messengers should also recognise – with all humility – that information continually changes and evolves.

Communicating the risks of climate change and our ability to act – believing and acting in 'constructive hope' – is critical (Maartensson and Loi, 2022). Despite the fact that the comet ultimately killed human civilisation in *Don't Look Up*, the film made it obvious that humanity had the potential to prevent its demise. Similarly, we still have the ability to address climate change, although time is running out as we postpone action.

Towards the end of the film, as the comet makes its impact, the two scientists, together with their families and friends, are having dinner amid profound conversations. It was a moment from which we can learn: battering people with facts is a weak communication strategy. Instead, it should be about listening more than speaking and lending a hand so that people can connect the dots between what matters most to them and climate action.

References

Ahmed, W., Vidal-Alaball, J., Downing, J., & Seguí, F. L. (2020). COVID-19 and the 5G conspiracy theory: Social network analysis of Twitter data. *Journal of Medical Internet Research*, *22*(5), e19458.

Casarões, G., & Magalhães, D. (2021). The hydroxychloroquine alliance: How far-right leaders and alt-science preachers came together to promote a miracle drug. *Revista de Administração Pública*, *55*, 197–214.

Cato, S., Iida, T., Ishida, K., Ito, A., Katsumata, H., McElwain, K. M., & Shoji, M. (2021). The bright and dark sides of social media usage during the COVID-19 pandemic: Survey evidence from Japan. *International Journal of Disaster Risk Reduction*, *54*, 102034.

Chang, D. C., Oseni, T. O., Strong, B. L., Molina, G., Ortega, G., Chen, H., & Rogers Jr, S. O. (2021). The other global pandemic: Scientific racism and the normality bias. *Annals of Surgery*, *274*(6), e646–648.

Crick, M. J. (2021). The importance of trustworthy sources of scientific information in risk communication with the public. *Journal of Radiation Research*, *62*(Supplement 1), i1–6.

Dang, H. L. (2021). Social media, fake news, and the COVID-19 pandemic: Sketching the case of Southeast Asia. *Austrian Journal of South-East Asian Studies*, *14*(1), 37–58.

Delina, L. L. (2022). Moving people from the balcony to the trenches: Time to adopt 'climatage' in climate activism? *Energy Research & Social Science*, *90*, 102586.

Deotto, F. (2021). How did we let this happen? *Massachusetts Review*, *62*(4), 800–808.

Di Giorgio, S. (2022). Misinformation in the time of COVID: Fighting the spread of fake news. *Journal of Mental Health*, *31*, 447–449.

Islam, R., Kamaruddin, R., Ahmad, S. A., Jan, S., & Anuar, A. R. (2016). A review on mechanism of flood disaster management in Asia. *International Review of Management and Marketing*, *6*(1), 29–52.

Leavitt, J. W. (2003). Public resistance or cooperation? A tale of smallpox in two cities. *Biosecurity and Bioterrorism: Biodefense Strategy, Practice, and Science*, *1*(3), 185–192.

Litman, L., Rosen, Z., Rosenzweig, C., Weinberger-Litman, S. L., Moss, A. J., & Robinson, J. (2021). Did people really drink bleach to prevent COVID-19? A tale of problematic respondents and a guide for measuring rare events in survey data. *MedRxiv*, 1–47.

Maartensson, H., & Loi, N. M. (2022). Exploring the relationships between risk perception, behavioural willingness, and constructive hope in pro-environmental behaviour. *Environmental Education Research, 28*(4), 600–613.

MacIntyre, E., Khanna, S., Darychuk, A., Copes, R., & Schwartz, B. (2019). Evidence synthesis – evaluating risk communication during extreme weather and climate change: A scoping review. *Health Promotion and Chronic Disease Prevention in Canada: Research, Policy and Practice, 39*(4), 142–156.

Millet, B., Carter, A. P., Broad, K., Cairo, A., Evans, S. D., & Majumdar, S. J. (2020). Hurricane risk communication: Visualization and behavioral science concepts. *Weather, Climate, and Society, 12*(2), 193–211.

National Academy of Sciences. (2018). *Emergency Alert and Warning Systems: Current Knowledge and Future Research Directions*. Washington, DC: National Academies Press.

Paulik, L. B., Keenan, R. E., & Durda, J. L. (2020). The case for effective risk communication: Lessons from a global pandemic. *Integrated Environmental Assessment and Management, 16*(5), 552–554.

Rabinovich, A., & Morton, T. A. (2012). Unquestioned answers or unanswered questions: Beliefs about science guide responses to uncertainty in climate change risk communication. *Risk Analysis: An International Journal, 32*(6), 992–1002.

Rocha, Y. M., de Moura, G. A., Desidério, G. A., de Oliveira, C. H., Lourenço, F. D., & de Figueiredo Nicolete, L. D. (2021). The impact of fake news on social media and its influence on health during the COVID-19 pandemic: A systematic review. *Journal of Public Health*, 1–10.

Seppänen, H., & Virrantaus, K. (2015). Shared situational awareness and information quality in disaster management. *Safety Science, 77*, 112–122.

Sun, F. (2022). Residents of Hong Kong's subdivided flats forced to sleep on rooftops or streets after catching COVID-19. *South China Morning Post*, 26 February.

Sylves, R. T. (2019). *Disaster Policy and Politics: Emergency Management and Homeland Security*. Thousand Oaks, CA: CQ Press.

Whelchel, A. W., Reguero, B. G., van Wesenbeeck, B., & Renaud, F. G. (2018). Advancing disaster risk reduction through the integration of science, design, and policy into eco-engineering and several global resource management processes. *International Journal of Disaster Risk Reduction, 32*, 29–41.

16
The Hubris of Control

Many responses to the COVID-19 pandemic and all other crises, including the climate catastrophe, are motivated by the belief that one can 'control' the course of events. But control is not only a fallacy: it is a hubris. What is needed, instead, are options that are considerate, mutualistic, and diverse in character, as well as those that take group capabilities into account.

Bellerophon, one of the most legendary Greek heroes, was thrilled about taming Pegasus, the winged horse. Before meeting Pegasus, the gods charged Bellerophon with slaying the fire-breathing Chimaera. This beast was a terrifying mix of animals, with a lion's body and head, a snake for a tail, and a goat's face protruding from its chest. The night before meeting the beast, Bellerophon sought help from Athena. She agreed, telling him where to find Pegasus and gave Bellerophon a golden girdle. Together, Bellerophon and Pegasus destroyed the Chimaera. The hero wanted to escape and visit Olympus, the home of the Greek gods, so he pushed Pegasus to fly even higher. The gods were upset and sent a fly to sting Pegasus, causing the horse to bolt and knock Bellerophon to the ground.

The deluge of opinions about how to deal with the COVID-19 pandemic was not unexpected, given that many self-proclaimed experts were holed up at home with their computers. In addition to news and commentary, numerous articles appeared across the media, assessing what the major crisis implied and recommending how it could be turned to positive ends. There has been, of course, no shortage of instruments that give the appearance of being effective in addressing the pandemic. Hubris of control, reminiscent of Bellerophon's hubris, however, is perilous.

Tools were available to the public via 'dashboards' that seemed to be 'in control' of the crisis (Stirling and Scoones, 2020). These dashboards included dispassionately assured experts, seemingly precise scientific metrics, rigorous technical models, massive hierarchical agencies, and almost seductively informative graphics (cf., Buštíková and Baboš, 2020; Jewell, Lewnard, and Jewell, 2020). However, what the pandemic seems to have shown is not merely that there is no reliable information, but that the dashboards have been constructed to a significant extent by human imagination; hence, they, too, demonstrate frailty.

Managing and controlling have always been the recipe for dealing with crises. The thirst for control is also evident in the vigorous pursuit to resist climate change (Stirling and Scoones, 2020). We see these attempts at control through a multitude of goals such as speeding up energy transitions, enhancing resilience, amplifying scientific partnerships, galvanising protest groups, enhancing social justice, reducing consumption, revitalising democratic values, realigning neoliberalism, and retooling the economy. Writers have articulated these – in some cases, overlapping – pursuits. I agree wholeheartedly and have even written papers and books about some of them (e.g., Delina, 2016, 2017, 2019).

However, another element comes to light from our experience of 'controlling' the pandemic that has implications for how we should attend to the climate crisis. Modifications insistently advised as a reaction to the pandemic seem almost identical to those urged in response to other issues and challenges before the pandemic began. Despite the aspirational rhetoric and language of progress, these suggested modifications appear 'fairly predictable'.

The concerns of the pandemic – and other future crises – are (and should be) about the numerous and genuine tragedies of people's lives and livelihoods, which were already fragile (Prakash and Borker, 2022), and of people who did not have the same opportunities to broadcast their opinions as the self-titled 'pandemic experts' or 'crisis experts'. The majority of these people live in the Majority World. We risk falling prey to yet another populist message, to media stereotypes, to academic pride, or to speedily managed policy tales if we disregard these fragile peoples and their lived concerns. This is true even in cases when the motivation being advanced is admirable.

There seems to be just one undeniable fact thus far. Despite the ever-present doubts that the COVID-19 pandemic has exposed in a harrowing manner, the fact that nobody is aware of the historical ramifications of the pandemic situation has been strangely overlooked among all the confident proclamations and forecasts that have been made. An almost infinite number of potential futures may arise from these monumental crossroads (e.g., Müller-Mahn and Kioko, 2021; Karjalainen et al., 2022). There is a high probability that competing points of view will continue to conflict in each of these possible futures, just as they do today. In my work on energy transitions, I have found that plural and cosmopolitan ways of viewing, facilitating, and arriving at energy futures are required, especially if we consider the voices from the margins in this exercise of future-making (Delina and Janetos, 2018).

Certain things, nevertheless, were quite evident as the pandemic raged. Both democracies and autocracies proved to be equally unprepared for the crisis. Decision-makers showed a lack of long-term vision. Indecisiveness was revealed and most articulated by both macho demagogues and plutocrats (Parmanand, 2022). Rich nations appeared to have scant resources available to them. Scientific organisations and expert advisors revealed themselves as generally poor in understanding the real world.

One can, therefore, reasonably conclude that even the most powerful, recognised, and self-confident governments and their agencies could badly mismanage, not just in attempts to 'control' but even to anticipate, a single variable of a particular illness. Considering authorities' failure to anticipate, one can find it difficult to trust other hubristic ambitions to predict, much alone valiantly steer, the destinies of human societies.

If we could not recognise the mystery and ambiguity of the universe during the crisis, when could we ever recognise and acknowledge it? Crisis after crisis occurred beyond the moment when the COVID-19 pandemic started raging in 2020. The whirling dervishes of our historical time are, without doubt, at their most turbulent.

The Russian war on Ukraine, the military re-takeover of Myanmar, and the landslide victories of populist politicians, including that of a dictator's son in my own country, coincided with our collective public health misery. The significance of the mysterious universe hits twice as hard, not as a result of any additional confident projections of what these ambiguities will entail, but rather in light of what we can already see unravelling right before our eyes and through our lived experiences.

Regardless of how the pandemic – and other crises – turned out, we witnessed at least one global hegemonic fatality. Crisis response requires more than just a particular conviction about how the world should be. The predictive and oracular pursuit of control is now experiencing catastrophic erosion.

This erosion of control affects the ordering of societies. Precarious power is brought to its knees by this weathering. It appears, time and time again, that the world is not 'controlled' by reassuring certainties and imperious deeds. Control, it seems, is a risky cast of power, which, the pandemic proved, is genuinely incapable of governing. Yet, those who command authority can sustain their privilege and even successfully thrive during this global misery.

Consider, for instance, the oft-repeated adages 'science-based' and 'evidence-based' policymaking. Evidence is vital in decision-making but it is not the sole requirement for action (Barnes and Parkhurst, 2014). On its own, evidence is inadequate. Actions cannot be 'based on' data or analysis alone (cf., de Campos-Rudinsky and Undurraga, 2021; Kaufman et al., 2022). At the very most, evidence can only enlighten us. Decision-making through 'science and evidence' is a convenient illusion serving those in positions of control. Put simply, the pandemic has demonstrated that there is no such thing as control in the larger, more expansive 'real world' of human affairs (e.g., Goodwin et al., 2021). This is not a critique but a simple statement of fact.

We cannot deny the significance of control. It is a powerful sensation – in our relationships with various types of machines, for example. We are pretty used to the concept of controlling things. We control when to switch on a light. We control when we use our mobile phones. In situations where things operate, we have grown very comfortable with what it means to control something. We are highly familiar with the sensation of control. Control – it seems – provides us with the spirit for the complete and exclusive achievement of our anticipated goal.

But regardless of the methods of control, it has been quite evident that we could not address the COVID-19 pandemic by using power (Kavanagh and Singh, 2020). We should translate the same lesson when tackling other monumental crises. In one nation after another, early responses to the pandemic – whether they consisted of autocratic coercion or arrogant superiority – have proved unsuccessful or even harmful (Stasavage, 2020, Windholz, 2020).

We are not even close to being at the end of the pandemic saga. As these words are written, in July 2022, *The New York Times* reports that new subvariants of the Omicron variant are raging in the United States. The unintended consequences of the control measures we have seen since day one of the pandemic might be even more significant than the sickness caused by the coronavirus itself.

On a greater scale, we still do not know the pandemic's social, behavioural, and economic impacts on our relationships and well-being (Fuster and Varieur Turco, 2020). We remain abstracted from any additional aspects this saga may bring. These unknown aspects could become clear – or they may remain opaque. We also could not comprehend with complete certainty how the coronavirus would respond. Because so many things have gone wrong, fallen short, occurred by accident, or are yet to occur, we are still far from the familiar sense of 'control' that the present failed attempts are supposed to mirror (Parviainen, Koski, and Torkkola, 2021).

Despite these insights into the open-endedness not just of the pandemic but a myriad of other crises, the concept of control continues to drive the globalising fantasies of modernity (Matravers, 2013). Now, more than ever, we continue to hear statements like 'zero COVID', at least in my part of the world (Hong Kong), when others have already faced the fact that the coronavirus will not go away. In the same way that holding a hammer may train its owner to see every situation as if it were a nail, these fantasies continue to blossom and, as a result, paradoxically imprison their believers to an unending desire to exert control.

Once one begins to look for these imaginations of control, one is driven to consider every aspect of control by other entities over one's own life. Examples include control by industry over production, control by capital over labour, and control by science over reason. In each realm, control has fallen short of expectations. Still, it has also resulted in many irrational forms of reaction that are often substantially harmful. The characteristic feature of the COVID-19 pandemic is not that it is unique, only that it is severe. A well-known pattern of unfulfilled expectations has been played out over weeks rather than decades or centuries.

The pandemic demonstrated, once and for all, that the 'real world' does not accept any kind of control. At first, the sequence of events seemed to make sense. But, as time has passed, one of the most important lessons that can be learnt from the history of the pandemic thus far – and this is provisional – is that it does not matter how devastating an event or a crisis is for people or the planet; what matters is that maintaining control is always going to be more difficult. What the pandemic brought front and centre is the fact that crises arise in undetermined, non-linear jumbles of actions and reactions, influences and responses, familiarities and surprises.

Before the COVID-19 pandemic, avian influenza caught the world by surprise in 2004. Bird flu spread despite significant influenza epidemics in the past. Once more, avian influenza diffused again in 2009 with the H1N1 virus. This history shows us that it is impossible to predict when or how a new disease will originate; it only assures us that it is highly likely that other epidemics and pandemics will occur in the future (Platje, Harvey, and Rayman-Bacchus, 2020).

Surprises emerge from imaginable and unimaginable sources. Following the avian influenza epidemics, much attention was paid to the chicken population in South East Asia (Rushton et al., 2005; Park and Glass, 2007). However, the next outbreak occurred in pigs, not in our part of the world but in Latin America, especially Mexico (Ear, 2012). Despite the significant resources put into pandemic preparation and epidemiological disease modelling, which Hong Kong has eventually mastered (Bauch et al., 2005), it remains impossible to know what disease will occur next or when it will occur. Even when an epidemic happens, there are still so many unknown factors in any model that any forecasts of what will take place are only educated guesses, regardless of how much information is available (Luo, 2021). Models, after all, are created by human modellers working with incomplete knowledge.

The same caution should be issued against the overuse and misapplication of climate mitigation models. A just energy transition necessitates lowering energy use in affluent nations to achieve significant emissions reductions while securing adequate energy for development in the rest of the world. Existing models, however, keep the Minority World's energy advantage at almost three times larger per capita than the Majority World. Most scenarios depend significantly on hazardous and unfair bioenergy-based negative emissions technology to balance the Minority World's high energy demand with the Paris Agreement objectives. These scenarios tend to rely on appropriating land in the Majority World to retain and expand the Minority World's energy advantage.

To be open to uncertainty and surprise, one must adopt a new strategy that involves a more pluralistic stance on modelling and sources of information, including relating to local understandings and experiences – especially those from the Majority World (e.g., Landström et al., 2019). The COVID-19 pandemic has demonstrated a potentially lethal dependence on inherently flawed models and, as a result, an unsafe dependence in science policy communities on restricted epidemiological data (Gurdasani and Ziauddeen, 2020). This is because this knowledge is not supplemented by other sources of expertise that are more wide-ranging and deeply embedded indigenously. In climate modelling for impacts, adaptation, and mitigation, local knowledge is important for users and producers; hence, modellers should include them in future models (e.g., García-del-Amo, Mortyn, and Reyes-García, 2020; Reyes-García et al., 2020).

Taking preventative steps against diseases may have unintended and severe consequences for vulnerable people. As I write these words, backyard pig producers are the primary target of containment efforts to address the African swine flu outbreak in my home province in the Philippines (Mighell and Ward, 2021). As a result, several pigs had to be killed or sold at prices lower than the prevailing market price. This had a terrible effect on people's livelihoods, especially those whose backyard piggeries supplement their precarious income sources. The same can be said of energy transition efforts, which are beyond the ability of many countries in the Majority World. Countries with financial and technological power in the Minority World should support energy transition in the Majority World.

Returning to the pandemic response, poor and marginalised populations often suffered most due to control measures (e.g., Nyashanu, Simbanegavi, and Gibson, 2020). We saw this in the case of quarantine and lockdowns. Poor and marginalised peoples were of the same demographic as those who had the least access to health assistance if they became ill with COVID-19 (Benfer et al., 2019; Al-Zaman, 2020). Although everybody has the potential to get infected with a virus, the effects of these pathogens, both the sickness itself and the preventative measures taken in the wake of a pandemic, are not uniformly distributed in inequitable societies. It is easy to forget about issues of equality that viruses bring about during a pandemic if one listens to rhetoric such as 'we will conquer' (Bambra, Lynch, and Smith, 2021).

The only time we pay attention to the dangers of diseases is when there is a major epidemic. In Hong Kong, this occurred when avian flu ravaged the city from 2004 to 2006 (Chen, 2009) and swine flu broke out in 2009 (Lam et al., 2011). During these times, the Hong Kong government provided funding (typically, at the last minute) and experts were contacted provide general advice.

In the case of the COVID-19 pandemic in 2020 and beyond, national responses took place first while the transnational apparatus painstakingly cranked into motion. With a global pandemic declared, we saw a rapid mobilisation of resources not seen since the Second World War (Chapman and Miller, 2020). Governments deployed funding and expertise rapidly, so that in less than a year after the World Health Organization declared the pandemic the first batches of vaccine became available. However, history also reveals that after major pandemics, things return to the way they were before.

The years that pass without an epidemic occurring are the ones that are the most significant. Viruses that might potentially spread from feral wildlife species are most likely to be proliferating at this time. In addition, as the world warms from intense and rapid global heating, new viruses may escape after their centuries, if not millennia, of being dormant in polar ice and mountain glaciers.

Zoonotic spillovers occur rather often, and the repercussions for human societies – as shown by the COVID-19 pandemic – may sometimes be quite severe. There is, potentially, a large number more. Viruses adapt quickly in response to selective pressure, which means there is always the potential for new viruses to emerge.

Thus, if we do not use the interregnum provided post-COVID-19 to follow viruses, investigate their genomes, and study their carriers, we might not be able to detect future pandemics, including those due to climate change. As a consequence of global heating in addition to our increasing agricultural output and expanding urbanisation, we need to make sure that we are always at the top of our game in adapting to the shifting ecosystems that are occurring all around us.

As we learn lessons from the pandemic, uncertainties provide us with significant difficulties for standardised systems based on the assumption of stability and control. Increasing reliability requires not just an awareness of the complexities and extensiveness of socioecological systems and the threats posed to these systems, but also a comprehension of the local settings in which these systems operate (Cox and Lázaro Gutiérrez, 2016). I observed this in my work on resilience rice farming in Indigenous landscapes in Bali in Indonesia and Ifugao in the Philippines.

Rice farming in terraced landscapes has existed for centuries in South East Asia. These communities show how people who interact with their environment can sustain and thrive. What we know about their persistent resilience is that as local communities scan their larger horizon for immediate and possible threats, they have to also look at their day-to-day routines and consider how they can quickly and flexibly react to any conditions. By doing so, they gain a solid understanding of their system. These communities also do not depend mainly on external experts; they create trustworthiness via their own networks. Communication and discussion remain essential, so that when a crisis hits, such as the COVID-19 pandemic, among others, it is possible for them to quickly mobilise their knowledge, resources, and labour and face the crises as a collective.

In crises, where situations change abruptly, without warning, most conventional, engineered systems created for 'stable' conditions are not very good at generating dependability and reliability. A health care system, for example, always depends on the consistent flow of patients suffering from a predetermined set of illnesses and needing a predetermined range of treatments. This is acceptable while things are considered 'stable'; however, as we have seen during the pandemic, 'stable' systems soon become overloaded and a shift in mentality is required to address the situation (Sanford, Blum, and Smith, 2020).

One essential component of system reliability is related to fundamental capability (Tabandeh, Gardoni, and Murphy, 2018). Capability is a crucial challenge, especially in underfunded systems, as in the case of many institutions and organisations in the Majority World. Capability extends beyond physical infrastructures; it also refers to the capabilities of engaged experts. Frontline public health employees like physicians, nurses, and pharmacists are often the ones who are expected to innovate and generate dependability while doing their jobs.

It thus appears that capabilities and the collective – not control – are essential in crisis response (e.g., George et al., 2016; Ansari, Munir, and Gregg, 2012). When all-encompassing acts speak louder than any seemingly controlling speech, the pandemic experience hinges on the argument of moving away from 'evidence-based policy' towards the emancipatory principles of knowing and doing (Stirling, 2016; Stirling and Scoones, 2020).

Attempts to alter the world are not simply laudable when inspired by ideals such as just energy transition and climate justice; they are profoundly vital. If we turn the dial towards the way of justice, it might be possible that even the illusions and delusions of control may be curved in new ways that are less hubristic. It might also be that the very impossibility of exerting control over a crisis may be seen as a good in that it can provide evidence of deceit, encouraging approaches that are far more humble, compassionate, and genuine in relation to the state of the real world.

But these are only possibilities. Humility suggests we have to acknowledge that nobody knows how things will turn out (Mazzocchi, 2021). The consequences of the COVID-19 pandemic – and any crisis, including the climate emergency – are not questions that can be answered in advance. Instead, they are something that must be fought for in their wake – and beyond.

My primary worry with some of the commentaries during the pandemic is that many of these voices are as confidently rigid and abstractly dominating as any sitting demagogue. They have nothing to do with the specific nature of any of the reforms that are called for. These hubristic voices starkly contradict the relatively little we know thus far about the pandemic. The same noises abound in commentaries about climate action, where climate denial reaches new levels with experts annotating the need to reduce greenhouse gas emissions through narratives of control. A cacophony of control-based noises glossing non-existent negative energy technologies and geoengineering techniques overwhelms what is imperative: ending energy poverty with renewable energy and, most importantly, replacing extant fossil fuel capacities with renewables.

Thus, the task is to drown out the empty assertions of control-based responses to emerging realities. The COVID-19 pandemic has shown that whatever futures we try to bring into existence, it is probable that they will turn out better if we structure them in ways that are antithetical to the failed impulse to control. This reinterprets the concept of crisis management not as a formalised process of administering and superintending, but as continuous mobilisations for access by the least powerful to their capacities to act. Let us not be Bellerophon, who to this day roams the world looking for Pegasus because of his hubris.

References

Al-Zaman, M. S. (2020). Healthcare crisis in Bangladesh during the COVID-19 pandemic. *American Journal of Tropical Medicine and Hygiene*, *103*(4), 1357.

Ansari, S., Munir, K., & Gregg, T. (2012). Impact at the 'bottom of the pyramid': The role of social capital in capability development and community empowerment. *Journal of Management Studies*, *49*(4), 813–842.

Bambra, C., Lynch, J., & Smith, K. E. (2021). *The Unequal Pandemic: COVID-19 and Health Inequalities*. Bristol: Policy Press.

Barnes, A., & Parkhurst, J. (2014). Can global health policy be depoliticized? A critique of global calls for evidence-based policy. In G. W. Brown, G. Yamey, & S. Wamala

(Eds.), *The Handbook of Global Health Policy* (pp. 157–174). Malden, MA: John Wiley & Sons.

Bauch, C. T., Lloyd-Smith, J. O., Coffee, M. P., & Galvani, A. P. (2005). Dynamically modeling SARS and other newly emerging respiratory illnesses: Past, present, and future. *Epidemiology*, *16*(6), 791–801.

Benfer, E. A., Mohapatra, S., Wiley, L. F., & Yearby, R. (2019). Health justice strategies to combat the pandemic: Eliminating discrimination, poverty, and health disparities during and after COVID-19. *Yale Journal of Health Policy, Law and Ethics*, *19*, 122–171.

Buštíková, L., & Baboš, P. (2020). Best in COVID: Populists in the time of pandemic. *Politics and Governance*, *8*(4), 496–508.

Chapman, C. M., & Miller, D. S. (2020). From metaphor to militarized response: The social implications of 'we are at war with COVID-19' – crisis, disasters, and pandemics yet to come. *International Journal of Sociology and Social Policy*, 40, 1107–1124.

Chen, H. (2009). H5N1 avian influenza in China. *Science in China Series C: Life Sciences*, *52*(5), 419–427.

Cox, A., & Lázaro Gutiérrez, R. (2016). Interpreting in the emergency department: How context matters for practice. In F. Federici (Ed.), *Mediating Emergencies and Conflicts* (pp. 33–58). London: Palgrave Macmillan.

de Campos-Rudinsky, T. C., & Undurraga, E. (2021). Public health decisions in the COVID-19 pandemic require more than 'follow the science'. *Journal of Medical Ethics*, *47*(5), 296–299.

Delina, L. L. (2016). *Strategies for Rapid Climate Mitigation: Wartime Mobilisation as a Model for Action?* Routledge.

Delina, L. L. (2017). *Accelerating Sustainable Energy Transition(s) in Developing Countries: The Challenges of Climate Change and Sustainable Development*. Routledge.

Delina, L. L. (2019). *Emancipatory Climate Actions: Strategies from Histories*. London: Palgrave Macmillan.

Delina, L., & Janetos, A. (2018). Cosmopolitan, dynamic, and contested energy futures: Navigating the pluralities and polarities in the energy systems of tomorrow. *Energy Research & Social Science*, *35*, 1–10.

Ear, S. (2012). Swine flu: Mexico's handling of A/H1N1 in comparative perspective. *Politics and the Life Sciences*, *31*(1–2), 52–66.

Fuster, V., & Varieur Turco, J. (2020). COVID-19: A lesson in humility and an opportunity for sagacity and hope. *Journal of the American College of Cardiology*, *75*(20), 2625–2626.

García-del-Amo, D., Mortyn, P. G., & Reyes-García, V. (2020). Including indigenous and local knowledge in climate research: An assessment of the opinion of Spanish climate change researchers. *Climatic Change*, *160*(1), 67–88.

George, A. S., Scott, K., Mehra, V., & Sriram, V. (2016). Synergies, strengths and challenges: Findings on community capability from a systematic health systems research literature review. *BMC Health Services Research*, *16*(7), 47–59.

Goodwin, R., Wiwattanapantuwong, J., Tuicomepee, A., Suttiwan, P., Watakakosol, R., & Ben-Ezra, M. (2021). Anxiety, perceived control and pandemic behaviour in Thailand during COVID-19: Results from a national survey. *Journal of Psychiatric Research*, *135*, 212–217.

Gurdasani, D., & Ziauddeen, H. (2020). On the fallibility of simulation models in informing pandemic responses. *The Lancet Global Health*, *8*(6), e776–777.

Jewell, N. P., Lewnard, J. A., & Jewell, B. L. (2020). Caution warranted: Using the Institute for Health Metrics and Evaluation model for predicting the course of the COVID-19 pandemic. *Annals of Internal Medicine*, *173*(3), 226–227.

Karjalainen, J., Mwagiru, N., Salminen, H., & Heinonen, S. (2022). Integrating crisis learning into futures literacy–exploring the 'new normal' and imagining post-pandemic futures. *On the Horizon: The International Journal of Learning Futures*, *30*(2), 47–56.

Kaufman, J., Bagot, K. L., Tuckerman, J., Biezen, R., Oliver, J., Jos, C., ... & Danchin, M. (2022). Qualitative exploration of intentions, concerns and information needs of vaccine hesitant adults initially prioritised to receive COVID-19 vaccines in Australia. *Australian and New Zealand Journal of Public Health*, *46*(1), 16–24.

Kavanagh, M. M., & Singh, R. (2020). Democracy, capacity, and coercion in pandemic response: COVID-19 in comparative political perspective. *Journal of Health Politics, Policy and Law*, *45*(6), 997–1012.

Lam, T. T. Y., Zhu, H., Wang, J., Smith, D. K., Holmes, E. C., Webster, R. G., ... & Guan, Y. (2011). Reassortment events among swine influenza A viruses in China: Implications for the origin of the 2009 influenza pandemic. *Journal of Virology*, *85*(19), 10279–10285.

Landström, C., Becker, M., Odoni, N., & Whatmore, S. J. (2019). Community modelling: A technique for enhancing local capacity to engage with flood risk management. *Environmental Science & Policy*, *92*, 255–261.

Li, N., & Molder, A. L. (2021). Can scientists use simple infographics to convince? Effects of the 'flatten the curve' charts on perceptions of and behavioral intentions toward social distancing measures during the COVID-19 pandemic. *Public Understanding of Science*, *30*(7), 898–912.

Luo, J. (2021). Forecasting COVID-19 pandemic: Unknown unknowns and predictive monitoring. *Technological Forecasting and Social Change*, *166*, 120602.

Matravers, M. (Ed.). (2013). *Managing Modernity: Politics and the Culture of Control*. London: Routledge.

Mazzocchi, F. (2021). Drawing lessons from the COVID-19 pandemic: Science and epistemic humility should go together. *History and Philosophy of the Life Sciences*, *43*(3), 1–5.

Mighell, E., & Ward, M. P. (2021). African swine fever spread across Asia, 2018–2019. *Transboundary and Emerging Diseases*, *68*(5), 2722–2732.

Müller-Mahn, D., & Kioko, E. (2021). Rethinking African futures after COVID-19. *Africa Spectrum*, *56*(2), 216–227.

Nyashanu, M., Simbanegavi, P., & Gibson, L. (2020). Exploring the impact of COVID-19 pandemic lockdown on informal settlements in Tshwane Gauteng Province, South Africa. *Global Public Health*, *15*(10), 1443–1453.

Park, A. W., & Glass, K. (2007). Dynamic patterns of avian and human influenza in east and southeast Asia. *The Lancet Infectious Diseases*, *7*(8), 543–548.

Parmanand, S. (2022). Macho populists versus COVID: Comparing political masculinities. *European Journal of Women's Studies*, *29*(S1), 43S–59S.

Parviainen, J., Koski, A., & Torkkola, S. (2021). 'Building a ship while sailing it': Epistemic humility and the temporality of non-knowledge in political decision-making on COVID-19. *Social Epistemology*, *35*(3), 232–244.

Platje, J., Harvey, J., & Rayman-Bacchus, L. (2020). COVID-19 – Reflections on the surprise of both an expected and unexpected event. *Central European Review of Economics and Management*, *4*(1), 149–162.

Prakash, A., & Borker, H. (2022). Pandemic precarity, life, livelihood and death in the time of the pandemic. *Economic and Political Weekly*, *57*(5), 40–45.

Reyes-García, V., Fernández-Llamazares, Á., García-del-Amo, D., & Cabeza, M. (2020). Operationalizing local ecological knowledge in climate change research: Challenges and opportunities of citizen science. In M. Welch-Devine, A. Sourdril, & B. Burke (Eds.), *Changing Climate, Changing Worlds* (pp. 183–197). Cham: Springer.

Rushton, J., Viscarra, R., Bleich, E. G., & McLeod, A. (2005). Impact of avian influenza outbreaks in the poultry sectors of five South East Asian countries (Cambodia, Indonesia, Lao PDR, Thailand, Viet Nam) outbreak costs, responses and potential long term control. *World's Poultry Science Journal*, *61*(3), 491–514.

Sanford, A. G., Blum, D., & Smith, S. L. (2020). Seeking stability in unstable times: COVID-19 and the bureaucratic mindset. In J. M. Ryan (Ed.), *COVID-19: Volume II: Social Consequences and Cultural Adaptation* (pp. 47–60). Abingdon, UK: Routledge.

Stasavage, D. (2020). Democracy, autocracy, and emergency threats: Lessons for COVID-19 from the last thousand years. *International Organization*, *74*(S1), E1–17.

Stirling, A. (2016). Knowing doing governing: Realizing heterodyne democracies. In J.P. Voss & R. Freeman (Eds.), *Knowing Governance* (pp. 259–289). London: Palgrave Macmillan

Stirling, A., & Scoones, I. (2020). COVID-19 and the futility of control in the modern world. *Issues in Science and Technology*, *36*(4), 25–27.

Tabandeh, A., Gardoni, P., & Murphy, C. (2018). A reliability-based capability approach. *Risk Analysis*, *38*(2), 410–424.

Windholz, E. L. (2020). Governing in a pandemic: From parliamentary sovereignty to autocratic technocracy. *The Theory and Practice of Legislation*, *8*(1–2), 93–113.

17
Mobilising the 3.5 Per Cent

Anyone who has been observing the activities of the ruling class – both in government and in business – can see that it is disorganised, and, when viewed in isolation, tactically incapable and unwilling to address even short-term crises, let alone a significant existential dilemma such as the climate crisis. A revitalised social movement could promote swift and equitable climate action: what it needs to do is to mobilise 3.5 per cent of the population – although, of course, whether this number is enough to address any particular world crisis is unknown.

Activists working within progressive social movements have come across significant obstacles during the COVID-19 pandemic (Fisher and Nasrin, 2021). During this time, in-person mobilisations were inappropriate moments for political action on the streets or in public squares. Freedoms were curtailed, and the physical distance between people made it hard to engage through traditional means of protest. Mobilisations were not only problematic in public areas but also in places of employment, given the very stringent constraints on the right to meet and the restricted opportunities for face-to-face interaction. Because of the pandemic, people's mental spaces were also constrained, making it difficult to be creative in the arena of climate activism. The effects of the pandemic on social mobilisation were that it became more difficult to maintain hope, a stimulant for any collective activity, while fear, which instils discouragement, increased.

Despite the challenges of mobilising during the COVID-19 pandemic lockdowns, it is essential to underline that it is very uncommon for social movements to take root during times of extreme crisis, disaster, and intense suppression of individual and communal liberties (e.g., Della Porta, 2017; Islam and Islam, 2016; Dodman, Mitlin, and Co, 2010). Throughout history, for instance, we find that wars have been the spark that ignited rounds of discontent (Della Porta, 2017). Dissent has also followed military battles – before, after, and sometimes during these conflicts. These kinds of uprisings are evidence of the resilience of civic engagement in times of severe adversity.

Moments of extreme crisis may – and often do – spark the creation of new forms of political opposition. The pandemic showed us that the widespread adoption of new technologies allows people to stage their dissent online (Libal and Kashwan, 2020). In many instances, people gathered on their balconies or at windows to send collective messages of protest or sympathy (Tomasini, 2021). And even during government-imposed lockdowns, activists still found their way out of their homes to participate in public demonstrations, as we saw in the anti-government protests in Thailand (Selway, 2022; Ockey, 2021) and in the Black Lives Matter mobilisations in the United States (Kampmark, 2020).

We should note that social movements take action through various methods, which are not solely limited to congregating in demonstrations (Delina, 2022). Social activities build upon pre-existing networks while simultaneously connecting and expanding those networks by their performative actions (Delina, 2019). Social movements can take advantage of the opportunities for creativity that arise during times of unpredictability by organising themselves in this fashion. The severity of the COVID-19 pandemic makes it abundantly clear that there is a need for change.

This necessary transformation must be profound enough to rupture the status quo. As we have previously learned from the histories of mobilisation, change must also be comprehensive so as to include all aspects of society and culture, from politics to economics (Delina, 2019). If, during times of relative calm, social movements gain momentum as a result of opportunities for incremental change, during times of extreme turmoil they gain momentum as a result of people's awareness of severe and widespread danger. In response to these dangers and the apparent shortcomings of the state and, even more so, of the neoliberal market in respect of pandemic response, organisations that represent social movements have been transitioning into mutual aid groups. These groups encourage direct social action by assisting those in their greatest need.

The need for public solidarity is brought into sharper focus by a crisis, which also makes room for new prospects for change (Libal and Kashwan, 2020). The pandemic has shown how solidarity can arise during a time of distress. Although emergencies have an immediate impact on central authorities, right up to and including the militarisation of that power (Passos and Acácio, 2021), the pandemic crisis has revealed that states are unable to solve problems by using violence only. There were attempts at militarising the pandemic response – as occurred in the Philippines, where military men, not physicians, were at the helm (Imbong, 2022; Hapal, 2021). However, social movements emerged to offer a counterbalance to the risks incurred by an authoritarian approach to the crisis.

The COVID-19 pandemic also highlighted the importance of access to essential public goods and the intricate management of these services, which requires the involvement of institutional networks and the engagement of citizens. The necessity of bottom-up efforts and participation in the administration of resources (e.g., Del Castillo and Maravilla, 2021) was illustrated. In addition, the pandemic showed the need to underline the rights of people to public health and to broaden theses rights to include those who are currently insecure. If claims for universal health protection as a public good have traditionally been the demands of progressive groups, then the pandemic proved why this is necessary (Galvani et al., 2022).

During the pandemic, we saw how strengthened demagogues and authoritarians utilised their newly granted extraordinary powers to solidify their authority, weaken human rights, and suppress civil society (Manson, 2020; Filsinger and Freitag, 2022). In my own country, the Philippines, for example, Rodrigo Duterte admitted in June 2022 that he had used his powers to stop the operations of a private broadcast corporation in 2020. Duterte's human rights record is also littered with the blood of Filipino citizens murdered during his war on drugs and through red-tagging efforts (Teehankee, 2021).

During times of crisis, social movements often rise to the forefront of public attention (Auethavornpipat and Tanyag, 2021). Even in nations where governments are hostile to social movements, civil society can stay robust, and activism may thrive as local activists and civil society leaders adapt to their new situation, as shown, for instance, in the Philippines' community pantry projects (Del Castillo and Maravilla, 2021) (see Chapter 12 for more details). At the community scale, the rise in unstructured organising via mutual assistance projects has created a new space for civic activity. In addition to mutual support, the goal of this organising is to put people who are ill, under quarantine, or otherwise vulnerable in contact with others in the community who live nearby and who can run errands and provide essential supplies or whatever else is needed. Some community organisations fought the pandemic head-on, providing essential services to vulnerable people and covering government response shortages.

The Maginhawa food pantries in Quezon City in the Philippines illustrated how ordinary citizens and community organisations could work in solidarity to meet these gaps (Del Castillo and Maravilla, 2021). Volunteering their time and donating essential supplies such as food and medicines, pantry organisers persevered despite efforts by the Duterte government to link them with communist groups (Lacsa, 2022).

In addition to giving immediate aid, activists continue to protect fundamental rights and liberties, a difficult task hampered by the pandemic's changing dynamics. Duterte's wanton targeting of individuals who criticise his administration and the militarisation of his government's response to the pandemic, assaulting free speech, and harassing independent media, was met with dissent (Teehankee, 2021). When Duterte portrayed the reaction to the pandemic as a war response, his government coerced many Filipinos into giving up their rights, liberties, and dignity to have any chance of surviving. Their last line of defence, it turned out in the story of food pantries, was the social cohesiveness of their communities.

Fostering solidarity in Filipino food pantries during the pandemic entailed rallying public support undergirded by Filipino values. Solidarity was accomplished by working with new allies outside the traditional human rights space. Moreover, food pantry volunteers and organisers achieved it by taking inspiration from Filipino traditions such as *bayanihan*, which means 'people working together out of kindness to accomplish a common objective', and *pakikipagkapwa*, which means 'a shared sense of belonging and showing respect to others'.

Extraordinary situations warrant extraordinary solutions. We saw and experienced this first-hand during the pandemic. Populists and authoritarians engaged in efforts to undermine the legitimacy of human rights activities, such as in India (Ghosh, 2020) and the Philippines (Docot, 2021; Anderson 2020). Typically, states of emergency imply a weakening of democratic freedoms, sending signals aimed at weakening the ability of civil society to dissent. However, such circumstances might also provide opportunities for experimentation that can broaden the boundaries of politically imaginable ways to stimulate the civic spirit. Despite the obstacles, members of civil society in the Philippines are still fighting back against the overreach of the government and state-sanctioned violence.

In the face of the climate emergency, one of the most critical tasks that civil society can continue to play – as it did during the COVID-19 pandemic crisis – is galvanising public support for more civic involvement and activities (Delina, Diesendorf, and Merson, 2014). Drawn to disruptions in new social and political realities, organisations, mobilisers, and activists can transform into agents of social change. They could pull and communicate ideas and inform the emergence and development of viable routes for social mobilisation.

As we have seen in the Maginhawa food pantries, the pandemic ushered in the formation of new types of community mobilisations. As this mobilisation emerged, civil society has presented an opportunity to recapture the public's sense of its worth and, by proving what it can do, to mobilise public support for future mobilisations. The story of community mobilisations in Maginhawa provides a peg on which to hang future mobilisations, especially as the climate crisis intensifies and the need for mobilisation to act on it at scale and speed ramps up. However, it remains to be seen whether this mode of organising and mobilising has the potential to grow into more long-lasting forms of community-building that are independent of the state.

In a way, the Maginhawa food pantries not only evoke feelings of solidarity but also underscore the concept of utopia. In this case, the community-led and volunteer-driven food pantries may be regarded as social counter-practices driven by the aspiration to improve everybody's state of being at a time when the government was perceived to be useless. Utopia has the prospect to create cracks within existing institutional and social arrangements and open up opportunities for new practices. The Maginhawa food pantries provided physical things – food, medicines, and other supplies – but also an intangible bequest: a different future when the present state of affairs is shaken up.

We would have addressed the climate emergency by now if we had put as much effort into averting it as we have in inventing excuses. When one turns one's head in any direction, one can see individuals furiously defending themselves against the ethical challenge of the climate crisis. Indeed, as the climate emergency worsens and climate action groups make it more difficult for powerholders in governments and businesses to ignore the challenges we face, individuals are coming up with more creative ways to cover their eyes and avoid taking responsibility for their actions. The foundation of these justifications is a deeply ingrained notion that if we are really in danger, someone, somewhere, will come to our rescue, or that 'they' will not allow it to happen. However, there is no them; there is just us. An environmental Armageddon can still be stopped, but only by the mobilisation of society now.

The assumption that voting is the only political activity necessary to alter the democratic political system is still widely held, although this is wilful ignorance. The Philippine national elections of 2022, in which I eagerly participated as a citizen voter, showed how voting, although necessary, will continue to be a dull and ineffective tool for emancipatory transitions. As long as elections are not accompanied by the focused strength of citizen protest, the articulation of specific demands for climate action, and the creation of spaces where new political forces can mobilise, altering political systems to align with the purposes of profound emissions reduction and decarbonisation seems futile.

The majority of the mainstream media is also deliberately antagonistic (Fischer, 2020), although there are a few rare exceptions. Even when journalists cover the climate crisis, they consciously avoid any reference to power. Instead, journalists speak about climate disasters as if strange, inert factors are driving them. The response then proposed is to use micro fixes for what is arguably a crisis requiring massive structural changes. Indeed, we can compare how comedies and dramas on television have got riskier while current affairs programming has become increasingly cautious. One example is Netflix's dystopian series *Squid Game* which became highly successful during the

COVID-19 pandemic due to its extensive depiction of how cash-strapped players would risk deadly high stakes over an enticing prize.

It is impossible to put our faith in those in governments to ensure the survival of life on Earth. We could also cannot presume the media to be on the side of survival. There is effectively zero authority looking out for our best interests and protecting us from danger. Nobody is going to come to our rescue. Yet, nobody among us can also escape the need to band together to preserve our lives, livelihoods, and communities.

My perspective is that melancholy is just another taste of repudiation. By refusing to acknowledge the tragedies that may one day befall us because of the climate emergency, we can cover up and remove these tragedies from our consciousness. Our tangible options are thus transformed into incomprehensible fear. By asserting that it is already too late to take climate action, we may be able to free ourselves of the responsibility of moral agency. Nevertheless, in doing so, we are putting other individuals in danger of starvation or death, especially those living in the Majority World.

People now suffer from a calamity. In contrast to people living in the Minority World, who can still afford to suffer in silence, those in the Majority World will be compelled to react pragmatically. It is not an option to give up hope in countries like mine, the Philippines, and those in the Pacific, which, almost every year, suffer from the ravages of more powerful and more frequent typhoons; or in Central America and sub-Saharan Africa, where crop failure, dry spells, and the breakdown of fish stocks have displaced people from their homes. Giving up hope is not an option. Climate migrants are already being pushed into moving due to climate inaction in the Minority World. Forced climate migrants are reacting to the horrific conditions generated mainly by the consumerism of the affluent world.

People have been caught off guard by every non-linear transformation that has occurred throughout history. Systems seem to be unchanging until these same systems are abruptly dissolved for no apparent reason. Many were caught in a similar situation when, out of the blue, a highly contagious virus appeared in Wuhan and then crept its way all over the world. As soon as systems are disturbed, it seems, in hindsight, that the disintegration was unavoidable.

Our system, characterised by unending economic expansion in a world that is not expanding, will ultimately collapse. This is because our planet is not increasing. Thus, our only option is to demand a new economic and political system founded on the concept that everyone has an equitable right to take pleasure in natural resources and participate equitably in decision-making. Demanding change requires that only a maximum of 3.5 per cent of the population need to participate in a non-violent mass movement for it to be successful (Chenoweth, Stephan, and Stephan, 2011).

People are generally sociable creatures who are aware of how social currents move and the direction in which they are moving. As soon as people become aware that the status quo has been altered, and when a determined and outspoken 3.5 per cent of the population rallies to the call for a new system, the subsequent cascades will become unstoppable. Despite the unfortunate events we have witnessed, it would be a defeat to give up before we have reached this point.

The global climate action movement continues its fight to protect the systems that make our lives on Earth possible. Climate mobilisation is climate action that is bold, radical, and non-violent. Ensuring that this mobilisation is successful depends entirely on us. The change will only cross the crucial barrier if a sufficient number of us – 3.5 per cent – can collectively let go of our climate denial and hopelessness and join this buoyant and ever-expanding climate action movement.

References

Anderson, W. (2020). The Philippine Covidscape colonial public health redux? *Philippine Studies: Historical and Ethnographic Viewpoints*, *68*(3), 325–337.

Auethavornpipat, R., & Tanyag, M. (2021). Protests and pandemics: Civil society mobilisation in Thailand and the Philippines during COVID-19. *New Mandala*, 29 July. www.newmandala.org/protests-and-pandemics-civil-society-mobilisation-in-thailand-and-the-philippine/.

Chenoweth, E., Stephan, M. J., & Stephan, M. (2011). *Why Civil Resistance Works: The Strategic Logic of Nonviolent Conflict*. New York: Columbia University Press.

Del Castillo, F. A., & Maravilla, M. I. (2021). Community pantries: Their role in public health during the COVID-19 pandemic. *Journal of Public Health*, *43*, e551–552.

Delina, L. L. (2019). *Emancipatory Climate Actions: Strategies from Histories*. London: Palgrave Macmillan.

Delina, L. L. (2022). Moving people from the balcony to the trenches: Time to adopt 'climatage' in climate activism? *Energy Research & Social Science*, *90*, 102586.

Delina, L. L., Diesendorf, M., & Merson, J. (2014). Strengthening the climate action movement: Strategies from histories. *Carbon Management*, *5*(4), 397–409.

Della Porta, D. (2017). Introduction: Social movements in civil wars. In D. Della Porta, T. Hidde Donker, B. Hall, E. Poljarevic, & D. P. Ritter (Eds.), *Social Movements and Civil War* (pp. 1–22). London: Routledge.

Docot, D. (2021). Carceral and colonial memory during pandemic times in the Philippines: A long letter of solidarity from the diaspora. *Commoning Ethnography*, *4*(1), 23–52.

Dodman, D., Mitlin, D., & Co, J. R. (2010). Victims to victors, disasters to opportunities: Community-driven responses to climate change in the Philippines. *International Development Planning Review*, *32*(1), 1–27.

Filsinger, M., & Freitag, M. (2022). Pandemic threat and authoritarian attitudes in Europe: An empirical analysis of the exposure to COVID-19. *European Union Politics*, *23*(3), 417–436.

Fischer, F. (2020). Post-truth politics and climate denial: Further reflections. *Critical Policy Studies*, *14*(1), 124–130.

Fisher, D. R., & Nasrin, S. (2021). Climate activism and its effects. *Wiley Interdisciplinary Reviews: Climate Change*, *12*(1), e683.

Galvani, A. P., Parpia, A. S., Pandey, A., Sah, P., Colón, K., Friedman, G., ... & Fitzpatrick, M. C. (2022). Universal healthcare as pandemic preparedness: The lives and costs that could have been saved during the COVID-19 pandemic. *Proceedings of the National Academy of Sciences*, *119*(25), e2200536119.

Ghosh, J. (2020). A critique of the Indian government's response to the COVID-19 pandemic. *Journal of Industrial and Business Economics*, *47*(3), 519–530.

Hapal, K. (2021). The Philippines' COVID-19 response: Securitising the pandemic and disciplining the pasaway. *Journal of Current Southeast Asian Affairs*, *40*(2), 224–244.

Imbong, R. A. (2022). Police power in the Philippines in the time of the pandemic. *Rethinking Marxism*, *34*(2), 240–254.

Islam, M. S., & Islam, M. N. (2016). 'Environmentalism of the poor': The Tipaimukh Dam, ecological disasters and environmental resistance beyond borders. *Bandung*, *3*(1), 1–16.

Kampmark, B. (2020). Protesting in pandemic times: COVID-19, public health, and Black Lives Matter. *Contention*, *8*(2), 1–20.

Lacsa, J. E. M. (2022). Community pantries initiatives: Community response to the deeper issue of poverty. *Journal of Public Health*, *44*(3), e415.

Libal, K., & Kashwan, P. (2020). Solidarity in times of crisis. *Journal of Human Rights*, *19*(5), 537–546.

Manson, J. H. (2020). Right-wing authoritarianism, left-wing authoritarianism, and pandemic-mitigation authoritarianism. *Personality and Individual Differences*, *167*, 110251.

Ockey, J. (2021). Thailand in 2020: Politics, protests, and a pandemic. *Asian Survey*, *61*(1), 115–122.

Passos, A. M., & Acácio, I. (2021). The militarization of responses to COVID-19 in Democratic Latin America. *Revista de Administração Pública*, *55*, 261–272.

Selway, J. S. (2022). Thailand in 2021: Demonstrations and discord in the depths of a pandemic. *Asian Survey*, *62*(1), 105–117.

Teehankee, J. C. (2021). The Philippines in 2020: COVID-19 pandemic threatens Duterte's populist legacy. *Asian Survey*, *61*(1), 130–137.

Tomasini, F. (2021). Solidarity in the time of COVID-19? *Cambridge Quarterly of Healthcare Ethics*, *30*(2), 234–247.

Index

#MeToo movement, 67
100 per cent renewable energy, 55
3.5 per cent, 152, 153

activism, 7, 68, 112, 147, 149
adaptation, xi, 4, 13, 14, 15, 54, 57, 97, 103, 104, 116, 120, 125, 126, 140
additionality, 57
affluence, 73, 85, 94
Afghanistan, 36, 56
Agenda 21, 52
agriculture, 13, 22, 51, 89, 95
aid, 20, 21, 29, 40, 57, 90, 96, 104, 111, 112, 148, 149
air conditioning, 20
air pollution, 20
Alaska, 40, 41
Amazon rainforest, 4, 63
Amazon.com, 4, 23, 33
America First, 48
American Civil Rights Act, 68
anxieties, 40
aparigraha, 76
apartheid, 21
apathy, 14
arctic tundra, 4
artificial intelligence, 27
Asian hate, 113. *see* racism
Aspen, 55
AstraZeneca, 51
Atlantic Meridional Overturning Circulation, 4, 63
Australia, 15, 20, 21, 36, 50, 54, 66, 86, 89, 103, 131
Austria, 68
authoritarian capitalism, 33

automation, 41
avian influenza. *See* bird flu
aviation, 7, 79
avocado, 97
ayuda, 111

Bali, 142
Balik Probinsya, 88
Bangladesh, 21
Batanes, 129
bayanihan, 150
Belgium, 35, 68
benevolence, 110, 112
Bezos, Jeff, 23, 120
Bhagavad Gita, 76
Biden, Joseph, 48
billionaires, x, 15, 23, 33, 52, 85, 120
biodiversity, 3, 52
bioenergy, 65, 140
biogas digesters, 76
biomass, 65
biometrics, 27, 28
bird flu, 139
Black Lives Matter movement, 67, 148
Bolsonaro, Jair, 132
border security, 28
borders, ix, 26, 27, 28, 41, 93, 103, 110, 113
boreal forests, 4
Boundary Dam coal-fired power plant, 65
Brazil, 40, 113
British Columbia, 15, 54
build the wall, 37
Burlington, 55

California, 15, 54, 131
Canada, 40, 54, 64, 65, 66, 97

Index

capitalism, 56, 74, 105, 106
carbon capture and storage, 5, 64, 65
carbon drawdown, 63, 64, 65
carbon sinks, 63, 65
caste discrimination, 77
cement, 5
central banks, 15
Chico River, 118, 119
Chile, 93
China, 2, 33, 36, 66, 67, 88, 106, 131
civil society, 53, 118, 124, 149, 150
climate denial, 62, 106, 143, 153
climate finance, 28, 36, 57, 103, 104, 105, 106, 141
climate justice, 104, 105
climate migrants, x, 27, 29, 152
climate reparations, 104, 105
cognitive bias, 130
collapse, ix, 1, 3, 11, 12, 13, 15, 16, 40, 62, 63, 124, 125, 152
colonialism, x, 95, 102, 105, 106, 116, 119
colonisation, 67, 101, 102, 104, 117, 117, 123, 126
Colorado, 55
community cohesion, 35
community pantry, 110, 111, 112, 149, 150, 151
compassion, 29, 62, 110
conspiracy theories, 132
consumption, vii, x, 6, 7, 13, 73, 74, 75, 78, 78, 80, 85, 85, 86, 87, 96, 107, 136
control, vii, ix, x, xi, 5, 11, 26, 27, 28, 36, 49, 76, 93, 102, 102, 135, 136, 137, 138, 139, 140, 141, 142, 143
cooling, 20, 55, 64
cooperatives, 36, 36
copper, 86
coral bleaching, 4, 6
coral reefs, 1, 3, 4, 6
Cordillera, 118, 119
COVAX, 49, 50, 51, 97
COVID-19 testing, 37
COVID-19 vaccine, 23, 37, 47, 50, 50, 51, 57, 96, 141
cultural identity, 117

Daguma Mountain Range, 125
Damon Centola, 68
dashboards, 135
data gap, 29, 30
Davao del Sur, 129
David, Randy, 110

Dayan, Datu Victor, 124
debt, xi, 39, 90, 102, 103, 105, 107
debt forgiveness, xi, 105, 107
decluttering, vii, 75, 75, 77, 80
decolonisation, vii, 116
decoupling, 38, 85, 86, 87
deep mitigation, 13
degrowth, 7
democracy, 33, 39, 53, 73, 77, 136, 150, 151
Democratic Republic of the Congo, 20, 74
deportation, 27
de-urbanisation, 88
digital nomadism, 75
direct air capture, 5, 6
domino dynamics, 66, 67, 68
Don't Look Up, 131, 132
drones, 28
droughts, 6, 13, 15, 93, 101, 129
Dulangan Manobos, 125
Duterte, Rodrigo, 30, 49, 111, 149
dystopia, 14

Earth Charter, 52
Earth Summit, 52, 53
Earth systems, 4, 6, 63
East Antarctic ice sheets, 4
East Asian monsoon, 63
ecological genocide, 34
Ecuador, 119
ego, 88
El Niño phenomenon, 15
El Salvador, 26, 113
electric mobility, 64, 66, 67
electric storage, 64
electric vehicles, 66, 67
Eliot, T. S., 4
energy transition, 6, 13, 16, 34, 36, 38, 39, 54, 55, 56, 57, 58, 62, 63, 64, 65, 66, 67, 68, 87, 106, 107, 136, 139, 140, 142
entrepreneurship, 40
Environment, Social, and Governance (ESG), 3
environmental governance, 52, 53, 57
Ethiopia, 56
Europe, ix, x, 4, 20, 21, 48, 49, 50, 56, 63, 67, 89, 102, 131
European Green Deal, 38, 39
European Union, 27, 28, 66, 97
excess profit taxes, 54
extinction of species, 11, 84
extractive industries, 39
extremely wealthy. *See* billionaires

factory farming. *See* industrial farming
fake prosperity, 93, 95
famine, 94
fat-tailed events, 22
fear, 14, 15, 111, 112, 132, 147, 152
Fiji, 19
Filipinos, 3, 15, 19, 47, 48, 110, 111, 112, 129, 131, 149, 150
Finland, 40
fish banks game, 2
fishing, 2, 3, 4, 152
flooding, 5, 15, 19, 21, 63, 93, 101
food insecurity, 20, 22, 94, 95, 96, 125
food security, 94
food systems, 93, 95, 96
forests, 1, 20, 65, 67, 73, 89, 97, 118
fossil fuel divestment movement, 28, 34
France, 36
free speech, 150
freedoms, 30, 54, 78, 88, 147, 149, 150
Fridays for Future, 68

Gandhi, Mahatma, 77
Gates, Bill, 23, 34, 120
Gaza, 56
General Santos City, 2
genetic testing, 29
genocide, x, 102, 124, 125
geoengineering, 11, 15, 124, 143
Germany, 68, 131
Ghana, 51
going-back-to-the-land, 89
Gotabaya Rajapaksa, 37
greed, 74, 76, 116, 120
Green New Deal, 38, 39, 40, 87
Green parties, 68
green pluralism, 53
greenwashing, 39
Guatemala, 113, 119
Guterres, António, 48

H1N1, 50, 139
heating, 4, 5, 6, 20, 23, 26, 33, 34, 37, 55, 57, 62, 63, 78, 93, 94, 95, 96, 103, 141
heatwaves, 20, 63, 94, 131
Himalayas, 94
homeless people, 20
Honduras, 113, 119
Hong Kong, ix, xii, 2, 3, 20, 26, 41, 132, 138, 139, 141

hope, 5, 6, 36, 48, 51, 55, 63, 64, 66, 67, 68, 97, 105, 132, 147, 152
hotter days, 20
hotter nights, 20
hubris, vii, 135, 143
human rights, 23, 27, 30, 50, 67, 73, 77, 78, 97, 117, 117, 120, 126, 149, 149, 150
humility, 143
hysteria, 112

Ifugao, 142
immigration, 28
independent media, 49, 150
India, 36, 40, 47, 51, 54, 68, 150
Indigenous epistemology, vii, 123, 125, 126, 127
Indigenous Peoples, xi, 14, 40, 116, 117, 118, 119, 120, 124, 125, 126
individualism, 78
Indonesia, 142
industrial agriculture, 1, 6, 96
industrial revolution, 102
inequality, 7, 14, 22, 33, 37, 38, 42, 73, 77, 80, 87, 94, 106, 113, 141
inflation, 37
innovation, 35, 36, 39, 55
insurance, 12, 22, 23, 104
Intergovernmental Panel on Climate Change, 12, 65
isolationism, 48

Japan, 3, 50
joy, 75, 89
just adaptation, 15, 16
just migration, 14
justice, x, 14, 23, 39, 56, 62, 78, 104, 104, 105, 106, 126, 127, 136, 142

Kenya, 40
Kolkata, 54
Kondo, Marie, 75

Lake Sebu, 124
Latin America, 39, 103, 139
limitarianism, 35
livelihoods, 11, 22, 26, 40, 65, 74, 76, 88, 89, 96, 101, 104, 113, 119, 120, 129, 130, 132, 136, 140, 152
lobbying, 28, 66
local knowledge, 140
London Heathrow, ix, 20

loss and damage, 104
Luzon, 118

male privilege, 88
Marcos, Ferdinand, 68, 118
Mars, 2
masculinity, 88
material footprint, 86
materialism, 7, 78
melancholy, 152
methane, 96
Metro Manila, 88, 118
Mexico, 26, 113, 139
Microsoft, 23
migrants, x, 26, 27, 28, 89, 113, 152
migration, x, 27, 37, 68, 113
militarisation, 27, 28, 37, 49, 148
military–industrial complex, 36, 74
Mindanao, 54, 125, 129
minimalism, 73, 75, 75, 76, 77, 80
mining, 1, 73, 74, 86, 87, 118
modelling, 30, 139, 140
moderation society, 35, 76, 78
monocropping, 96
Montreal Protocol, 53
multilateral development banks, 57
multilateralism, 47, 48, 49, 51, 52, 53, 54, 56, 58
multinational corporations, 97, 104, 106
multiple breadbasket failures, 11, 94
Musk, Elon, 23, 120
Myanmar, 21, 27, 48, 56, 137

national security, 28, 28
nationalism, vii, 37, 47, 48, 49, 50, 51, 53, 57
neocolonialism, x, 105
neo-liberalism, vii, 33, 35, 36, 37, 38, 73, 74, 77, 78, 79, 84, 88, 105, 120, 136, 148
net zero, 5, 38
Netflix, 74, 131, 151
New England, 55
New South Wales, 21
New York, 54, 131, 138
New York City, 54
Newark, 54
Non, Ana Patricia, 110
normalcy bias, 130, 131
Norway, 66
nuclear winter, 11

ocean acidification, 3
oligarchs, 35, 120
Omicron variant, 138
Ontario, 64
outsourcing, 78
overfishing, 6
Oxfam, 23

Pa Deng, 35, 76
Pacific, 19, 20, 56, 129, 152
Pacific bluefin tuna, 3
Pacific Ring of Fire, 129
pakikipagkapwa, 150
Palawan, 129
panic, 111, 112
Paris Agreement, 5, 49, 52, 53, 54, 56, 57, 63, 68, 95, 140
patents, 88, 96
patriarchy, 88
people–place relationships, 124
perpetual economic growth paradigm. *See* neo-liberalism
perpetual growth paradigm. *See* neo-liberalism
persons with disabilities, 20
Peru, 119
pets, 77
Pfizer–BioNTech, 51
Philippines, ix, xii, xiii, 1, 3, 3, 19, 26, 30, 36, 41, 47, 49, 54, 56, 68, 75, 86, 88, 93, 101, 102, 110, 111, 112, 117, 118, 119, 124, 125, 129, 140, 142, 148, 149, 150, 151, 152
planetary boundaries, 14
planetary systems, 62, 66
plant-based diet, 97
plastics, 74, 84
political right, 28, 77
pollinators, 94
polycentrism, 53
populism, ix, 47, 136, 137
precautionary principle, 12, 14
preppers, 15
privatisation, 27
psychology, 14, 15, 34
public opinion, 36

quarantine, ix, 26, 140, 149
Quezon City, 110, 149

racism, 67, 77, 113, 116
Rakhine state, 21
Rama IX, 76

Index

rare earth elements, 39, 67
recreancy, 113
red-tagging, 111, 149
refugees, 20, 21, 26, 27, 28
renationalisation, 107
residential electricity use, 20
restorative justice. *See* climate justice
rewilding, 97
rice farming, 75, 93, 94, 96, 142
Rio de Janeiro, 52, 54
risk, xi, 2, 12, 12, 13, 14, 15, 20, 21, 22, 49, 110, 114, 117, 120, 123, 124, 125, 126, 127, 129, 130, 131, 132, 136
Robeyns, Ingrid, 35
Rohingya, 21, 27
Roosevelt, Franklin Delano, 38
rural economy, 89
Russia, ix, 21, 36
Russian war on Ukraine, 21, 137

San Miguel Corporation, 125
Sarangani Bay, 2
sarvodaya, 78
Saskatchewan, 65
satyagraha, 77
sea level rise, 54
seawalls, 13
Second World War, xi, 21, 38, 56, 107, 141
security threat, 28, 48
self-sufficiency, 35, 67, 73, 75, 76, 77, 78, 88, 90
Serum Institute of India, 51
sethakit por piang, 35
sexism, 77
Sinovac, 47
social media, 28, 48, 75, 132
social movements, xi, 147, 148, 149
solar home systems, 35, 76
solidarity, 110, 111, 112, 113, 114, 119, 148, 149, 150
South Africa, 97
South Cotabato, xiii, 86, 125
Southern Ecosocial Deal, 39
space escapism, 15
Spain, ix, 20, 49, 101
Squid Game, 151
Sri Lanka, 37
state of exception, 54, 55, 56
steel, 5
stewardship, 88, 116, 120
Stockholm, 52, 53, 56, 57

Stockholm+ 50, 52, 53, 56
subjugation. *See* colonialism
sub-Saharan Africa, 103
subsidies, 79, 96, 103, 107
sufficiency economy, 35
surprise, 3, 139, 140
surveillance, ix, 26, 27, 28
Sustainable Development Goals, 52
sustainable farming, 96
swaraj, 78
Sweden, 68
swine flu, 139, 140, 141
Switzerland, 40, 68
Syria, 27, 95

T'boli-Manobo peoples, 124
taxation, 38, 39, 66, 79, 87, 107
technofixes, 6, 15, 64, 65, 96
technology transfer, 57
Tesla, 23
Texas, 55
Thailand, 35, 76, 148
Thunberg, Greta, 68
Tigray, 48
tiny houses, 75
tipping points, ix, 4, 11, 14, 62, 63, 66, 67, 68, 84
Tonga, 19
trauma, 104, 126, 131
trawling, 3, 6, 96
Trump, Donald, 48, 49, 132
typhoon, 13, 15, 19, 38, 54, 63, 93, 101, 111, 129, 152
Typhoon Haiyan, 111
Typhoon Harold, 19
Typhoon Rai, 129, 131
Typhoon Vongfong, 19
Typhoon Yasa, 19

Ukraine, ix, x, 21, 27, 56, 137
uncertainty, 12, 30, 114, 140
United Kingdom, 36, 50, 106
United Nations, 15, 27, 48, 48, 51, 52, 94
United Nations Decade of Action, 52
United Nations Environment Programme, 52
United Nations Framework Convention on Climate Change, 52, 57, 103
United Nations High Commissioner for Refugees, 27
United Nations Security Council, 48

United States, 26, 28, 36, 39, 40, 48, 50, 51, 54, 56, 66, 68, 79, 86, 97, 102, 113, 138, 148
United States–Mexico border, 26, 113
universal basic income, 39, 40, 41, 90
universal health protection, 149
university endowments, 28

vaccine nationalism, 50
Vanuatu, 19
Victoria, 54
visa, 26
Visayas, 54, 129
vulnerable populations, 14, 20, 21, 23, 33, 34, 53, 95, 95, 101, 104, 137, 140

wartime mobilisation, 56, 63

West Antarctic ice sheets, 4
West Philippine Sea, 3
white rhinos, 97
white supremacy, 67
wildfires, 15, 20, 54, 97, 131
work, xi, xii, 12, 13, 20, 30, 33, 35, 36, 37, 38, 39, 41, 42, 51, 53, 54, 55, 56, 63, 78, 80, 84, 88, 111, 112, 118, 132, 136, 142, 149
work from home, 41
World Health Organization, 50, 113, 141
Wuhan, 66, 125, 152

xenophobia. 113 *See* racism

YouTube, 75

Zimbabwe, 20

Printed in the United States
by Baker & Taylor Publisher Services